LATIN AMERICA
AND THE CARIBBEAN

FIRST EDITION

LATIN AMERICA AND THE CARIBBEAN

READINGS IN CULTURE, GEOGRAPHY, AND HISTORY

Virginia Ochoa-Winemiller

New Jersey City University

cognella®

SAN DIEGO

Bassim Hamadeh, CEO and Publisher
John Remington, Executive Editor
Gem Rabanera, Senior Project Editor
Jeanine Rees, Production Editor
Emely Villavicencio, Senior Graphic Designer
Trey Soto, Licensing Coordinator
Natalie Piccotti, Director of Marketing
Kassie Graves, Vice President of Editorial
Jamie Giganti, Director of Academic Publishing

Cover image copyright © 2012 Depositphotos/yuriy61.

Printed in the United States of America.

cognella® | ACADEMIC PUBLISHING
3970 Sorrento Valley Blvd., Ste. 500, San Diego, CA 92121

CONTENTS

SECTION III THE 19TH AND 20TH CENTURIES: INDEPENDENCE AND REVOLUTIONS 67

SECTION IV POPULATION, MIGRATION, AND URBANISM 111

INTRODUCTION

Latin America and the Caribbean are regions geographically close to the United States, but they are poorly understood historically and culturally. This statement is more relevant today as exemplified by the abundance of preconceptions and confusion clouding the current discourse in the media. As a result, learning to contextualize the cultures and history of these regions becomes a challenge for those interested in the complexities of the Latin American and Caribbean landscapes and their people.

Since the arrival of Christopher Columbus in the latter part of the 15th century, these regions have been closely linked to the developed world as sources of raw material and labor, and at the same time beset by lasting social, religious, and political transformation. A lasting consequence of such an uneven relationship has been the perception of Latin America and the Caribbean as underdeveloped third world regions ridden with poverty, crime, diseases, and their populations unable to take care of themselves. To add to this distorted view, the geography, boundaries, diversity, and self-identification of their residents via national and ethnic labels remain poorly understood. In the United States, the influx of immigrants from Latin America and the Caribbean has become an important issue in the political discourse. Latin America and the Caribbean are regions facing constant postcolonial challenges derived from a long history of conquest, colonization, economic dependency, corruption, and globalizing forces. Yet, the push-and-pull factors behind these migration flows are widely obscured by the spread of misinformation leading to subsequent intolerance toward the newcomers.

Textbooks such as this anthology are a venue to students and the general public to reinforce their knowledge by enhancing their exploration of the history, cultures, and global relevance of Latin America and the Caribbean. This anthology aims to contribute to the discussion of some of the issues already outlined. The underlying principle behind the selection of readings and their organization was the inclusion of multiple disciplinary approaches and voices to the debates surrounding these regional and global issues. By incorporating multiple voices, the goal is to encourage civil discussion, critical thinking, and reflection, not memorization.

A thematic sequence of readings helps to contextualize and critically assess the history, cultures, and global relevance of Latin America and the Caribbean regions. Sequentially organized, the readings represent a current overview of scholarly research on topics such as environmental and climate-related issues, 19th- and 20th-century revolutionary movements, social development, poverty, neoliberalism, drugs, migration, gender, culture changes, and religion. To aid the reader in the exploration of this book, this anthology includes pedagogical tools such as bold-font keywords, additional suggested readings, and relevant readings listed at the end of each topic.

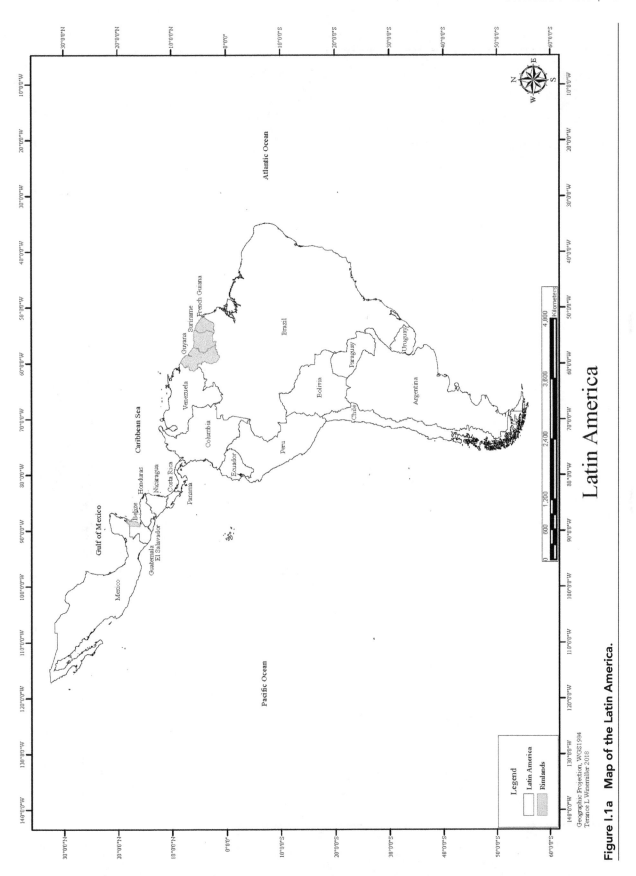

Latin America

Geographic Projection, WGS1994
Terance L Winemiller 2018

Figure I.1a   Map of the Latin America.

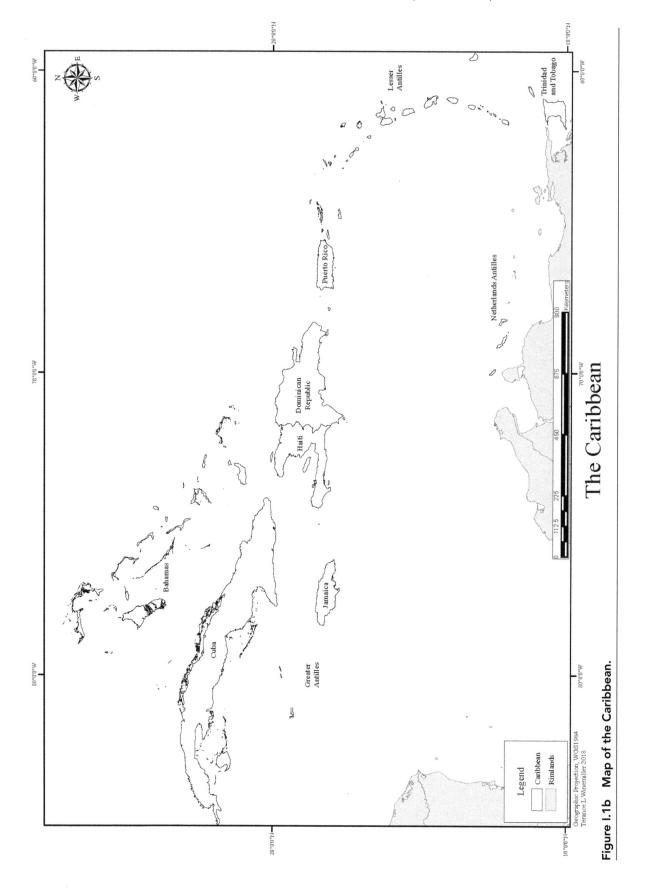

The Caribbean

Geographic Projection, WGS1984
Terance L Winemiller 2018

Figure I.1b Map of the Caribbean.

SECTION I

ENVIRONMENT

Editor's Introduction

Climate change, environmental degradation, and the strategies implemented to reduce their socioeconomic impact are the subjects of the readings in this section. The physical geography and the anthropogenic effects of agricultural and mining practices, as well as high pollution levels from urban areas are changing local weather patterns in striking ways. These changes are leading to the increase of life-threatening storms, water scarcity, and lasting droughts in Latin America. The subsequent impact on human lives and local economies has been staggering, revealing the vulnerability of this region to climatic conditions. Although several Latin American countries supported both the 1997 Kyoto Protocol and the 2016 Paris Agreement, which aimed to reduce greenhouse gases by setting internationally binding emission reduction targets, their implementation still faces resistance and criticism from agricultural businesses, local mining companies, and industry.

Moreno's (2010) article conveys the need to understand the direct connection that exists between climate change and the supply of freshwater in Latin America. The economy of Latin America, heavily reliant on the production and export of agricultural (coffee, soybeans, and sugar), animal protein (cattle and poultry), and mineral commodities (copper and ore), utilizes vast quantities of water. Extreme weather events and droughts, a direct result of changes in climatic patterns, are also threatening the water supplies of major urban areas. For Moreno (2010),

Latin American leaders are adopting new strategies aimed to protect the water wealth of the region. Waty's (2015) contribution focuses on the advantages and drawbacks of Mexico's 2014 introduction of a carbon taxing policy, part of a General Climate Change Law, which aims to successfully reduce CO_2 emissions and generate revenue to support the development of renewable energy.

References

UNFCCC (1997). *Kyoto Protocol to the United Nations Framework Convention on Climate Change.* Adopted at COP3 in Kyoto, Japan, on 11 December 1997.

United Nations Framework Convention on Climate Change (2017). The Paris Agreement. Retrieved from http://unfccc.int/paris_agreement/items/9485.php

Section I: Key Terms

carbon tax

climate debt

climate stabilization policies

commodities

Cordillera Blanca

dieback

drip irrigation

El Niño

emission trading system (ETS)

extreme weather events

glaciers

greenhouse gases

renewable energy (RE)

sustainable development

Water

To Tackle CO_2, Start with H_2O

How Latin America's Water Problems Could Affect Climate Change Negotiations

Luis Alberto Moreno

Ask the mayor of a city in the Andes Mountains about the outcome of the December 2009 climate negotiations in Copenhagen and you may be met with a shrug. Ask about the drought that has left parts of his city without drinking water, and you will almost certainly get an earful.

The notion that climate change and local water supplies may be connected comes as no surprise to mayors, governors, and presidents in Latin America. But like politicians everywhere, they must respond to immediate problems while keeping an eye on the polls. Not surprisingly, the plummeting level of a local freshwater reservoir can seem like a higher priority than rising concentrations of atmospheric CO_2.

This perennial tension between immediate and long-term priorities was one of several factors that prevented a more ambitious agreement out of the United Nations Climate Change Conference in Copenhagen. The tasks of negotiating an emissions-reduction framework and finding ways to finance mitigation and adaptation measures were daunting in and of themselves. But delegates from developing countries faced an additional challenge. Simply put, they had to persuade their citizens that the abstract risks of climate change were just as important as the tangible imperatives of health, food, education, jobs, and safety in countries where millions of people still lack these essentials.

Very few leaders were willing or able to make that argument last December, but this may be starting to change. In Latin America, water issues may soon bring climate change policy into municipal politics and local elections. Moreover, the intersection of water and climate could help to reconcile some of the disagreements that emerged in Copenhagen, opening a new path towards North–South collaboration on climate issues.

The Blessings of Abundant Water

Water is more tightly linked to human potential and economic competitiveness in Latin America than almost anywhere else. If water were petroleum, Latin America would be considered a hydrological Middle East. While holding only 8 percent of the world's population, Latin America and the Caribbean control roughly 31 percent of the planet's freshwater resources.

This vast water advantage has yielded benefits on several fronts. Latin America as a whole gets around 68 percent of its electricity from hydroelectric sources, compared to a global average of less than 17 percent. The steady expansion of this clean, renewable, and comparatively inexpensive energy source has been crucial to the region's economic expansion over the past half century.

Latin America's lucrative commodity exports—primarily in mining and agriculture—depend on extraordinary quantities of water. The region exported nearly $68 billion worth of metals and minerals in 2008, including more than one-third of the world's copper. As mining executives in Chile's copper-producing northern region are quick to point out, their industry could not exist without the millions of cubic meters of water that are used to process ores and to refine metals.

Latin America has cemented its role as a global breadbasket over the last decade, with the value of its agricultural exports doubling to more than $100 billion in 2008. Millions of people in Asia, Europe, and Africa now depend on Latin American food imports. The region dominates the production of crops like soybean (60 percent of global exports in 2008), sugar (51 percent), and coffee (52 percent) that require vast quantities of predictable rainfall. And Latin America has become the leading exporter of animal protein, such as beef (50 percent of global exports) and poultry (36 percent), partly because countries like Brazil, Argentina, and Uruguay have abundant rain-fed grass and can cheaply grow the grains needed for animal feed.

In contrast to geographic regions where land and water for agriculture are severely constrained, Latin America has the potential to vastly expand food production. For example, while the Near East/North Africa region uses 53 percent of its water resources for irrigation, Latin America can rely almost entirely on rain. In fact, barely 1 percent of the region's freshwater is used for irrigation.

The Dangers of Water Volatility

Latin Americans are so accustomed to cheap and abundant water that they have been stunned in recent years to see how quickly this blessing can turn into a vulnerability.

In 2001, the Brazilian state of São Paulo, the country's industrial heartland, was hit by a drought that sharply reduced power generation at critical hydroelectric complexes. The government was forced to impose restrictions in order to cut electricity consumption by 20 percent, which had steep consequences on economic output.

In 2008 and 2009, one of the worst droughts in half a century killed an estimated 1.5 million head of cattle in Argentina and destroyed nearly half of the country's normally prodigious wheat crop. Across the Andes Mountains, the same drought crippled hydroelectric facilities in Chile's central region, where most of its population is concentrated. Hydroelectricity production plunged by 34 percent, forcing the government to rely on diesel–and gas–powered generators at a time when fuel prices were reaching historic highs.

At various points in 2009, major cities in Venezuela, Ecuador, Colombia, and Paraguay were forced to ration water, cut electricity generation, or both. Large sections of Mexico City, home to some 17 million people, survived without water for days at a time, and the country's corn and bean harvests were severely affected. In Guatemala, President Álvaro Colom was forced to declare a "state of calamity" because of hunger and malnutrition in parched rural areas.

Unfortunately, some countries have also been plagued by hurricanes or torrential rains, which have further damaged water supply and sanitation systems, among other infrastructure. Meteorologists cite linkages between these extreme weather events and quasi–periodic climate patterns such as *El Niño* and *La Niña*. But climatologists also warn that in a warmer planet, these extremes will become more frequent and more severe. In other words, today's droughts and hurricanes may portend what is to come.

Though long-term changes in rainfall patterns are notoriously difficult to predict, there are concrete signs that climate change is starting to threaten Latin America's water wealth. Annual measurements of tropical glaciers in the Andes Mountains of Peru and Ecuador show that these glaciers have lost around 30 percent of their total mass in the last 30 years, and the melting rate appears to be increasing. In 2006, for example, glaciologists monitoring Bolivia's Chacaltaya glacier estimated that it would survive until at least 2015. But by the summer of 2008, this glacier—once the location of the world's highest ski resort—had disappeared altogether.

Glaciers are a vital component of the hydrological systems that supply water for drinking, agriculture, and electricity to some 80 million people in the Andean region. The glaciers act as reservoirs, building up mass in the form of snow and ice during the rainy season, and then slowly releasing meltwater that feeds rivers and springs during the dry summer months. If the glaciers continue to shrink, water supplies could be severely disrupted, particularly in the arid Pacific coastal regions of Peru and Chile.

In addition to their negative effects on exports and employment, these disruptions could exacerbate the inequality and the social exclusion that have long characterized the distribution of Latin America's water wealth. An estimated 115 million people—around one out of every four Latin Americans—still live without a water connection in their homes. With some exceptions, the public utilities that supply water and sanitation services to around 90 percent of the region's people are inefficient and underfunded. The average utility loses 50 percent of its water production to wasteful events such as leaks, theft, or non-payment. Furthermore, should climate change threaten their water supplies, many of these service operators would not be able to finance the development of alternative public utility sources.

Making the Global-Local Connection

All of these factors are gradually convincing Latin America's leaders that water can no longer be treated as a free and limitless commodity, and that changes in water supplies may be the first and most disruptive consequence of climate change.

This shift is evident in the demand for more detailed estimates of the potential impact of climate change at the local level. Over the past two years, Mexico, Brazil, and Chile have sought assistance from the United Nations, the Inter-American Development Bank (IDB), and Great Britain to carry out the first country-level studies of the regional economic impact of climate change. Similar studies are now underway in Colombia, Peru, Bolivia, Ecuador, and most Caribbean and Central American countries.

As these studies are completed, governments can begin to anticipate the impact of various climate change scenarios within their territories and to determine how individual industries and populations may need to adapt.

In some cases, adaptation may imply building new infrastructure to redirect water from places where it abounds to places that are increasingly dry. In Peru, for example, the IDB is underwriting a project to divert water from a small mountain river that currently drains into the water-rich Amazon basin. A percentage of the river's water will soon flow instead to the country's dry Pacific coastal region, where it will be used to irrigate up to 150,000 hectares, generate hydroelectricity, and meet the needs of local communities.

In other cases, adaptation may require a shift to smarter water use in existing agricultural sectors. Latin American farmers have only begun to apply technologies such as drip irrigation that enable producers to get "more crop per drop." Some specialists estimate that the region could easily double its total food output—using the same amount of water—by investing in efficient irrigation systems.

For the cities in which 80 percent of Latin America's population lives, adaptation will likely mean prioritizing investments and reforms in public utilities in order to reduce waste, extend coverage to those who lack utility services, and eliminate water-borne diseases among the poor.

But if they seek to adopt a truly strategic approach to protecting their water wealth, Latin American governments will also need to make concessions regarding global emissions reductions. A political shift on emissions will reduce the risk of water crises in the decades ahead.

Climate Change Negotiations Going Forward

This is where water offers an opportunity to bridge some of the disagreements that crippled negotiations in Copenhagen. In the months leading up to the next UN Climate Change Conference, to be held this November in Cancún, Mexico, the international community will wrestle with how to make progress on emission reductions without alienating poor and developing countries.

For Cancún to be more successful than Copenhagen, industrialized countries that prioritize emission reductions and clean energy will need to persuade people in the Global South that the North cares as much about the near-term health of children as it does about the long-term health of the planet. Developing nations, for their part, will have to show that they are willing to share in the sacrifices necessary to mitigate climate risk.

The government of Spain has been a pioneer in showing how these divergent priorities can be reconciled. Spain has become a leading international investor in wind and solar power as a part of its national strategy to develop green energy companies and preemptively meet emission targets. But last year, Spain also created a $1.5 billion grant fund that finances water and sanitation projects in the poorest communities in Latin America and the Caribbean.

These grants are helping to jump start critically needed infrastructure projects in countries such as Paraguay, Guatemala, and Bolivia, and have leveraged hundreds of millions of dollars in additional funds from the IDB. In Haiti, a $39 million grant for water and sanitation projects, jointly financed by Spain and the IDB, is being reprogrammed to help rebuild Port-au-Prince's shattered water and sanitation infrastructure.

The highland city of La Paz, Bolivia, offers another example of the benefits of this approach. Spain, the IDB, and other donors are helping to finance the expansion of water and sanitation networks to low-income neighborhoods that primarily house Aymara Indians in the city's outskirts.

Since the glaciers that supply a significant percentage of the city's water supply are melting rapidly, some of this aid will also be used to help the city plan ahead, secure new sources of water, and reduce leaks in the existing network.

As a country with large tropical forests, Bolivia could be an important participant in future programs to reduce CO$_2$ emissions caused by deforestation. By honoring the aspirations of Bolivians who wish to have water in their homes today, international donors may improve the odds that Bolivia, like other developing countries, will help forge a global climate pact in the future.

There is no reason why this kind of climate-focused international aid cannot be practiced on a much larger scale. Despite the disappointment that greeted the Copenhagen Accord last year, the agreement included a commitment by developed countries to provide $30 billion in financing for the 2010–12 period, and a pledge to mobilize $100 billion by 2020. These funds will be used to help developing countries cope with the impacts of climate change and to achieve the deep cuts in global emissions required to hold the increase in global temperatures below 2 degrees Celsius.

Money, though important, will not necessarily be the biggest obstacle. The challenge for donors is to effectively communicate the link between short-term investments in quality of life and the long-term sacrifices necessary to make that life sustainable. Only then will ambitious mayors in drought-stricken Andean cities start paying closer attention to climate negotiations that unfold on the other side of the planet.

Is Mexico the Emerging Leader of Latin America in Post Carbon Politics?

Eddy Waty

Abstract

Air pollution is a serious threat to the health and economic development of Latin America, where over 100 million people breathe dangerously polluted air. More than 14,700 deaths were caused by air pollution in 2010 in Mexico alone. Thus, the Mexican government has pledged to reduce CO_2 emissions by 30% by 2020. To reach this goal, the Mexican government has several options including: 1) a straight carbon tax, to remain in force; 2) a carbon tax evolving to a market-based cap-and-trade system; or 3) a carbon tax evolving to a market-based system, with resultant revenues dedicated to supporting clean energy initiatives. The argument is made that European Union countries and others have shown that a carbon tax can work, with certain safeguards in place, but it should transition to a market-based system over time, as this is favored by industry. In addition, to support long-term clean air goals and showcase ongoing successes, revenues should be used to support the development of renewable energy (RE), which can enroll citizens as stakeholders.

Option 3 has the potential to support emissions reduction goals, generate economic investment and jobs, and improve the population's health. Mexico has announced firm initiatives in this direction. Other Latin American countries are making progress. Brazil has expanded clean energy to 15% percent of its total, Chile plans to increase RE to 20% by 2020, and Uruguay is inviting solar and wind projects. But no other Latin American country appears to have a plan as comprehensive as that of Mexico. Its leadership and example could thus serve as a model for Latin America, if its government follows up on its promises.

Eddy Waty, "Is Mexico the Emerging Leader of Latin America in Post Carbon Politics?" *Pepperdine Policy Review*, vol. 8, pp. 1–10. Copyright © 2015 by Pepperdine University School of Public Policy. Reprinted with permission. Provided by ProQuest LLC. All rights reserved.

1. Introduction

Mexico is the second most populous country in Latin America, with a population of 118.4 million as of 2013. Brazil is the largest country, with 203 million people. Mexico's nominal GDP was $1.26 trillion in 2013, and its GDP per capita was $10,310 in that year (The World Bank, 2014a). It has an EPI (Environmental Performance Index) score of 55.03 in 2014, ranked 65 out of 178 countries which is ahead of other Latin American countries with large urban populations such as Brazil (77) and Argentina (93) (Yale, 2014).

According to the World Bank, Mexico's GDP growth rate has been declining. It was 5.1% in 2010, but only 1.1% in 2013 (The World Bank, 2014b). As Mexico seeks to return to faster rates of economic growth, the pollution-prone exploitation and commercialization of its natural resources threaten its environmental sustainability. Costs of pollution were estimated at approximately 5% of GDP in 2011, primarily due to the impact of air pollution on health in Mexico. According to the World Health Organization, more than 14,700 deaths were caused by air pollution in 2010, and nine of Mexico's cities are among the 20 most polluted on the planet. Mexico is thus highly motivated to reduce air pollution, not just to reduce climate change (which was made a goal when Mexico signed and ratified the Kyoto Protocols) but to save thousands of its citizens lives (Richter, 2013).

The healthcare and related costs of pollution do not include the costs of government subsidies to the fossil fuel industry, which are not made public. However, fossil fuel subsidies are estimated to be many hundreds of millions of dollars annually (Makhijani, 2014).

In recent years, Mexico has taken major steps toward a greener economy. The current President of Mexico, Enrique Peña Nieto, has spoken about adopting the Inclusive Green Growth paradigm. He said, "The great promise of a better future for humanity is the ability to grow and create wealth without damaging our environment or our natural heritage" (RTCC, 2014). In 2014, it was a first-mover country in Latin America to implement a carbon tax and consider an Emission Trading Scheme (ETS) as shown in Figure 1.2.1 (World Bank, 2014c).

President Nieto believes it is possible to both tackle climate change and achieve economic growth, implying he believes the often-stated "either-or" dilemma between increasing economic growth and improving the environment is false. [...] The question then becomes: What viable options are there for achieving all three of these goals for Mexico, followed by other Latin American countries?

2. Literature Review

Many countries have tried various options to reduce air pollution and provide a rich source of experience of workable alternatives, as well as lessons learned about unintended consequences and their accompanying possible mitigating actions. Countries have tried simple carbon taxes,

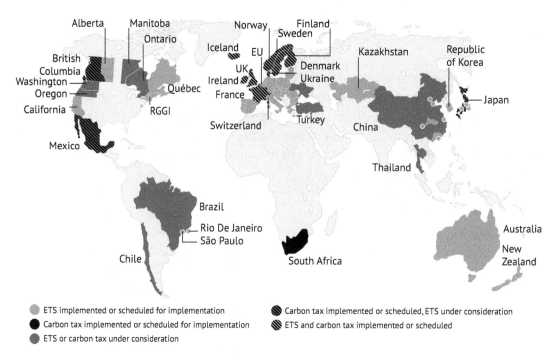

Figure 1.2.1   Map of Existing, Emerging, and Potential Regional, National and Sub-National ETS and Carbon Tax Pricing Instruments

Source: The World Bank, 2014

various types of cap-and-trade schemes that allow companies to gain credits by supporting the reduction of pollution outside of their immediate area, and investments in clean energy projects. Since government-imposed carbon taxes are much simpler to implement than cap-and-trade schemes that need free-market inputs, many countries have started with straight taxes and then transitioned to cap-and-trade.

The Secretariat of Environment and Natural Resources (Semarnat, 2014) introduced a carbon tax in Mexico in 2014 on the use of fossil fuels. The tax is, strictly speaking, not on total carbon content, but on the additional amount of emissions that would be generated if the subject fossil fuel were used instead of natural gas. The tax on natural gas is, therefore, zero. The rate is capped at 3% of the sales price of the fuel (The World Bank, 2014d). This policy aims at increasing awareness of CO_2 emissions and encouraging the use of cleaner fuels and other green alternatives. The approximate carbon emissions price was set at $3.50/$tCO_2$e (tons of carbon dioxide equivalents). The estimated revenue is roughly $1 billion per year. This price is relatively low. The 2013 cost per tCO_2e in the European Union was about $6.70, $11.50 in California, and $15.75 in the United Kingdom for fuels to generate electricity.

Many companies are using even higher prices, called internal carbon prices, to plan for future investment decisions. For example, Shell uses a price of $40 per ton for projects with long lifetime, and it uses this number to plan budgets. Many companies anticipate that some governments may charge social costs of carbon in the future. The American government recently estimated the social cost at $37 per ton (The Economist, 2013).

The Mexican government is considering additional policies to reduce pollution, including investment in clean energy research and development (R&D) and various market-based cap-and-trade mechanisms. Three such schemes are discussed below.

2.1 Carbon Taxation

A carbon tax is a tax levied on the carbon content of fossil fuels (e.g., coal, oil, and natural gas). It provides a carbon emissions price in the economic system. Carbon taxes are intended to control emissions by establishing a fixed price that polluters must pay. High prices discourage pollution.

The Nordic countries first announced carbon taxes in the 1990s. Denmark started its program in 1992. The Danish carbon tax's aim was to, "Increase the climate change profile and provide an economic incentive to consume less energy from carbon-intensive sources" (World Bank, 2014c). Although performance results have been mixed in other Nordic countries, Denmark showed a strong decline in energy use, 26% from 1990 to 2010 and a 25% decrease in CO_2 emissions from 1993 to 2000 (World Bank).

The Danish carbon tax covers all consumption of fossil fuels and was introduced gradually to minimize effects on the competitiveness of industry. It was presented as part of a larger environmental tax package that includes energy taxes and subsidies for green investments. Since the purpose was not to increase the overall tax burden, the energy tax was lowered to offset the introduction of the carbon tax. Norway implemented a similar tax in 1991, to include coal, oil, and natural gas. It was found that a few industries had to be exempted, to preserve competitive positions, but the tax covers more than half of the total Norwegian CO_2 emissions (World Bank, 2014c).

Switzerland also has a carbon tax. Companies are allowed to switch to a cap-and-trade system but not many companies have done so. The tax has enabled it to meet its Kyoto Protocol commitments. Proceeds from the tax are returned to citizens, in the form of discounts on health insurance and building renovations to make them "greener."

Two benefits of a "pure" carbon tax are that it is relatively simple to administer and it gives the state immediate revenue. In contrast, market-based systems can take years to define and implement. During a conference on the economics of carbon taxes at the American Enterprise Institute, Williams (2012) presented his research results on choosing among carbon mitigation policies, including carbon taxes, emissions trading, and traditional environmental policies (including clean energy standards, electricity emission taxes, efficiency policies, higher motor fuel taxes, phased oil taxes, and tighter fuel economy standards). He found that a carbon tax has the least management costs per ton, with the highest relative emissions reduction.

Critics of a carbon tax, which may include powerful industries, have made accusations that it can make companies non-competitive and may force industries to leave the country and set up in untaxed locations (a consequence known as "leakage"). Fischer et al. (2012) provided options for mitigating adverse carbon tax impacts on manufacturing industries and examined partial or full exemption from carbon taxes, output based rebates (OBR), border carbon adjustment (BCA), and other options. They found border carbon adjustment to be an effective method of addressing leakage. An import-based BCA requires importers to pay a carbon tax equivalent to that of local production and can thus avoid the loss of exports.

Studies showed that other safety mechanisms should also be considered, including phasing in the tax slowly so industry can adapt to it, and meeting with industry to consider tax reductions or exemptions for any companies that would in fact become uncompetitive. Studies by the World Bank, the United Nations (UN), and others have shown that the impact on a country's GDP of a carbon tax that is carefully implemented is normally very minor (Bowen, 2011; Carolyn et al., 2012).

In general, it was found that a carbon tax shows promise in improving the environment, but other policies may have a more positive impact on economic growth, as well as social benefits in Mexico. In 2013, 14 countries had a fixed carbon tax. Prior to 2013, more countries had fixed taxation but transitioned over time to a market-based system (World Bank, 2014d).

2.2 Market-Based Systems

The World Bank's (2014c) *Report on the State and Trends of Carbon Pricing* follows the evolution of carbon pricing, and explains different instruments and approaches. Two common market-based mechanisms are the European Union Emission Trading System (EU ETS) and the Clean Development Mechanism (CDM). Both of these are commonly called an ETS or cap-and-trade program. They are managed by the governing jurisdiction that sets an emissions limit, the "cap," but leaves it to the negotiations of the market (i.e., the "trade") to set the price of the carbon. It was first used in the U.S., as a part of the Clean Air Act Amendments of 1990, to reduce dangerous levels of SO_2-caused acid rain resulting from coal-fired power plants.

This type of pollution reduction system provides permits for pollution, and a spot market to trade such permits. A cap-and-trade system generally has a set goal and schedule for the total amounts of carbon emissions across a wide area, but the price for a specific pollution source can remain flexible. It can thus reduce the economic impact that a pollution quota might have on a specific business, while ensuring that quotas are met at regional and international levels.

There may be circumstances where a totally free cap-and-trade system may be harmful. For instance, companies in Norway (where emission reduction tends to be expensive) could choose not to curtail their own pollution at all, but to simply buy carbon credits from far-away countries where pollution reduction is far cheaper; this could lead to excessive local carbon emissions. For such cases, and for occasions when there are wide swings in economic conditions (e.g., inflation and deflation), a floor (i.e., a minimum level) for local reductions may be beneficial.

Another problem with market-based systems was evinced by the EU ETS, established in 2005. The carbon price started at $38/tCO$_2$e and remained fairly stable for a while, but then underwent a wild downswing as a result of the international economic crisis that started in 2008, which caused a supply-demand imbalance. The reduced emissions in the system due to less fossil fuel usage led to an overly high supply of allowances and a carbon price drop of over 80%. The EU is now looking for long-term solutions to this problem. Its short-term measure to strengthen the ETS was to implement "back loading" of 900 million allowances, that is, to defer assessing payments due until the end of a significant time period. The EU Allowances system is an extremely complex financial infrastructure and has led companies to buy "futures" in credits in case their prices rise or they may not be available at certain periods.

The Clean Development Mechanism (CDM) works similar to the EU ETS. Generally, a polluting entity from a developed country can earn Certified Emission Reduction (CER) credits for investing in projects in a developing country, and each credit is equivalent to a ton of CO_2. CER credits are intended to count towards meeting Kyoto Protocol targets. As is the case for the EU ETS, CDM credits can be bought and sold. Though the EU ETS is run by the EU, the CDM and its related Joint Implementation (JI) mechanism is administered by the UN. The four chief benefactors of the CDM in 2013 were China, India, Brazil and Mexico; the largest investor into the system is the UK (United Nations, 2014).

The World Bank examined the CDM, EU ETS and other market-based systems, and found that such carbon pricing instruments can be effective. However, market-based systems do not always work in the manner or to the extent expected. It reported that instruments can be designed to be more cost-effective and flexible; linking can influence market behavior; levers that work for the private sector do not always deliver at government level; and that policy designers need to take systemic overlaps and interactions into account (World Bank, 2014c).

By 2013, 35 countries (including 28 in the EU) and a total of 20 states and provinces had enacted emissions trading programs; together, these cover about 8.5% of global Green House Gases (GHG) emissions (World Bank, 2014c).

2.3 Revenue Distribution from Carbon Levies

Some claim that environmental protection policies are regressive because they raise prices for the lower income classes and eliminate jobs. Slogans such as, "This will raise prices!" and, "Jobs will be lost!" have been popular in TV campaign ads by industries when fighting environmental initiatives. A recent example of such accusations took place when the oil and gas industry spent millions to attack anti-fracking initiatives in Santa Barbara and San Bernardino counties in California (Cart, 2014). Similarly, Australians recently voted a prime minister out of office on the issue of carbon taxation.

Industry opponents played up the word "taxes" pejoratively, and the opposition candidate promised to, "Ax the tax." The new government promptly got rid of the country's anti-carbon program, although two-thirds of Australian voters believe there should be a limit on carbon emissions. The California and Australia cases illustrate that voters may be emotionally swayed against carbon limits unless they can see near-term and understandable benefits, especially if powerful interests (oil companies in California and coal companies in Australia) use massive media buys to fight anti-pollution initiatives (Baird, 2014).

Although levies on carbon (whether a straight tax or ETF) can be regressive, there are ways to mitigate impacts. Williams (2014) and Gonzales (2012) found that the major determinant of the distributional effects of a carbon tax across income groups arises from the methods by which that revenue is recycled. For example, voters in California and Germany, where energy taxes are recycled to benefit the populace, have been supportive of carbon reduction initiatives, which have created many new jobs. Similarly, Costa Rica's revenues from its recently initiated carbon trading program are being used to pay thousands of landowners for reforestation and green energy projects. They also fund a bank (aptly named BanCO2!) for low-cost financing of energy-efficient cars and home energy retrofits. These are examples of high-visibility benefits that proved popular.

Gonzales (2012) examined other options for spending the proceeds from carbon emissions in Mexico, including a manufacturing tax-cut and food subsidies. He determined that costs are distributed regressively when revenue is recycled as a manufacturing tax and progressively when it is recycled as a food subsidy for the less wealthy. However, studies have shown that providing subsidized foods to poor or rural areas can negatively affect crop prices of local farmers and damage the economy (Oxfam, 2005). Neither of these two policies, thus, appears to be an attractive way to spend carbon revenues, compared to the strategy employed by Costa Rica and others, to stimulate local green initiatives.

Bowen (2011) analyzed different carbon pricing strategies. His policy recommendations included investing in R&D to promote innovation and appropriate infrastructure improvements, and funding for renewable energy projects.

3. Policy Analysis and Options

Mexico is moving ahead on carbon tax initiatives in order to reduce global climate change and its own high level of pollution. Its emissions level in 2010 was about 661 megatons of CO_2e, and its pledged emissions level for 2020 is 672 megatons, which is 30% below Business as Usual (BAU) levels. The current trajectory (unless the planned actions are actually put in place) for 2020 indicates a level of 800-845 $MtCO_2e$, which would substantially increase health costs and deaths from air pollution and other greenhouse gas effects. This is, therefore, a high-priority issue for Mexico. Major portions of its economy and tens of thousands of lives are at risk.

As stated, the strategic objective of Mexico's government is to achieve sustainable development, defined as a condition when climate stabilization policies trigger innovative solutions that drive economic growth and offer social benefits. As a result, the evaluative criteria for climate policy options should include: economic growth (renewable energy investment and job creation), social benefits (better health), and environmental improvement (reaching the desired CO_2 emission level and reducing air pollution). The aforementioned literature indicated three major policy options for Mexico that could achieve these criteria. These are reviewed below, with the assumption that similar conclusions could be drawn for other, though not necessarily all, Latin American countries.

3.1 A Carbon Pricing Option

A carbon tax has many advantages. First, the tax provides immediate revenue for the government, estimated at over $1 billion for Mexico. Second, it can be simple, transparent, and cost efficient. Third, a carbon tax provides an incentive to reduce emissions from present fossil fuel energy sources and encourages the use of more efficient alternatives. Finally, it can be an effective first step to carbon reduction before getting into the full complexities of an ETS.

Disadvantages include the possible decline of industrial competitiveness, uncertain emissions target, and the potential pushback of industry and consumers if they perceive they are being "taxed" only for vague, futuristic goals. The present Mexican implementation of a carbon tax appears to encourage moving to natural gas rather than green energy, since gas is not taxed, and is often cheaper than renewable energy alternatives. An inclusion of natural gas (as is practiced by Norway, Denmark, and others) in the taxation should be considered for the future. Without such an inclusion, Mexico cannot grow with "sustainable" energy, as is the stated goal.

The experience of other countries with a carbon tax, evaluated by the aforementioned criteria, is as follows: a) it is effective for environmental improvement (it reduced air pollution but may not have reached desired CO_2 emission level); b) it creates social benefits (better health); but c) it has little or no impact on economic growth, especially job creation.

3.2 An ETS Option for Mexico

An ETS can help achieve meaningful reductions in greenhouse gas emissions levels, since it is goal-oriented toward a maximum pre-determined emissions level. An ETS can be cost-effective because it recognizes that some companies can be more effective at reducing emissions than others and allows competitive market forces, rather than bureaucracy, to make adjustments while assuring the final goal. An ETS can also generate revenue for the government, although the amount may not be as predictable as income from a pure-form carbon tax.

One ETS disadvantage is that it can encourage industries that are addicted to fossil fuels to pollute more because it is possible to purchase cheap offsets or carbon credits rather than switch from fossil fuels to renewable energy. An ETS is complex to setup and administer, even with initial experience with a carbon tax system. It is also subject to major external shocks such as recessions, which can result in unpredictable carbon pricing and planning difficulties for industry.

For the three criteria, an ETS would a) benefit the environment (by decreasing air pollution, and presumably reach a desirable CO_2 emission level); b) would offer the social benefit of better health, from better air; and c) it has minor effects on economic growth, with negligible job creation.

The experience of other countries with an ETS that reacts purely to prices has been that no new or innovative technology has been produced, and the cheapest off-the-shelf renewable energy systems are usually imported and used. Without government support, the advancement of sustainable energy in Mexico with this option is liable to be limited, especially in rapidly evolving green technologies, such as renewable energy (RE) storage, micro-grids, RE linked to water purification or desalination, and non-opaque solar cells.

3.3 An ETS with Revenues Dedicated to Clean Energy

The benefits of an ETS, as well as its challenges, were aforementioned. If Mexico evolved from its carbon tax system to an ETS and earmarked the resultant revenues for true green energy (not natural gas) projects, that could provide many potential opportunities. This is the only option that meets all three criteria. It a) supports environmental improvement (both by reducing CO_2 to the desired level and air pollution); b) offers social benefits, including better health; and c) supports significant economic growth, including creating jobs by providing the tax revenues for green energy projects, including innovative research for pollution reduction via carbon storage or water purification systems. R&D funding of RE projects could advance the goal of making Mexico's economic growth sustainable.

Such funding could be greatly leveraged by not having the government pay the entire bill, but by forming Public Private Partnerships (P3) with industry. Experience has shown that leverage of 10:1 for green energy projects is possible with this schema; that is, the provision of $1 million by government for a project could attract $10 million from private industry (Cellucci & Grove, 2011). Energy is an especially good candidate for this, as RE is often marginally 10% more expensive than fossil fuel competitors. With the P3 support from government making up the difference, industry could be assured of successful competition for projects.

In short, Option 3 appears to have the greatest payoff for Mexico, and the best chance of helping it meet its goals for increasing economic growth sustainably, obtaining social benefits and reducing pollution both within the country and on a global basis.

4. Conclusion

Air pollution is a serious threat to the health and economic development of Latin America. Over 100 million people are breathing dangerously polluted air; over 14,700 deaths were caused by air pollution in Mexico alone in 2010 (Maxwell, 2013). The new government of Mexico, under President Nieto, has pledged to accelerate the drive to cut pollution, increase clean energy use, and reduce emissions by 30% by 2020 (Leme, 2014). To reach this goal, the Mexican government has implemented a carbon tax and is examining a market-based ETS. A carbon tax has been shown to be effective—if it is carefully managed and does not hurt the competitiveness of local industries (EU, 2013).

An even better energy policy option appears to be a transition to an ETS, with resultant revenues dedicated to developing green projects in Mexico, including innovative R&D to reduce pollution and produce clean energy on a continuous basis. The funding's effect could be multiplied by creating a P3 for R&D, critical to the nation and profitable for the investors.

If Mexico follows through on its announced initiatives, it could provide a model for other Latin American countries, which have made progress in some, but not all, of these areas. Brazil has expanded its clean energy, to 15% of its total consumption. Chile plans to increase RE to 20% of its total by 2020. Uruguay is starting major solar and wind projects. However, none of the other Latin countries appears to be as advanced as Mexico, with its comprehensive ambitions for pollution reduction and renewables support. It could, thus, serve as a model for success, if its leadership follows up on its promises. Vig et al. (1999) remind us that environmental policy develops under leadership rather than by public opinion. Mexico is showing Latin America and the world that it is becoming a leader in the post-carbon economy.

References

Baird, J. (July 24, 2014). A carbon tax's ignoble end: Why Tony Abbott axed Australia's carbon tax. *The New York Times*. Retrieved from: http://www.nytimes.com/2014/07/25/opinion/julia-baird-why-tony-abbott-axed-australias-carbon-tax.html?_r=0.

Bowen, A. (2011). *The case for carbon pricing*. London: Grantham Research Institute on Climate Change and the Environment.

Carolyn, F. et al. (2012). *Options for mitigating adverse carbon tax impacts on EITE industries*. Washington DC: American Enterprise Institute.

Cart, J. (November 29, 2014). Election win puts rural San Benito County on anti-fracking map. *Los Angeles Times*. Retrieved from: http://www.latimes.com/local/california/la-me-san-benito-fracking-20141129-story.html#page=1.

Cellucci, T.A., & Grove, J.W. (2011). *Leveraging public-private partnership models and the free market system to increase the speed-of-execution of high-impact solutions throughout state and local governments*. Washington, DC: Department of Homeland Security, Office of Science and Technology. Retrieved from: http://www.dhs.gov/xlibrary/assets/st-leveraging-partnerships-for-state-and-local-governments-August2011.pdf

The Economist. (December 14, 2013). Carbon copy. *The Economist Online*. Retrieved from: http://www.economist.com/news/business/21591601-some-firms-are-preparing-carbon-price-would-make-big-difference-carbon-copy.

Galbraith, K. (2013). A carbon tax by any other name. *New York Times*. Retrieved from: http://www.nytimes.com/2013/07/25/business/global/a-carbon-tax-by-any-other-name.html?

Gonzales, F. (2012). *Distributional effects of carbon taxes: The case of Mexico*. Energy Economics, 34, 6, 2102-2115.

King, E. (2014). *Mexico eyes economic benefits of landmark climate law*. Responding to Climate Change. Retrieved from: http://www.rtcc.org/2014/06/30/mexico-eyes-economic-benefits-of-landmark-climate-law/#sthash.7ggjndSh.dpuf.

Koronowski, R. (May 8, 2013). *A price is right: Carbon tax has very broad, bipartisan support (outside of Congress)*. Climate Progress. Retrieved from: http://thinkprogress.org/climate/2013/05/08/1702861/price-carbon-tax-broad-bipartisan-support-congress.

Makhijani, S. (2014). *Fossil fuel exploration subsidies: Republic of Mexico.* Washington, DC: Oil Change International.

Maxwell, A. (2013). *Outdoor air pollution is officially linked to cancer: What it means for Latin America and Mexico.* Switchboard. Retrieved from: http://switchboard.nrdc.org/blogs/amaxwell/outdoor_air_pollution_is_offic.html

Oxfam. (2005). *Food aid or hidden dumping? Separating wheat from chaff.* Oxford, UK: Oxfam International.

Richter, C. V. (2013). *Green growth challenges and the need for an energy reform in Mexico.* Paris: OECD.

Secretaria De Medio Ambiente y Recursos Naturales. (2014). *Carbon tax in Mexico.* Mexico: Semarnat.

United Nations. (2014). Clean Development Mechanism. *United Nations Framework Convention on Climate Change.* Retrieved from: http://unfccc.int/kyoto_protocol/mechanisms/clean_development_mechanism/items/2718.php.

Vig, N. J. et al. (1999). *Environmental policy: New directions for the twenty-first century.* Washington, DC: CQ Press.

Williams III, R. C. et al. (2014). *The initial incidence of a carbon tax across income groups.* Resources for the Future, 14–24.

Williams III, R. C. et al. (2012). *Choosing among carbon mitigation policies: Carbon tax, emissions trading, or traditional regulation.* Washington DC: American Enterprise Institute.

World Bank. (2014a). *Mexico.* Retrieved from http://data.worldbank.org/country/mexico

World Bank. (2014b). *GDP growth (annual %).* Retrieved from http://data.worldbank.org/indicator/NY.GDP.MKTP.KD.ZG

World Bank. (2014c). *State and trends of carbon pricing.* Washington, DC: International Bank for Reconstruction Development.

World Bank. (2014d). *Putting a price on carbon with a tax.* Retrieved from: http://www.worldbank.org/content/dam/Worldbank/document/SDN/background-note_carbon-tax.pdf.

Yale. (2014). *EPI Index 2014.* Newhaven, CT: Yale University.

Section I: Recommended Readings

Al-mulali, U., Lee, J. Y. M., Hakim Mohammed, A., & Sheau-Ting, L. (2013). Examining the link between energy consumption, carbon dioxide emission, and economic growth in Latin America and the Caribbean. *Renewable & Sustainable Energy Reviews, 26*, 42–48.

Carruthers, D. V. (2008). *Environmental justice in Latin America: Problems, promise, and practice*. Urban and Industrial Environments Series. Cambridge, MA: MIT Press.

López-Vallejo, M. (2017). A fragmented continent: Latin America and the global politics of climate change. *Review of Policy Research, 34*, 134–136.

Shawn, W. M. (2007). *An environmental history of Latin America*. New Approaches to the Americas Series. New York, NY: Cambridge University Press.

Vitz, M. (2018). *A city on a lake: Urban political ecology and the growth of Mexico City*. Radical Perspectives Series. Durham, NC: Duke University Press.

Section I: Post-Reading Questions

1   Discuss the link between climate change and Latin America's water wealth. What strategies are Latin American leaders using to secure freshwater resources in the region?

2   What are the positive and negative outcomes of a carbon tax as a policy aiming to reduce CO_2 emissions? Provide examples for both.

SECTION II

PREHISTORY AND EUROPEAN CONQUEST

Editor's Introduction

The readings in Section II provide a chronological and geographic exploration of the prehistory of Mesoamerica, the Caribbean Tainos, and the arrival and contributions of African slaves during Colonial times. Variations in environmental contexts, e.g., weather patterns, topographically derived altitudinal zonation, and biotic resources, enabled a long history of occupation, dating back at least 20,000 years ago. An array of particular human adaptations, from hunter-gatherers to sedentary communities, allowed for the development of multiple cultural regions and modes of sociocultural integration within particular ecological zones. Middle America gave rise to the cultural region of Mesoamerica encompassing an array of cultures and some state-level societies, including the Olmec, Maya, and the Aztecs. Walker's (2017) article concisely explores the major sociocultural developments and contributions of these Mesoamerican cultures.

The geographic region of the Caribbean was the setting of South American migrants, known as Taino or Arawak, who occupied the archipelago more than 7000 years ago. Hispaniola and Puerto Rico were the largest setting for these Taino chiefdom-level societies by the time of Columbus's arrival in 1492. The subsequent conquest and colonization of the Taino, along with the sociocultural and environmental devastation introduced by Europeans, is the topic discussed in Sued-Badillo's (2011) contribution to this section. With the inclusion of archaeological and historical sources, including Spanish administrative documents housed at the Archivo General de Indias in Seville, Sued-Badillo integrates a native's perspective in her narrative that strikingly differs from traditional accounts based on observation and riddled with biases.

Morgan's (2011) article addresses the Caribbean history of Africans arriving as slaves via the transatlantic slave trade. Variations in the magnitude and coastal origin of slaves imported throughout the Caribbean led to the development of diverse slave cultures shaped by imperial needs, a plantation economy, and timing. African slaves reached peak population numbers in the 18th century. The Middle Passage led to cultural transformation and adaptation, resulting in the formation of Creole cultures, new African ethnicities, and syncretic religions such as Vodou and Santeria. Systemic rebellion, resistance, and maroonage were symptomatic of the tensions and power struggles afflicting Caribbean slavery until the end of the institution of slavery in the 19th century.

Section II: Key Terms

Aztec

cabildos

caciques

Caribs

chiefdom

Cimarrones

Creole

inter-African syncretism

Libertos

Maroons

Maya

Mayan

Mesoamerica

Olmec

quinto real

repartimiento

shaman

Vodou

The Olmec, Maya, and Aztec

Renee Walker

Early Mesoamerica

Mesoamerica is an area of the New World that includes Mexico, Belize, Guatemala, El Salvador, Nicaragua, and Honduras. Similar to North America, Mesoamerica was settled by Paleoindian people during the Ice Age. Hunter-gatherers lived in seasonal camps and moved frequently to take advantage of regional resources. By around 6,000 years ago, many groups had domesticated maize (corn) from a wild plant known as teosinte (Flannery, 1976). Other early domesticates included beans, amaranth, and chili peppers. This period was known as the Formative period and was characterized by permanent villages with wattle and daub structures (wood and mud/clay), the appearance of pottery and specialized crafts, increased social stratification, increased population, increased trade, and the beginnings of a writing system (Flannery, 1976).

One early Mesoamerican village is San Jose Mogote, located in the Valley of Oaxaca and dating to around 3,400 years ago. The site covers around five acres and contains both domestic and public structures (Flannery, 1976). In addition to maize, amaranth, and chili peppers, avocados were also cultivated at San Jose Mogote. Excavations of the structures revealed that they were made from wattle and daub; they contained hearths, earth ovens, and stone tools for processing plants, known as manos (hand stones) and metates (bottom stones). Pits dug into the soil were used to store surplus crops, and pottery vessels were used for cooking and storage. Craft specialization at San Jose Mogote was focused on producing magnetite mirrors. Magnetite was acquired locally, manufactured into mirrors, and then traded as far away as the Gulf Coast.

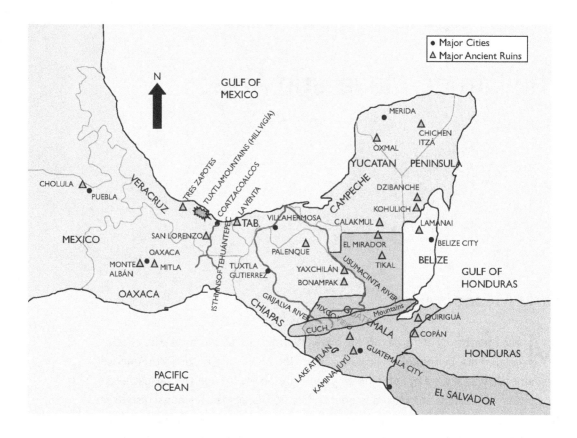

Figure 2.1.1   Map of Mesoamerica showing ancient sites and modern cities.

Some of the earliest writing also appears at the site of San Jose Mogote in the form of a glyph. Mesoamerican script uses glyphs (images) that represent words or sounds. It is often referred to as hieroglyphic writing, but Egyptian hieroglyphics and Mesoamerican script are not related (Coe, 1992; Scarre, 2013). Unlike Egyptian writing, there has not been a Rosetta Stone recovered for Mesoamerican script, so not all Mesoamerican writing has been deciphered. However, it is often depicted on stone monuments. In the Mayan and Aztec periods, discussed below, books called codices recorded religious rituals, dynastic information, and astronomical observations.

At the beginning of the Pre-Classic period, around 3,000 years ago, a culture known as the Olmec exhibited the earliest evidence of emerging political complexity (Evans, 2008). Located in the current area of Vera Cruz, along the Gulf Coast, the Olmec constructed a series of towns that had public architecture and populations of several thousand people. The Olmec people were known for their art, particularly, the carving of jade and other stone, elaborate ceramic vessels, and mirrors of polished iron ore (Evans, 2008). They are also known for erecting large stone head sculptures (known as colossal stone heads) in their towns that may have represented their leaders (Figure 2.1.2). The architecture of Olmec towns—such as San Lorenzo, La Venta, and Tres Zapotes—includes basalt tombs, central plazas and ceremonial platforms, and pyramids (Scarre, 2013). However, around 2,400 years ago, the Olmec towns were abandoned, many of the public structures were destroyed, and most of the colossal head monuments were mutilated and pushed over. It is unclear what caused this abandonment, but theories such as political unrest, external pressure, and climate change have been postulated.

Elsewhere in Mesoamerica, the large settlement at Monte Alban, located in the Oaxaca Valley, grew to a population of over 15,000 people by around 2,300 years ago. Known as the first city in Mesoamerica, the site was built on a ridge and included a city center with a central plaza, upper-class residences, stone platforms, and tombs. The site also had a stone wall built around the edge of the ridge. Many of the stone structures show human figures engaged in various activities, including dancing (called the Danzante figures), religious rituals, and conquests. Most of the population lived in houses built at the base of the ridge and there is also evidence of markets and craft specialization areas (Flannery, 1976).

Figure 2.1.2 Colossal Stone Head Monument at San Lorenzo.

Bibi Saint-Pol/Wikimedia Commons/Public Domain

Teotihuacan

In the Valley of Mexico, near present-day Mexico City, an enormous city developed to cover seven square miles. It was home to almost 125,000 people by around 1,500 years ago and was the dominant political structure for the entire basin (Scarre, 2013). Teotihuacan may have grown due to its strategic location with access to natural resources, such as obsidian for trade, springs for fresh water, and rich agricultural land. The site was laid out in a very strict grid pattern with a main street (known as the Avenue of the Dead) that went from north to south and an east-to-west cross street. Pyramids and temples were made from limestone then faced with lime plaster and painted. One of the main buildings is the Temple of Quezalcoatl (Temple of the Feathered Serpent), which contained over 200 sacrificial victims buried to consecrate the building.

Figure 2.1.3   Pyramid of the Sun, Teotihuacan, Mexico.

User: Jackhynes/Wikimedia Commons/Public Domain

The pyramids located along the Avenue of the Dead are similar in size and overall shape to Egyptian pyramids, but were made by piling up rubble then facing it with limestone in a "stepped" pattern, known as talud-tablero (an architectural style with a flat platform, or the tablero, and a sloped surface, or talud).

The largest is the Pyramid of the Sun (Figure 2.1.3.), located on the east side of the Avenue of the Dead, with the staircase facing west and aligned with the setting of the sun during the summer solstice (Evans, 2008). The pyramid was built over a cave that contained offerings, such as ceramic bowls and obsidian. Construction of the pyramid was conducted in two phases, the first completed approximately 1,900 years ago and the second completed around fifty years later, which resulted in an original height of 246 feet (although today it stands around 200 feet high) and a width of 738 feet (Scarre, 2013). The talud-tablero construction was probably covered with plaster and painted, though this has since eroded away.

The second-largest structure at Teotihuacan is the Pyramid of the Moon, which was built slightly after the Pyramid of the Sun at the northern apex of the Avenue of the Dead. The pyramid was around 140 feet tall after the fifth and final stage of construction was completed. Associated with this final stage is a burial that includes four human skeletons, animal remains, jewelry, ceremonial vessels, a turquoise mask, and obsidian blades.

Surrounding the ceremonial center of the city are over 2,000 residential structures. Many of these structures are laid out like compounds with houses and storage buildings connected with inner courtyards. Some were so large, they most likely housed up to 100 individuals who were probably related (Scarre, 2013). These buildings had adobe or stone rooms connected with passageways, plaster-lined floors, and drainage systems. In addition to residential buildings, some areas of the site suggest an artisan area where ceramic vessels, statues, turquoise and coral jewelry, and obsidian artifacts were made. Some artifacts from Teotihuacan are found as far away as Guatemala and Belize.

Beginning around 1,400 years ago, the population of Teotihuacan diminished and most construction at the site ceased. Archaeological evidence suggests that some of the central buildings and temples were burned around this time. By around 1,300 years ago, the site was abandoned. Theories for the decline and the abandonment of the city include external causes (warfare), internal strife, and drought. Warfare has been largely ruled out, because it was mainly the structures in the city center that were burned and not surrounding apartments and markets.

Internal causes may have been a factor. The destruction is similar to the case of the Olmec Culture, where people may have revolted against the ruling elite. Drought occurred in the area and may have been the reason behind a revolt. In any case, the city was completely empty by the time the Aztecs arrived. Hence, the name Teotihuacan means "City of the Dead" in the Aztec language, Nahuatl.

The Maya

Mayan cities developed in multiple ecological zones in southern Mesoamerica around 1,800 years ago. The Mayan cities were independent city-states, similar to the Mississippian cities of North America, and each had their own hereditary rulers, priests, armies, merchants, artisans, and farmers. The population was supported by trade and farming. Trade was facilitated by navigable river systems throughout the interior and also movement of goods up and down the Gulf and Pacific coasts. Farming was done by creating wetlands (often by flooding swamps and river floodplains) and planting up to three crops a year. Although the city-states were independent, the Maya shared a common written and spoken language, religion, and sociopolitical systems.

As mention previously, Mayan script is formed by glyphs that represent words and sounds. The Maya developed writing primarily to record the events in the lives of rulers, rituals, and astronomical events. In addition to written script, the Maya also had numbers and a calendar system. Numbers were recorded as an "eye" for zero, a dot for one, and a bar for five. The calendar system (also called the Calendar Round) consisted of two calendars, rotating together. The first was the astronomical calendar, which was 365 days long, composed of 18 months of 20 days each and five extra days at the end of each year. Another other calendar, known as the sacred almanac, was 260 days long and included 20 day names and 13 numbers (Evans, 2008). Each began at the same point, which marked the beginning of a "cycle." The conclusion of each cycle occurred after 52 years when the dates matched up again. When a cycle ended, it was an important event for the Maya and was marked by rituals, sacrifice, and the construction of monuments.

The Maya worshipped many different gods, and each day, month, city, and occupation had its own special deity. Some of the more important Mayan deities included Itzamna (the lord of the heavens), Kinich Ahuau (sun god), Chaac (rain god), Yun Kaax (god of corn), Ah Puc (god of death), and Ix Chel (goddess of the moon) (Evans, 2008). There were many different festivals and ceremonies in the Mayan religion and some of the rituals included blood sacrifice. Sometimes the kings would pierce their tongues or foreskin with stingray spines, bleed onto bark paper, and then burn the paper as an offering to the gods. In other cases, sacrifice was more drastic and involved human sacrifice. Some Mayan sculptures and bas-relief carvings on monuments show individuals being decapitated (Evans, 2008).

Another important ritual for the Maya was the ball game. While this game was probably invented in the Olmec region, the Maya incorporated the game into their myth of the "Hero Twins" who played the underworld gods in a ball game and won. The game was usually played in an I-shaped court with a solid rubber ball and between three and five players, though the rules varied throughout Mesoamerica (Scarre, 2013). Stone markers in the center of the ball courts may have been goals, but some ball courts have stone rings on the sides, like hoops in basketball, though the Mayan stone rings were vertical. Players wore special gear (depicted on stone monuments), including belts padded with cotton and helmets. The ball was moved by hitting it with the hips and maneuvering it to the goal. Ball courts are found through Mesoamerica and in some cases the game was probably more of a sport than a ritual ceremony, but there is evidence on some monuments of ball players being decapitated as part of rituals.

There were many important cities of the Classic Mayan Region. One of these was Copan, located in Honduras. It was a large city with two pyramids and a ball court. The pyramid at the north of the city center has a stairway (called the hieroglyphic staircase) that inscribes the history of the rulers. At the base of the staircase is a stela (stone marker) dated 756 A.D. that was dedicated by the fifteenth ruler of Copan, a man named "Smoke Shell" (Evans, 2008). Another important city was the city of Tikal, located in Guatemala. The city center contains multiple pyramids, palaces, north–south and east–west avenues, royal tombs, and a ball court (Figure 2.1.4). Tikal covers an area of around six square miles and was home to approximately 60,000 people at its height. It is located today in Tikal National Park, which preserves the city, and is also a nature preserve. The city of Palenque, located in southern Mexico, contains multiple buildings, monuments, temples, tombs, and a ball court. It is best known for the burial of Pacal in the Temple of the Inscriptions. Lord Pacal, whose name means "shield," ruled for 68 years and died at the age of 80. His tomb contained a massive stone coffin carved with Mayan script that celebrated his rule and he was interred with an elaborate jade mask.

Around 1,200 years ago, many of the Maya cities were depopulated and monumental construction ended. By 1,100 years ago, most of the cities were abandoned. Several factors may have caused the collapse including warfare, disease, peasant revolt, and drought. While drought has been well documented in the region at around the time of the Mayan collapse, not all of the cities were abandoned at the same time. Some cities have archaeological evidence to suggest warfare was the cause, some show disease and malnutrition (perhaps associated with the drought) caused a decline, and some sites indicate internal political unrest. It is likely that all

Figure 2.1.4 Temple I, Tikal, Guatemala (Image by Raymond Ostertag).

of these causes were factors and as cycles of warfare, drought, and disease erupted in the region, it weakened the power of the rulers. The Classic Mayan era cities were abandoned, but outlying villages and agricultural areas continued to be populated into historic times.

After the collapse of the Classic Maya in Southern Mexico, Belize, Guatemala, and Honduras, several cities evolve in the northern Yucatan. This begins the Post-Classic period of Mesoamerica. The largest city in the area is the site of Chichen Itza, which covers an area of five acres (Coe, 1999).

Figure 2.1.5 El Casitllo, Chichen Itza, at the spring equinox.

User: ATSZ56/Wikimedia Commons/Public Domain

The largest structure is named El Castillo, a stepped pyramid that is almost 100 feet high and around 180 feet wide at the base (Evans, 2008). Each side has a staircase; at the bottom of the northern staircase is the carved head of a serpent. The pyramid is aligned so that during the setting of the sun on the spring equinox, the sun casts a shadow on the northern staircase that resembles a serpent going down the side of the structure (Figure 2.1.5). Other structures at Chichen Itza include the Great Ballcourt, which is 551 feet long by 230 feet wide and has two stone rings on the sides of the court. There are also temples, including the Temple of the Warriors and the Temple of a Thousand Columns. Finally, the Sacred Cenote is part of the underground river system in the Yucatan, where frequently "sinks" or "wells" form and the water is accessible from the surface. There are other cenotes at the site that provided fresh water, but the Sacred Cenote contains sacrificial remains, including statues, gold, jade, and human remains.

Aztec Empire

In central Mexico during Post-Classic times, we see the development of a well-known culture called the Aztec. Prior to the Aztec, however, a group known as the Toltecs lived in the region north of Mexico City between 1,100 and 800 years ago. The capital of the Toltecs was Tula Grande, which covered four square miles with a population of 30,000–60,000 residents (Evans, 2008). The city is characterized as being focused on trade and there are many areas where craftspeople and merchants lived and worked. The city also contained stepped pyramids and structures of columns shaped like warriors called Atlantean figures. Tula Grande was burned and looted 800 years ago, possibly by civil war or conflicts with outside groups, and thus the Toltec empire collapsed.

At around the same time of the collapse of the Toltec, the people known as the Mexica, who originated to the north of Tula, began to move south into the Valley of Mexico. The mythical homeland of the Mexica was Aztlan. One Mexica legend tells that a leader named Tenoch had a vision from the war god Huizilopochtli who told Tenoch to lead his people until he found an eagle sitting on a cactus eating a snake. Once Tenoch found this site, he was to build a great city to honor the gods and the gods in turn would make the Aztec. Thus, the city was called Tenochtitlan and became the capital of the Aztec Empire in A.D. 1325 (Scarre, 2013). Now Mexico City, Tenochtitlan was located on an island in the middle of Lake Texcoco in the Valley of Mexico, and the city was connected to the mainland by a series of causeways. In addition to the causeways, the city had multiple canals that people navigated by canoe. The city center contained a great pyramid known as the Templo Mayor (Figure 2.1.6). The Templo Mayor had two shrines at the top, one to Huitzilopochtli and one to Tlaloc (the rain god). At the base of the pyramid was a sculpture of Coyolxauhqui (goddess who was leader of the star gods). On either side of the Templo Mayor are pyramids dedicated to the Huitzilopochtli and Tlaloc. In addition to the temples, there were also palaces and a central marketplace known as the Tlateloco. At its height the city was occupied by around 125,000 people and covered five square miles (Scarre, 2013).

The Aztec economy was based on agriculture and trade. The agricultural fields, called chinampas, were artificial islands built up between long, straight drainage canals along the shores of the lake. As the empire expanded (largely through military conquests), tribute from conquered territories was brought into the capital. Each Aztec town had markets and, according to records, they were open on certain days of the month. The Tlateloco, in Tenochtitlan, was probably open every day, however. According to the Spanish conquistador Bernal Diaz del Castillo (who arrived

Figure 2.1.6   Reconstruction of the Tenochtitlan.

User: Thelmadatter/Wikimedia Commons/Public Domain

with Cortés in the early 16th century), items exchanged in the market included agriculture products, ceramics, flowers, crafts, dogs (for food), and slaves (1956).

The Aztec kept track of trade and exchange, tribute paid to the rulers, and religious rituals in books called codices. Very few pre-conquest books survived, but there are also records compiled by the Spanish. One of the most famous is the Florentine Codex, which was compiled by the Spanish Priest Bernardo de Sahagun. The Florentine Codex consists of interviews Sahagun carried out with Aztec informants written both in Nahuatl, the native Aztec language, and Spanish (Evans, 2008). The text has twelve chapters, called books, and covers three themes: religion, sociopolitical issues, and natural history. One of the most disturbing things the codex records is the critical role of human sacrifice in Aztec ritual. The Florentine Codex provides detailed descriptions of how sacrifice is carried out and how it varied depending on what god was being honored.

Aztec society was organized with the kings and their families at the top of the hierarchy, then merchants, commoners and slaves in descending order to the bottom of the hierarchy. The records of the rulers begin in A.D. 1376, with a leader called Acamapichtli who ruled until A.D. 1391. The last ruler was Cuauhtemoc, who ruled from A.D. 1520–1525. The ruler at the time of the Spanish arrival was Moctezuma II, who ruled from A.D. 1502–1520 and expanded the empire to its maximum extent (Evans, 2008). Hernán Cortés arrived on the coast of Vera Cruz in A.D. 1519, sent by his cousin, the governor of Cuba, to explore Mexico. At the coast, he was given a female translator named Malinche (she knew Nahuatl and Mayan) who learned Spanish (Evans, 2008). Malinche is known as a traitor in Mexico today for helping Cortés in conquering Mexico, although some say she saved people by helping Cortés negotiate peacefully with some of the cities they visited. Moctezuma II heard of the Spanish arrival and sent gifts to them. Some scholars think that Moctezuma II may have thought that Cortés was the return of the god Quetzalcoatl (the feather serpent god), who was prophesied to return the same year that Cortés arrived, but other scholars dispute this claim (Restall, 2003). Eventually, Cortés made his way to Tenochtitlan where he was greeted by Moctezuma II and his nobles. At one point, Cortés had to leave the city to deal with another expedition of Spaniards that had arrived at the Coast of Vera Cruz. While he was away, there was fighting in the city between the Spaniards and the Aztec, so Cortés returned. Soon after his return, in A.D. 1520, Moctezuma II was killed (either by his own people or the Spaniards) and the Spanish were forced from the city. Cortés was joined by people from Tlaxcala, who were enemies of the Aztec, and together they laid siege to Tenochtitlan. The siege lasted for 85 days and ended when the Spanish captured the northeast section of the city and the last king of the Aztec, Cuauhtemoc, surrendered in A.D. 1521.

Bringing It Together

Mesoamerica is an area with a rich archaeological history. Beginning around 6,000 years ago, corn was domesticated and people began to settle in sedentary villages. One of the earliest of these villages is San Jose Mogote in the Valley of Oaxaca. Towns soon evolved, particularly in the Olmec area (gulf coast) and took on a characteristic layout with a town center, central plaza, pyramids, temples, stone monuments, and tombs. Some of the Olmec towns include San Lorenzo, La Venta, and Tres Zapotes. These cities often had colossal stone heads that may have been representations of their leaders. In western Mexico, a city called Monte Alban evolved and became home to around 15,000 people. Another large city, located in central Mexico, was Teotihuacan. Teotihuacan covered a large area and the city center included two large pyramids (one pyramid, the Pyramid of the Sun is the largest stone structure in the Americas), temples, tombs, and a central plaza, all connected by a main avenue laid out on a north–south axis. In southern Mexico, the Maya were a group of people who shared common language, writing systems, and religious beliefs. They built large independent city-states that contained pyramids, temples, palaces, tombs, and stone monuments. The Mesoamerican writing system flourished during the Mayan era and the Maya recorded astronomical events, had an advanced calendar system, and also recorded religious rituals and the history of their kings. After the collapse of the Classic Maya 1,100 years ago, large cities evolved in the northern Yucatan, including Chichen Itza, which has a large, astronomically aligned pyramid (known as El Castillo) and a ball court. In central Mexico, the Toltec Culture flourished beginning around 1,100 years ago. The Toltec built their capital, Tula Grande, in the Lerma and Tula river valleys. The Toltec were replaced by people from the north, known as the Mexica initially, but who later became the Aztec. The Aztec built a capital city in the valley of Mexico called Tenochtitlan, which had great temples to their war god and rain god and ruled over a vast territory covering much of northern and eastern Mexico. Despite their great power, in A.D. 1521, the Aztec people were conquered by the Spanish led by Hernán Cortés and Mexico became a Spanish ruled colony. The Aztec influence lives on in the modern Mexican people through language, culture, and traditions.

Discussion Questions

1   Who were the Olmec? Why were they known as the "mother of all Mesoamerican civilizations"?

2   What was the construction and development at the site of Teotihuacan?

3   Were the Maya a civilization or city-states? Explain why they should be categorized in the way that you chose.

4   What happened to cause the collapse of the Maya?

5   When and how did the Aztec civilization arise? What were some of the Aztec's accomplishments?

6   What do we know about Aztec religion?

7   What were the circumstances that led to the end of the Aztec empire?

Recommended Videos

Teotihuacan (Protele Inc, 1983).
In Search of History: Mexico's Great Pyramids (History Education, 1997).
The Maya: Death Empire—Engineering an Empire (History Education, 2006).
Montezuma: Twilight God of the Aztecs (BBC, 2009).
The Aztecs: Engineering an Empire (History Education, 2006).

Key Terms and Concepts

Mesoamerica	An area of the New World that roughly includes Mexico, Belize, Guatemala, El Salvador, Nicaragua, and Honduras.
Maize	Corn domesticated from a wild plant known as teosinte.
San Jose Mogote	An early Mesoamerican village, located in the Valley of Oaxaca and known for its production of magnetite mirrors.
Olmec	A culture known to exhibit the earliest evidence of emerging political complexity, located in the current area of Vera Cruz, along the Gulf Coast of Mexico.
San Lorenzo, La Venta, and Tres Zapotes	Olmec towns.
Colossal Head Monuments	Large basalt carvings of human heads, thought to represent Olmec leaders.
Monte Alban	A city in the Valley of Oaxaca.
Teotihuacan	A city located near the Valley of Mexico that covered seven square miles and was home to almost 125,000 people by around 1,500 years ago.
Talud-Tablero	Mesoamerican method for constructing pyramids that involved piling up rubble and then facing it with limestone in a "stepped" pattern.

Pyramid of the Sun	Located on the east side of Teotihuacan, the pyramid's staircase faces east and aligns with the setting of the sun during the summer solstice. The tallest stone pyramid in the Americas.
City-states	Independent Mayan cities had their own hereditary rulers, priests, armies, merchants, artisans, and farmers.
Mesoamerican Script	Uses glyphs (images) that represent words or sounds.
Mayan Calendar System	A calendar system (also called the Calendar Round) that consisted of two calendars, rotating together, called the sacred almanac (260 days) and the astronomical year (365 days).
Mesoamerican Ball Game	A game that is usually played by between three and five players in an I-shaped court with a solid rubber ball, though the rules varied throughout Mesoamerica. Stone markers in the center of the ball courts may have been goals, but some ball courts have stone rings on the sides.
Copan	A Mayan city, located in Honduras, that contains a large pyramid, which has a stairway that inscribes the history of the rulers and is called the hieroglyphic staircase.
Tikal	A Mayan city, located in Guatemala that contains multiple pyramids, palaces, north–south and east–west avenues, royal tombs, and a ball court.
Palenque	A Mayan city, located in southern Mexico, which contains multiple buildings, monuments, temples, tombs, and a ball court.
Pacal	Lord of Palenque, he ruled for 68 years and died at the age of 80; his tomb is in the Temple of Inscriptions.
Chichen Itza	A Post-Classic city in the Yucatan, Mexico, that covers an area of five acres and has a large pyramid (named El Castillo) that is almost 100 feet high and around 180 feet wide at the base.

Toltecs	A culture located in the Tula and Lerma river valleys north of Mexico City.
Tula Grande	The capital of the Toltecs, which covered four square miles with a population of 30,000–60,000.
Mexica	Originated in northern Mexico and eventually moved south to form the Aztec civilization.
Aztlan	Mythical homeland of the Mexica.
Tenoch	An Aztec leader who had a vision from the war god Huizilopochtli, who sent him on a quest to find an eagle sitting on a cactus eating a snake where he founded the city Tenochtitlan in honor of the gods.
Tenochtitlan	Capital of the Aztecs with a main temple (called the Templo Mayor) that had two shrines at the top, one to Huitzilopochtli and one to Tlaloc (the rain god).
Tlateloco	The marketplace in Tenochtitlan.
The Florentine Codex	A book by the priest Sahagun that consists of interviews with Aztec informants written both in Nahuatl, the native Aztec language, and Spanish.
Moctezuma II	The ruler at the time of the Spanish arrival who ruled from A.D. 1502 to 1520.
Hernán Cortés	Spanish conquistador who conquered the Aztecs in A.D. 1521 after arriving on the coast of Vera Cruz in A.D. 1519.
Malinche	Cortés's native female translator, who is considered a traitor in Mexico today.
Cuauhtemoc	The last king of the Aztec, who surrendered to Cortés in A.D. 1521 after an 85-day siege of the city.

References Cited

Coe, M. D. (1992). *Breaking the Maya code.* London: Thames & Hudson.

Coe, M. D. (1999). *The Maya.* (6th ed.). London and New York: Thames & Hudson.

Evans, S. T. (2008). *Ancient Mexico and Central America: Archaeology and Culture History* (2nd ed.). London: Thames and Hudson.

Flannery, K. V. (1976). *The Early Mesoamerican village.* Walnut Creek, CA: Left Coast Press.

Restall, M. (2003). *Seven myths of the Spanish Conquest.* Oxford: Oxford University Press.

Scarre, C., ed. (2013). *The human past: World prehistory and the development of human societies.* London: Thames and Hudson.

From Tainos to Africans in the Caribbean

Labor, Migration, and Resistance

Jalil Sued-Badillo

U ntil fairly recently, historians have based their research concerning the native societies and cultures of the Caribbean on two major types of sources—contemporary chronicles and histories, and Spanish administrative documents. While both are still considered invaluable fonts of data, their very nature is deeply problematic—a situation that has shaped traditional portrayals of Amerindian life in the precontact and immediate postcontact periods.

Chronicles have long been considered the starting point for Amerindian history and culture. Beginning with the writings of Christopher Columbus himself, this category of sources comprises wide-ranging observations made by contemporary travelers and other writers. But information from these sources is decidedly partial, contradictory, and problematic, particularly in regard to the native Tainos.

Of equal importance are the voluminous writings of the first "historians of the Indies," who recorded the process of conquest and colonization. One of the earliest, Peter Martyr, author of *De orbe novo* (in two volumes, the first published in 1511), never set foot in America but wrote from a privileged position at the Spanish court with access to important reports. In contrast, Gonzalo Fernández de Oviedo, author of the *General and Natural History of the Indies* (in five volumes, the first of which appeared in 1535), lived most of his life on Hispaniola, served important official positions, and wrote as a champion of Spanish colonial rule. Friar Bartolomé de las Casas, the most prolific of these historians, is best known for his brief *Account of the Destruction of the Indies* (1552), but less so for his major published works *History of the Indies* (1875) and *Apologetic History of the Indies* (1909). Although he was a witness to much of what he wrote about, he drafted much of it late in life, in constant struggle with his memory.

Jalil Sued-Badillo, "From Tainos to Africans in the Caribbean: Labor, Migration, and Resistance," *The Caribbean: A History of the Region and Its Peoples*, ed. Stephan Palmié and Francisco A. Scarano, pp. 97–113. Copyright © 2011 by University of Chicago Press. Reprinted with permission.

Of particular interest is *An Account of the Antiquities of the Indians*, a brief but significant account of some religious beliefs of the Tainos in Hispaniola, written by Friar Ramón Pané in 1494. This very first "ethnographic" report drafted on American soil has had an erratic history. The Taino *caciques* (chiefs) were interviewed through interpreters, and the work itself was published in an Italian translation only in 1571. Even aside from the great confusion admitted by Pané in the organization of his early notes, or the different versions of key Amerindian names and place names in each subsequent translation or transcription, the reliability of this work is obviously questionable.

The same can be said of all the other chronicles. They were not systematic studies, and they were often based on casual observations. Many are riddled with cultural biases, exaggerations, omissions and, worse yet, contradictions. This becomes obvious when, for example, comparing Oviedo's work with that of Las Casas. These authors were at opposite ends of the political spectrum of their times, yet no serious historian can do without them.

Far more important than the writings of early chroniclers and travelers are the Spanish administrative archives—primarily the Archivo General de Indias in Seville, which remains the most important source of information on Spain's colonial empire. Containing extensive but rigorous records of everyday affairs, judicial documents, official and private correspondence, reports, testimonies, policy papers, census records, and other facts and figures, its holdings include invaluable data on Amerindian cultures, particularly those on Hispaniola. But, like the chronicles, these documents were created by Spanish officials with at best an imperfect understanding of the people whose lives they were documenting, and often with patently ideological motives.

Only recently have archaeologists and ethnohistorians begun to reconstruct Amerindian societies from a perspective aimed to approach that of the natives themselves. Although contemporary knowledge of the Caribbean as it existed in 1492 is becoming more sophisticated and interdisciplinary, it is still one-sided at best.

The Tainos

Historians do not know what the native populations of the Caribbean named themselves. The designation *Taino* is a modern label now applied to a variety of ethnic groups coexisting in the Caribbean archipelago at the end of the 15th century. The term, recorded first off the coast of Haiti and later in Guadeloupe as hearsay, is said to have meant "good or noble Indians," but this meaning has not been linguistically confirmed. The application of this term to the original inhabitants of the Greater Antilles has been a recent practice by historians and archaeologists, mainly those in the Spanish-speaking Caribbean; their North American counterparts have usually preferred the term *Arawak,* also a modern label. Whatever its origin, the collective term at least acknowledges that, in spite of their diversity, the people of the Caribbean region had more characteristics in common than differences.

The islands had been inhabited for more than 7,000 years, having been populated initially in several waves of migration from South and Central America. The last of these migrations occurred from 500 BCE to 300 CE, bringing horticulturalists and proficient pottery makers from Amazonian and Andean backgrounds. They introduced lasting cultural essentials such as language (Arawak), religious symbolism, family structure, economic strategies and products, animals, and metallurgy and pottery making, all to be further developed on the islands. The term *Taino* has been reserved for the people of the last stage before the European conquest and limited to the regions where more social and cultural complexity was achieved; their predecessors are referred to in the archaeological literature as *pre-Tainos*. By the middle of the first millennium CE, pre-Tainos were establishing a new cultural scenario reflecting their progress in adapting to the insular environment and its challenges. The ethnic fusion of the new continental horticulturalists with the original and poorly understood "Archaic" population of the islands transformed the latter's cultures and ushered in new social formations.

Perhaps the most conspicuous center for this process of transculturation, as the Cuban scholar Fernando Ortiz was to call it, was the island of Borinquén (today's Puerto Rico). The smallest of the Greater Antilles, Borinquén was the foremost boundary of the last wave of continental migrations to the insular Caribbean. Its territory proved suitable for slowing down migratory expansion and allowing for the effective integration of newcomers with natives. Borinquén thus experienced ethnic admixtures more comprehensively than other islands, and produced the formative social configurations for the future Taino culture. Migration and other forms of influence from Borinquén toward the Greater and Lesser Antilles acted as a cultural vector and induced a basic cultural uniformity throughout the archipelago.

Two islands were the prime centers of Taino social complexity in the Caribbean: Haiti-Quisqueya (today's Hispaniola, including Haiti and the Dominican Republic), whose sphere of cultural influence also included eastern Cuba and Jamaica, and Borinquén, whose social formation extended into eastern Quisqueya and the Lesser Antilles as far back as Guadalupe. The diffusion of pre-Taino cultural traits from Borinquén, probably beginning around 400 CE, was made possible by the emergence of a chiefdom-like political formation on that island. This regional form of government, transcending smaller tribal boundaries, first appeared in the southern coastal valleys of the island, slowly spreading to the mountainous interior and outward to the neighboring islands.

This type of social arrangement is often considered a forerunner to state formation and has been extensively discussed by modern anthropologists, but its operation remains elusive. Agreement seems to exist that among the Tainos and others like them, a chiefdom was a thickly populated region with multiple communities that were organized politically and hierarchically and subordinated to a center. Such political formations are considered to have been geographically expansionist and war-prone while zealous of their formal frontiers; their paramount chiefs are also considered to have acted as high priests, with religion more than force as the basis of their authority. Such chiefs, known as *caciques*, were polygamous (as attested to by most chroniclers) and highly respected figures who mainly acceded to their positions through inheritance.

The governed communities paid tribute mainly in the form of services rendered to the chiefs in agricultural labor, occasional ceremonial constructions, and conscription in case of war. But the chiefs did not control productive activities. They had neither standing armies nor permanent bureaucracies, and close family members acted as occasional administrators, envoys, and key allies.

Kinship structure was matrilineal—that is, the succession to inheritance and rank ran through the mother's side in an arrangement that permitted women to participate in public activities and assume political status as *cacicas*. In Puerto Rico, 12 cacicas have been identified in the historical sources. In Hispaniola, dozens are listed in census reports dating from the early years of colonial occupation, and Anacaona, sister of a former high provincial chief from Jaragua, inherited the rank and ruled over a large number of vassal polities. The participation of women in the political and religious realm makes the Tainos heirs to an ancient and conspicuous Andean practice traceable from Peru to the Antilles and abundantly observed and recorded in the 16th century (Sued-Badillo 1985, 2007).

In Puerto Rico, only one chiefdom governing about two-thirds of the island appears to have existed in 1492. Its central enclave, known as Cayabo, was in the modern southern region of Ponce, and the reigning family bore the name of Agüeybana. The rest of the island apparently remained in the hands of local tribal chiefs, who sought Spanish protection from the lead chiefdom's encroachment. In Hispaniola, most of the island was divided among five large polities— Jaragua, Maguá, Maguana, Marién, and Cayacoa or Higüey—while some of its more isolated regions remained locally independent. In the principal islands, then, the chiefdoms apparently had not yet realized the formation of a political status, which would have implied a much wider and more effective integration beyond the immediate region. A permanent bureaucracy and army, a religion with temples and priests engaging in practices beyond traditional shamanic ceremonies, and forced regular tributes on production and on services (beyond occasional ones) were all things that did not yet exist.

In the absence of formal social classes, public inequalities and an elite structure beyond nuclear kinship were beginning to develop in Haiti and Borinquén, and the fabrication and circulation of sumptuary goods were likely controlled by the caciques for prestige and social status. But a state system organized to control and exploit the general population existed only in parts of Mexico and Peru. In Cuba and Jamaica there is evidence not even of chiefdoms, but only of a still-dominant "tribal" (or kinship-based) social structure and a very limited political geography. Most Spanish observers concurred that Hispaniola had a population of more than a million inhabitants by 1492. Along with Puerto Rico—perhaps the more densely populated of the two principal islands—it harbored the Tainos' most impressive material and artistic expressions, which validated their political significance.

But the Tainos' main social achievements came in their effective and ingenious management of their environment. Tropical lands are not paradisiacal; the welfare of their inhabitants depends on their ability to utilize diverse resources efficiently. The Tainos had evolved from horticulture or food gardening to intensive and diversified agriculture with strategies including raised fields, mound planting (*conucos*), crop rotation, water canals, fish traps, and slash-and-burn techniques,

Figure 2.2.1 A cacique on the island of Cuba leads his people in negotiations with Columbus. Engraving by Benjamin West and Francesco Bartolozzi (1794). *Source:* **The John Carter Brown Library.**

and they went on to exploit varied ecological niches for different crops, like mangroves and reefs (Newsom and Wing 2004). In Puerto Rico the Spanish observed a Taino preference for cultivation on hillsides, contrary to practices in Hispaniola. The result was a rich and diverse production of staple foods, grains, and vegetables that, coupled with successful hunting and fishing, provided a balanced caloric intake, definitely superior to that of most Europeans.

The Tainos also had varied animal assets, both wild and domesticated. Marine species came to the island mangroves or estuaries and were caught in fish traps for consumption over time. Domesticated animals included guinea pigs, bush rats (*hutías*), dogs, and doves and other exotic birds. Edible wild resources included crabs, shellfish, iguanas, seals, manatees, land and sea turtles, and birds. The forests supplied rich woods for construction and fuel, resins, medicines, fruits, seeds, fibers, narcotics, dyes, and a long list of other resources. Of complementary importance, the islands were rich in all types of rocks: chert and quartz, granite, marble, jadeite, jasper, and a fair share of semiprecious stones. This permitted a long tradition of superb stonework, including unsurpassable religious icons, petroglyphs, and numerous stone artifacts.

The Tainos substantially modified their environment, making the land and sea work for them. In contrast, lack of prior experience in tropical environments greatly limited Spanish agricultural colonization of the islands. Many of Iberia's main native farming techniques and products were not reproduced for decades, and some foods—like wheat, olives, and grapes—would not be introduced successfully for centuries, thus allowing the survival of many Taino food products and even their planting techniques. Taino root crops, as well as cultigens such as maize, tobacco, peanuts, native fruits and herbs, drugs, and beverages, are still common in the modern Caribbean. The Taino world has been an intrinsic part of Caribbean historic memory and modern national identities—if not biologically, then certainly culturally and spiritually. Today it represents the world before colonialism, a kind of idealized, mythical past suggesting that if life was better in the past, it can also be better in the future.

The Encounter

Beginning with the conquest of the Caribbean islands, European expansion to the New World was one of the first chapters of modern colonialism. The Tainos were fated to be among the first Amerinidans to be conquered and directly exploited by a distant and culturally distinct power. The political and economic forces responsible for this major thrust naturally transcended the microcosm of Columbus's life and Castilian politics. They encompassed a massive transformation of the Old World itself. In only 60 years after 1492, Europe shifted from a multiplicity of small warring kingdoms into a handful of strong monarchies building competitive nation-states and expanding frontiers. Commercial cities dominated the seas and established ties with hitherto unthinkable partners. The fragmentation of Christianity, the intense rivalry with the emerging Ottoman Empire, population growth, recurrent agricultural crises, and the need for currency to compete commercially—all these factors were involved in the forces in Europe that took Columbus to the land of the Tainos in 1492.

It is no exaggeration to say that the fate of the New World was sealed by the few golden trinkets Columbus found on the necks and ears of the first Amerindians encountered in the Lucayan islands—not because of any unique Spanish obsession with gold, as Black Legend advocates traditionally argued, but because gold and silver were the Old World's commercial lubricants at a time when trade was reshaping economic and political geography. In the 15th century, precious minerals were as important as crude oil is today. The same interest groups that drove Columbus and others to explore far and wide were motivated by an accepted bimetallic monetary system (gold and silver) that permitted trade among the most diverse economies. Europe lacked gold deposits, and depended for them on unreliable intermediaries. The kingdoms of the Spanish Peninsula, notably Castile, had a notably disorganized monetary system supported by too little gold.

Prior to Columbus's voyages, Castile had been bracing to conquer territories in North Africa to obtain the precious mineral then filtering from the interior of that continent into the hands of Italians, Arabs, and Portuguese merchants. The Catholic Monarchs had devoted much effort to monetary reforms and economic enterprises that could assure them a more competitive position. So, when Columbus returned and informed the monarchs of new lands—greatly exaggerating the first amounts of gold found—their response was immediate and positive. A mere nine months after the first voyage, Columbus returned to the islands in command of 17 ships carrying a variegated crew of nearly 1,500 passengers.

The promise of gold determined the fate of the new lands. Ethnic groups were classified according to the mineral importance of their lands and their disposition to collaborate with exploration ventures or hinder them. If lands were labeled as "useless"—that is, with no tangible assets to be obtained—their populations could be removed by force to places where labor was needed. Such were the cases of Jamaica, Aruba, Curaçao and Bonaire, the Bahamas, and large stretches of the Venezuelan coast during the early 16th century. The prior cultural identities of native communities perished under these coerced migrations. The most notorious case of such identity theft was that of the "Caribs," a label that came to be used to criminalize different groups throughout the Caribbean and on the American mainland in order to legally justify violent measures against them.

Beginning in the first years of the 16th century, Hispaniola, Puerto Rico, and Cuba became primary mining centers, their native populations coerced into exploration, porterage, clearing and constructing, extraction, and smelting and shipping of ore. The costs of conquest and exploitation were nearly unmanageable for a poor and distant Catholic kingdom with a weak agricultural tradition that was primarily oriented toward livestock. Although the earlier Spanish conquest of the Canary Islands had set a limited precedent, no kingdom in Spain possessed significant experience with tropical environments or large forced-labor enterprises. Consequently, agriculture and animal husbandry were initially neglected, and food and tools came primarily as cheap imports from Seville—salted sardines, wine, oil—sold at highly inflated prices in the Caribbean.

Some time later, interisland trade slowly began to provide substitutes for some imports. Cassava replaced wheat bread, lard supplanted oil, and local fishing and animal husbandry—mainly swine—supplanted salted meat products. Iberian diets reflected in the early import trade of the islands did not replicate the variegated foodways of the large, ethnically mixed Andalusian population. Instead, the traditionally sober diet of Christians in the countryside of central and northern Spain—which lacked grains like rice, contained very little meat, and rejected spicy products—was imposed on the insular populations, to their despair and considerable suffering.

Meanwhile, the high cost of metal implements led to the practice of forcing Amerindian workers to till, dig, and labor with their own stone tools, greatly increasing their hardship—a practice denounced by Las Casas and his followers. Finally, the *encomienda* system, which distributed natives as workers among the colonizers, removed them from their traditional food collecting and agricultural activities. When they returned from the mines to their villages nine or ten months later, they had no food available. Rest periods were times of widespread famine. At least during the conquest period, natives also seem to have rejected Spanish salted meat products, and there is no evidence that they raised or consumed animals brought by the Europeans.

After 1508, coinciding with the conquest of Puerto Rico—the second island after Hispaniola to be occupied—private merchants were allowed to trade with the colony, and the encomiendas (also known as *repartimientos*), a system of Indian labor allocation, in essence transferred the administration and care of the natives (including in the spiritual realm) to the private sector. These encomiendas effectively signaled the monarchy's admission of its inability to assume full responsibility for colonial enterprises. With the subsequent conquest of other islands, the task of organizing the economic exploitation of the new territories fell to an ill-equipped assortment of persons and groups, including soldiers of fortune, clergymen, artisans, merchants, part-time urban laborers, and overseers of leading administrators, locally and abroad. The monarchy reduced its required share of benefits to the famous *quinto real* (royal fifth, or 20% of gold minted) and withdrew from directly participating in mining.

Much attention has been given to the study of the encomienda system in the Antilles without rooting it in mining, the primary economic activity of the period. However, subtle differences in its implementation on the different islands were entirely irrelevant to the fate of the natives: all the mining islands experienced significant population decline. When the islands inhabited principally by Tainos were afflicted around 1518–20 by smallpox epidemics, apparently brought into the Caribbean by the first direct slave shipments from Africa, their populations had already dramatically diminished. The census of 1514 on Hispaniola gave ample proof of this, as did the intensity of the slave raids sent from the mining islands to seek replacements.

As the underfed and overworked natives perished, armadas were sent to loot and capture slaves in the region in a way much like the earlier practice of pillage and plunder throughout the Mediterranean. Between 1510 and 1542, tens of thousands of enslaved natives were violently extracted from the Guianas to the region of present-day Colombia, and also from Costa Rica to Florida. The legal excuse covering most of these expeditions was the capture of "Caribs" (a name etymologically equivalent to "cannibals"), who supposedly were a menace to "peaceful" natives and had proven reluctant to accept Christianity. Indians who had resisted relations with the Spaniards were also labeled "Caribs." Slaves were even brought from Mexico in exchange for cattle raised on the islands.

The amount of gold extracted from Hispaniola, Puerto Rico, and Cuba—in that order of importance—and legally exported to Spain between 1500 and 1550 has been estimated at 50 to 60 tons, and it probably represented one-fifth of all the gold shipped from the Spanish empire during the 16th century. But as the first colonial venture of their kind, the islands suffered from metropolitan inexperience, lack of capital, and absence of the infrastructure necessary for mining activities, which Mexico and Peru would both possess decades later. Lack of mining implements, experienced technicians, and roads, along with poor logistics, plagued the mining experience on the islands. Of equal importance was the lack of labor legislation and work regulations that only later were put into practice on the continent. The wealth extracted from the Taino islands by Taino hands, in a relatively short period under such brutal conditions, explains the truly genocidal population decline in the region, openly admitted by Charles V in 1526 when he blamed the repartimiento/encomienda system for its share in that human tragedy and tentatively barred its implementation in Mexico.

Gold mining remained the primary economic activity in the major Taino islands until past the mid-16th century, when it was overshadowed by gold and silver mining in Peru, Colombia, and Mexico. This economic phase lasted much longer than was once believed by historians, who assumed, for example, that with the conquest of Mexico the new territory immediately opened up its mineral wealth. Mexican ores were discovered and exploited only decades after the fall of Tenochtitlan, so that initial conquest did not displace the insular Caribbean as the main gold producer. Nor did the conquest in Central America, from Panama to Guatemala, yield profitable colonies until the second half of that century. Instead, during the initial phase, much of this geographic expanse became rewarding for Amerindian slavers who aimed to supply the labor needs of mining industries in the insular Caribbean. During the late 1530s, Colombia and Peru began to reorient this human traffic away from the islands, forcing gold miners and sugar planters to take recourse in African slavery.

Establishing the factual chronology of conquest and colonization permits a more realistic and holistic understanding of these events and their consequences. Taino societies were subjected to a massive alteration of their existence and culture for nearly half a century. They were victims of forms of violence ranging from forced labor to population displacements; of deliberate dismemberment of communal structures and warfare; and of the often overstated factors of disease, hunger, deprivation, and mistreatment. Their tragedy was not the result of unavoidable forces of nature at play. Dramatic human consequences can come about from natural causes, such as ecological changes triggering population displacements, epidemics, and the like. But the Taino tragedy was the result of an organized economic venture, planned and executed quite consciously by its continental planners, who deliberately took the human costs involved into consideration. The Taino people did not succumb on contact with the first colonizers; their physical and cultural constitution was not as frail as has often been claimed. They perished under the onslaught and callous demands of an internationally ramified economic system, which, while still evolving, was nevertheless proving its capacity to conquer and subdue people and extract significant material benefits. The Tainos were thus the first victims of the social experiment of modern capitalism, and the native Caribbean was where the dynamics between "core" and "peripheral" regions of what became the capitalistic world system were first effectively experienced.

This first capitalistic enterprise in the Antilles was not limited to mining operations, but also generated complementary activities and a well-knit economic network. Pearls were extracted from the fringe islands of the eastern Caribbean—Cubagua, Margarita, and Coche—to which hundreds of Tainos were forcefully removed. The traffic in slaves became an economic enterprise of its own, intermingling dozens of ethnic groups while depopulating vast coastal regions in Venezuela, the Lesser Antilles, the Bahamas, Guyana, Panama, and Nicaragua. Ponce de León's "discovery" of Florida was accomplished during a slaving expedition in which the governor of Cuba, Velázquez, also participated. The need for local food supplies forced large contingents of Tainos to spend their very short periods of rest away from the mines in agricultural tasks or animal husbandry, both of which were very profitable activities for the white elite. Salted fish was traded on the Venezuelan coast, along with slaves. Wooden plates (*bateas*) used to pan gold in the rivers were handmade by natives in Hispaniola and sold in Puerto Rico. Jamaican Tainos ended up on other islands. And of course, an extremely rewarding commerce that involved the coming and going of dozens of ships every year to the Antilles to supply the growing number of colonizers was maintained through Andalusian intermediaries. This was an activity that produced important customs taxes (*almojarifazgo*) for the crown and a large array of goods for the settlers.

Blacks and Gold

Tainos and other Amerindian slaves brought from different parts of the Caribbean region also participated in the first labor-intensive sugar plantations created in Hispaniola around 1520 and in Puerto Rico in the 1540s. The traditional view that mining labor was limited to Amerindians and sugar labor to black slaves is far from correct. Blacks began their ordeal in the Caribbean by working in the mines, and natives lasted long enough to be forced into plantation agriculture, another economic venue that proved as profitable in Europe's progressive accumulation of wealth as it was painful for its coerced labor forces in the New World. By the 1560s, more than 50 sugar mills in Hispaniola and Puerto Rico exported more sugar to Andalusia than did their much larger Mexican counterparts. Being closer to Seville, the islands had a competitive advantage which permitted them to satisfy the demand for sugar in the only legal market in Spain. Aside from this geographical advantage, their greater importance as sugar exporters can be explained only by the intensity of the productive operations that rested on the backs of Africans and Indians.

Although Tainos helped the Spaniards locate the gold-producing regions and became the primary workforce in them, the general logistics associated with placer mining were strained by the Spaniards' inability to communicate effectively with the natives. This factor, more than any other, probably prompted the early introduction of black slaves from the Iberian Peninsula. Being fully assimilated into Christian culture, and fluent in the colonizer's language—many of them having been born in Castile or Portugal—these *ladino* slaves became an important asset in the new colonial scenario. Together with the ladinos also came free blacks (*libertos*), who were not socially different from other poor Spanish Christians migrating to the new frontier in search of a better life. The libertos fared quite well, but for the black slaves life on the islands was a nightmare. Toiling in a harsh tropical environment far from home proved tragic for them.

Figure 2.2.2 Slaves mining for gold under the watch of Spanish soldiers. Engraving from *Americae pars quinta* **(1595). Source: The John Carter Brown Library.**

As early as 1503, ladino slaves were reported to have run away in Hispaniola and were described as exerting a negative influence on the native inhabitants. And in 1514, the first of several ladino uprisings occurred quite unexpectedly in Puerto Rico, where gold production was reaching very high levels. Probably a strong hurricane that year was a precipitating factor. In any case, the event clearly represented the first black slave uprising in the New World. In 1521 another one occurred in Hispaniola, and thus began a tradition of resistance throughout the slaveholding Americas.

Slave labor of the scale and intensity organized in the first Caribbean colonies had no counterpart or antecedents in Europe. Mining and sugar making were both labor-intensive, a fact that imposed a distinctly new style of slavery throughout the Americas—more ruthless, more demanding, and insensitive. The Antilles had not been its first laboratory. The practice of using African slaves to produce sugar in large quantities had originated on Atlantic islands such as Madeira or São Tomé, but the Caribbean islands were where this economic combination acquired much of its historic force and social characteristics.

Modern plantation systems began to take shape in the Spanish Antilles during the 16th century based on enslaved Indians and Africans, who often were intermingled in an ethnic cauldron of hitherto unknown proportions. By 1560, for example, Hispaniola and Puerto Rico had a combined African slave population of some 45,000, not including clandestine groups of Amerindians of various origins. Such numbers of enslaved workers, applied primarily to operations like mining or sugar, were not to be found elsewhere in the hemisphere during that century.

Indians and black slaves—who began to arrive directly from Africa in 1518, according to very exact Spanish documentation—formed a variety of relationships with each other. Some ladinos and enslaved Africans sided with the Tainos and other ethnic groups against the Spaniards; some allied themselves with conquistadors against the Indians. Their life expectancy was terribly short. Few enslaved Africans were able to form families or survive long enough to transform their wretched existence into lasting forms of collective life. Given the high death toll in the mining camps and sugar fields, African slaves were constantly replenished in a vicious transcontinental economic cycle. Nonetheless, personal names of noted maroons (escapees) were always heard throughout the islands, and strong clues about the survival of many black runaways among the "Caribs" (surviving and regrouping Amerindians) of the Lesser Antilles are being uncovered. Only small groups of Creole or mulatto slaves were able to survive, but while they eventually came to constitute an important segment of Caribbean colonial societies during the late 16th century, that process was painfully slow. The overall creolization of Caribbean societies had to wait until almost a century after the conquest, when the dynamic export economies of the larger islands had collapsed and the large cattle ranches (*hatos*) that sprang up throughout the Spanish Greater Antilles significantly attenuated slavery's importance and established a less harsh and demanding life for the enslaved.

Resistance to Conquest

The myth of the easy conquest of the Caribbean islands, the submissive character of their inhabitants, their hospitable nature, and their dire need for protection against invading barbarians bent on devouring their victims has persisted to this day. This colonial version of the events and relations between the European invaders and the Tainos has become entangled with latter-day historical and anthropological accounts to a degree where it has gained widespread acceptance, both abroad and in the Caribbean itself. Yet the original facts of the European-Amerindian encounter have long been distorted and deformed for ideological reasons. This is so because that same period witnessed the forging of the colonial justifications for the conquest of America itself, and the emergence of political discourses used to legitimize European rule in the New World.

The Greater Antilles were the first battleground in the European conquest of the Americas. Many lives were lost in military encounters that lasted for decades. Resistance began with the burning of Columbus's first settlement in Hispaniola, La Navidad, and the killing of all 39 of its residents by warriors of the chief Caonabo in 1492. Most provinces in every island have

Figure 2.2.3 Spanish conquistadors burning a resistant native at the stake. Engraving based on an account by Friar Bartolomé de las Casas (1620). *Source:* **The John Carter Brown Library.**

their tales of local heroic caciques and brave or desperate deeds in defense of their home-lands. After Caonabo, the epic figures in Hispaniola are Guarionex, Cotubanama, Guarocuya, Mayobanex, and Enriquillo. In Puerto Rico, where official commemorations have traditionally downplayed Amerindian symbols, popular recognition of local caciques represents an almost intuitive respect for the precolonial past, thus challenging official discourses. For more than 200 years, poets and political dissidents have kept alive a strong sense of admiration for the warring caciques Agüeybana el Bravo, Urayoán, Guarionex, Comerío, Humacao, and others. And long-overlooked, newly discovered documents from the Archivo de Indias in Seville attest to the intense resistance in Borinquén and a high toll of lives on both sides, with evidence of the burning of the first Spanish towns of La Aguada (1511), Caparra (1513), and Santiago (1513), followed by relentless guerilla warfare which, as on the other islands, lasted until the 1530s. In Cuba, meanwhile, Hatuey and Guama have long been recognized as national figures.

Chronicles and administrative documents, furthermore, confirm the conquest's policy of violence, followed from the outset, against the reluctant caciques. Beginning with Columbus's

Figure 2.2.4   Natives committing suicide to escape Spanish brutality. Engraving from Theodoro de Bry, *Americae pars quarta* (1594). *Source:* The John Carter Brown Library.

reaction to Caonabo's rebellion in Hispaniola and the subsequent enslavement and shipment to Spain of several thousand Tainos, some native victims of Spanish reprisals were even condemned to row in the infamous galleys of the Mediterranean.

Events such as these reveal the falseness of the image of the Tainos' supposedly docile character and their incapacity to defend their lands—a trait applied to Puerto Ricans in colonial discourse to this very day. But the violent nature of the "encounter" also reveals and dramatizes the intolerance and bigotry of the conquistadores toward culturally different groups, their historical record of hostility to cultural dissidence, and their turbulent religious experience with non-Christians. It dramatizes the limitation of material resources at the onset of their historic entrance to the New World and their inclination to treachery and deceit.

Las Casas denounced the early practice in Hispaniola of killing local chiefs to provoke uprisings that justified punitive and enslaving measures. In 1500, Governor Nicolás de Ovando planned and executed the death of more than 80 caciques in the kingdom of Jaragua (Haiti) who had been assembled by the high chieftainess Anacaona to welcome him, in a deceitful move to reduce Anacaona as a potential threat to the conquest of the island. The event has gone down in history as the Massacre of Jaragua. Anacaona herself was publicly hanged some weeks later.

Reports of subsequent strategic slaughter to instantly subdue rebellious natives on other islands are associated with the locations where the events took place: Higüey in Hispaniola, Caonao in Cuba, Daguao and Vieques in Puerto Rico. In 1513, 17 caciques from Puerto Rico were abducted and shipped to Hispaniola without confirmation of their ever having reached the destination. Reports indicate that the practice of killing local chiefs was also carried out in Jamaica.

But resistance to conquest followed many paths and involved different events. Every island reported suicides, escapes, and violent behavior. Many women chose to kill their offspring or resort to abortion rather than see their children live as slaves. In Cuba, the chief Anaya hanged himself and his teenage daughter when he was unable to rescue her from a privileged settler. Collective suicide is also reported to have taken place in Cuba. In Puerto Rico, many Tainos escaped to the neighboring "Carib islands," shattering the myth of their traditional enmity with the inhabitants of those islands. In Cuba and Hispaniola *ranchos de indios alzados*, or maroon camps, were reported as early as the 1520s. The first *cimarrones,* a term generally associated with runaway blacks, were actually Taino escapees. But resistance also took nonviolent forms. Refusal to accept the Christian faith was constantly cited by clergymen. And in secret, the outlawed ancestral religions were kept alive.

Works Cited

Newsom, Lee A., and Elizabeth S. Wing. 2004. *On Land and Sea: Native American Uses of Biological Resources in the West Indies*. Tuscaloosa, AL: University of Alabama Press.

Sued-Badillo, Jalil. 1985. "Las cacicas indoantillanas." *Revista del Instituto de Cultura Puertorriquena* 87, enero a mayo.

Sued-Badillo, Jalil. 2007. "¿Guadalupe: Caribe o taína? La isla de Guadalupe y su cuestionable identidad Caribe en la época precolonial. Una revisión etnohistórica y arqueológica." *Caribbean Studies* 35, no. 1.

Slave Cultures

Systems of Domination and Forms of Resistance

Philip Morgan

The Caribbean received more enslaved Africans than any other region in the New World. Slavery took a highly exploitative form in the region, yet enslaved Africans and their descendants there created some of the most vibrant cultures anywhere in the Americas. One of the paradoxes of slave life in the Caribbean is therefore the harshness of its material conditions coupled with the resilience of its sociocultural forms.

The Caribbean gave rise to a bewildering variety of slave cultures. There were imperial variants: slave culture in the Spanish sector differed from that in the Dutch, British, French, and Danish sectors. There were great differences between the slave cultures of big and small islands, lowlands and highlands, terrestrial and maritime worlds, sugar-dominated and diversified economies, urban and rural settings. Spatial variations were complicated by temporal changes. Slave life differed in the early and mature stages of a society's development, in frontier and settled phases of growth, from slave-owning societies to slave societies, from eras of consolidation to ages of revolution and emancipation.

Slave cultures were also shaped by a complicated array of factors: the timing, magnitude, and coastal origins of the African slave trade; birth and death rates of enslaved Africans; demographic proportions of whites, blacks, and people of mixed racial ancestry; gender ratios; the type and intensity of the work performed by slaves; the constraints set by the masters' power and institutions; religious structures; and imperial frameworks—just to mention some of the most important variables.

Slave Trade

Between 1500 and 1870, the Caribbean region (construed as the islands and associated mainland rim) was the destination of about 5.75 million Africans, about 46% of all captives involved in the transatlantic slave trade. Four years after the first black slaves came from Seville in 1501, 17 African slaves arrived in Hispaniola to work in its copper mines and 100 or so in its gold mines. In 1525, 213 captives from São Tomé landed in Santo Domingo, marking probably the first slave voyage from Africa to the Americas. For the next century Africans continued to arrive in small numbers (perhaps 7,000 total) in the Spanish Caribbean islands. Not until the second quarter of the 17th century did a significant number (about 27,000) arrive in the British Caribbean. The 18th century was the high point of the trade, accounting for two-thirds of all Africans shipped to the Caribbean, although Cuba received most of its slaves (710,000) in the 19th century. The British Caribbean received the most Africans—almost 2.8 million—with the French next at 1.3 million, the Spanish about 1 million, the Dutch about 500,000, and the Danish just 130,000. About 15% to 20% of Africans arriving in the Caribbean were subsequently traded within the Americas.

The origins of these Africans varied. Overall, West-Central Africa supplied the most slaves—about 1.6 million. After 1595 Angola became the leading source of slaves for Spanish America; later it contributed about one-third of Africans brought into Cuba. The next most important region was the Bight of Biafra, which supplied about 1.3 million slaves, while the Gold Coast supplied just over a million, mostly to the British West Indies. The Bight of Benin exported just under a million, over a third of them to the French West Indies. The three regions of Upper Guinea—Senegambia (500,000), Sierra Leone (300,000), and the Windward Coast (300,000)—were minor suppliers despite being geographically the closest to the Caribbean. South East Africa sent fewer than 200,000.

Particular islands drew on specific regions of Africa for considerable periods of time. Before 1725, about three-quarters of Africans in Jamaica came from the Gold Coast and the Bight of Benin, accounting for the early prominence of so-called "Coromantees" from the former coastal region and Adja-speakers from the latter on the island; later, however, Jamaica received most of its Africans from the Bight of Biafra. In the first quarter of the 18th century, 60% of African arrivals in Saint-Domingue were from the Bight of Benin; by the third quarter of the century, 60% came from West-Central Africa. Overall, about half of Saint-Domingue's Africans came from Angola and the Congo. When the slave trade into Cuba began in earnest in the late 18th century, about a third of its Africans were from the Gold Coast. Thereafter, West-Central Africa and the Bight of Biafra predominated.

Slave Populations

The scale of the demographic disaster among Caribbean slave populations was staggering. By 1790 about 3.5 million Africans had arrived in the Caribbean, but the slave population, then at its peak, stood at only 1.5 million. This number represented a doubling of the population since 1750—primarily due to the remarkable intensification of the Atlantic slave trade and the constant infusions from Africa, since the existing slave population failed to self-reproduce. Annual rates of natural decrease in this population were about −5 or −6% in the late 17th century, gradually improving to about −1% in the early 19th. Throughout the 18th century, rates averaged about −2%, although they worsened in the latter half of the century as the numbers of Africans rose markedly, and they were always higher in the British and Dutch Caribbean than in the Danish and French Caribbean—a difference probably best explained by the greater British and Dutch focus on sugar.

The Spanish Caribbean—where slave populations were growing naturally by the 18th century, if not before—represented an obvious exception to these trends. In the first half of that century, the slave populations grew about as fast on these islands as on the North American mainland; later in the century, as the number of African arrivals rose significantly, the rate of natural increase dropped to less than 1%, but the continued positive rate was nevertheless a striking achievement in larger Caribbean terms. Births exceeded deaths not only in Cuba, Santo Domingo, and Puerto Rico during the pre-plantation era but also in Barbados and Antigua during the late slave era. Possibly the sugar economies on these two British islands became less onerous by this period and their slave populations, increasingly comprised of creoles, with more equal sex ratios, began to grow naturally. Other smaller islands where sugar production never took hold, such as the Bahamas, also had slave populations growing by natural increase.

As abolition of the slave trade made itself felt—first in the Danish islands, and then in the British, French, Dutch, and finally Spanish—the African proportion of the slave population declined. African arrivals represented about 45% of Jamaica's slave population in 1807, but only 25% in 1832. A classic divide in any slave society occurs when a majority of its population comprises not forced immigrants but the native-born. This transition happened earliest in the Spanish Caribbean, during the 17th century. Of major Caribbean slave societies, Barbados was the first to exhibit a creole majority by about the 1760s. Jamaica followed by the turn of the century. Even with the staggering influx of Africans just before its revolution, Saint-Domingue's slave population was then about 40% creole. Cuba followed an inverse trajectory: it went from a creole majority by the early 18th century to an African majority a century or so later.

Slaves in most mature Caribbean territories constituted demographic majorities, except in the Spanish Caribbean, where whites and free coloreds almost always outnumbered slaves. In 1750 slaves represented from 85% to 88% of populations in the British, French, Dutch, and Danish territories, but only 15% in the three Spanish Caribbean islands. By 1830, the proportion of slaves rose to 31% in the Spanish Caribbean but dropped everywhere else—to 81% in the British Caribbean, 80% in the French (not counting newly free Haiti), 73% in the Dutch, and 65% in the Danish. The major reason for these declining proportions was marked growth in the numbers of free persons of color. In 1830, almost two-thirds of the region's free persons of color resided in the Spanish Caribbean, a percentage that would decline as emancipation spread across the Caribbean.

African Influences and Creolization

How much of African culture was lost in transit or retained in some fashion is a contentious and complex issue. Few scholars would now argue that the Middle Passage was so traumatic that it stripped Africans of all their cultural assets. Conversely, few would claim that large elements of any one African culture could survive intact in the New World. No group—certainly not an enslaved one—can transfer its way of life from one locale to another. Much inevitably was jettisoned in the transition. But while the loss was great, the opportunity to reformulate and reinterpret elements of homeland cultures in new settings remained. Some merging, blending, and combining was inevitable, but precisely how this happened and to what extent is subject to debate.

New African ethnicities undoubtedly came into being in the diaspora. "Coromantee" in the British Caribbean and "Caramenty" in the French were new ethnic terms acknowledging the African port city of Kormantin that came to be applied rather indiscriminately to any slaves from the Gold Coast. Similarly, "Mina" referred to persons brought from the Gold Coast generally (Costa da Mina in Portuguese), not just from the port Elmina, and it encompassed speakers of many distinct African languages. Africans in the Biafran interior would not have understood themselves as "Igbo," but so labeled at the coast by their captors, many embraced the term. Only through the process of enslavement—and its profound sense of alienation and dislocation—did these Africans develop the need to form new patterns of identification. The process was predicated on loss, but also on the forging of new bonds both at the coast and aboard slave trade vessels.

In some places and times, African ethnicities clearly played vital roles, as in the "Amina" slave revolt of 1733 on the Danish island of St. John. The participants in this revolt were former members of the Gold Coast state of Akwamu, which had been in the forefront of slave-raiding and selling. In 1728, opposition to Akwamu from its conquered provinces led to its destruction, and large numbers of slave-trading Akwamu became slaves themselves. In launching their rebellion on St. John, they aimed to recreate elements of their Akwamu state. Not surprisingly, fellow Africans who had once been victims of Akwamu failed to join the revolt. This was an "ethnic" revolt, not a pan-African coalition.

Perhaps a more typical process was extensive inter-African syncretism. Even when Africans from one region dominated in a particular Caribbean territory, they came from different locales and interacted with other Africans from other regions. This process happened among the Saramakas, one of the many maroon peoples of Suriname and French Guiana. Different African ethnic groups certainly contributed beliefs, knowledge, and rituals to the larger collectivity; no single group dominated. Compared to other African American societies, Saramakas built their culture fairly autonomously, drawing little from Europeans and Native Americans. Intermarriage among Africans of different origins was common, and by the mid–18th century most maroons were native-born. Thus, anthropologist Richard Price notes, early Saramaka society "was far

Figure 2.3.1   **A spiritual healer in Suriname attempts to heal her client of an illness. Lithograph by Pierre Jacques Benoit and Jean-Baptiste Madou (1839). Source: The John Carter Brown Library.**

closer to Saramaka today, in terms of cultural development, than it was to Africa." Saramakas are one of the African American diaspora's most creolized people (Price 2006, 140).

Plantation slaves in Suriname and many other parts of the Caribbean undoubtedly maintained African practices and identities more strongly than did maroons. In 1750, for example, about three-quarters of Suriname plantation slaves were African-born, more than half having left Africa only within the previous decade. Constant infusions of Africans kept memories and practices of the homelands alive. Nevertheless, even the slave population of early 19th-century Trinidad, nearly two-thirds of which came from Africa, exhibited rapid inter-African syncretism, in part because the Africans were drawn from territories extending from Senegambia to Mozambique, in part because the island was demographically urban, and in part because slaveholdings were small. Consequently, few Africans found conjugal partners of their own ethnic group or region, and ethnic identity dissolved rapidly due to extensive intermarriage.

African influences also depended on timing. Although the Adja-Fon from the Bight of Benin ultimately represented a minority of Africans in Saint-Domingue, they arrived in large numbers in the first quarter of the 18th century. In other words, they constituted a charter group, creating many of the cultural norms and contributing the major deities, the ceremonies, and most of the African vocabulary to Haitian vodou. Later, as the Kongo region increasingly became the major supplier of slaves to the island, vodou began to incorporate various Kongo rituals.

If Haitian vodou owed much to first-comers, Cuban Santería derived heavily from latecomers. One of its major components was the worship of Yoruba deities known as orisha, yet not until the fall of the Oyo empire (1835) did extremely large numbers of Yoruba end up in Cuba, where they became known as Lucumí. Along with Yoruba-derived forms of worship, Santería incorporated notions deriving from West-Central African *minkisi* cults—hardly surprising, since 135,000 "Congos" flooded into Cuba in the last 15 years of the slave trade. Urban environments in western Cuba also became crucial to Santería's development, offering slaves a less regimented existence than in rural areas. Urban slaves and freed people created Afro-Cuban *cabildos,* or lodges, and mutual aid societies. By the end of the 18th century, 21 cabildos existed in Havana alone. One or more Lucumí cabildos—neo-African ethnic formations—provided the crucible out of which Santería emerged.

This process of cultural adaptation and transformation in which all Africans were engaged—which involved continuities and discontinuities, gains and losses, inventions and borrowings—usually goes by the name *creolization.* As to whether Africans reproduced at least part of their homeland cultures or largely adopted the customs of their host societies, the best answer would be that they did both, depending on many local circumstances. Slaves frequently accepted European institutions and civic and religious rituals, insinuating themselves into various social frameworks or niches—whether fraternities, festival cycles, or churches—and reworking them to their own ends. In other words, Africans selectively appropriated aspects of new cultures even as they remained faithful to aspects of their homeland cultures.

Ultimately, Africans in the Caribbean had to adapt to survive. They had no time for debates about cultural purity or precise roots, nor any necessary commitment to the societies from which they had come. They were denied much of their various cultural heritage and the institutions that socially anchored and maintained them. And even what they brought was sometimes ruthlessly jettisoned because it was no longer applicable or relevant to their new situations. Slaves had to be forward-looking. No wonder, as anthropologist Sidney Mintz puts it, when we think of the history of the people of African descent, "we are speaking of mangled pasts." For that reason, he continues, "It is not the precise historical origins of a word, a meaning, a phrase, an instrument, or a rhythm that matters, so much as the creative genius of the users, molding older cultural substances into new and unfamiliar patterns, without regard for 'purity' or 'pedigree' " (Mintz 1970, 9; Mintz 1974, 17).

Slave Economies

Perhaps the two greatest determinants of the slaves' economic lives were whether they grew sugar and whether they were primarily responsible for growing their own provisions. Perhaps as many as 8 of 10 Africans arriving in the region came initially to work on sugar plantations, which always employed the most slaves. Yet while sugar was the great consumer of labor, many slaves in the Caribbean worked at other jobs and with other crops. Moreover, slaves worked to provide not only for their masters but for themselves. The precise balance between sugar and non-sugar and master's and slave's economies varied greatly by place and time.

Few other regions in the world were more exclusively committed to a single economic activity than the Caribbean. Some islands were little more than vast sugar plantations. By the early 19th century, 9 in 10 enslaved workers in Nevis, Montserrat, and Tobago toiled on sugar estates, as well as three-quarters of enslaved workers on Guadeloupe and two-thirds on Martinique. Over time, sugar began displacing alternative export crops such as tobacco, indigo, and cotton, which required less capital. Nevertheless, in some places, especially after 1750, cotton, cacao, indigo, and particularly coffee became more prominent, although the overall trend was not away from but toward sugar monoculture. Cuba is the last great example of an island turning to full-scale sugar production late in its history.

Sugar involved labor far more onerous than that required by any other crop. Working in gangs, overseen by a driver with whip at hand, toiling in shifts at harvest time, sugar slaves experienced a draconian labor regime. Perhaps 90% of all 18th-century Caribbean slaves worked on sugar estates—probably one of the highest labor participation rates anywhere in the world. Women soon comprised the majority of most gangs, since they usually outlived men and skilled jobs were denied them. The one advantage of working on a sugar plantation was the opportunity to develop a craft—sugar plantations usually had twice as many skilled personnel as did coffee or cotton plantations—but such jobs were the preserve of men.

The large islands of the Greater Antilles generally encompassed a wider range of economic activities than did their smaller counterparts. Slaves on Hispaniola, Puerto Rico, and Cuba raised cattle for their hides; grew ginger, cacao, and tobacco; and raised provisions even after these islands turned intensively to sugar cultivation. Jamaica, Britain's largest sugar island, was always quite diversified. In the late 18th century, the proportion of Jamaica's slaves on sugar estates was about 60% and declining. Saint-Domingue, too, was notable for its large number of cotton, coffee, and indigo plantations. Coffee plantations, which tended to become important on mountainous islands, often were smaller and more diverse than sugar estates, provided less occupational variety, and were usually more isolated and healthier because of their highland locations.

Although sugar was the archetypal slave crop, many Caribbean slaves worked at other activities. A few marginal colonies grew no sugar at all. In British Honduras and Belize, most slaves were woodcutters. In the Cayman Islands, Anguilla, and Barbuda, a majority of slaves lived on small, diversified agricultural holdings. On the Turks and Caicos and on Bonaire, many slaves raked salt. On the Bahamas, cotton cultivation was important for some decades, and fishing and shipping occupied a significant minority of slaves. Indeed, on islands known for their entrepôts, such as St. Eustatius and St. Thomas, most slaves worked at sea or on the docks. Even in a monocultural economy such as Barbados, about 1 in 10 slaves produced cotton, provisions, ginger, arrowroot, and aloes. Slaves built forts, churches, and other essential public buildings as well as private dwellings.

By the late 18th century, the proportion of urban slaves ranged from about 1 in 20 on French Saint-Domingue (where they congregated in three large towns) to 4 in 10 on Danish St. Thomas

Figure 2.3.2 An urban market in Saint-Domingue, 1770s. Engraved print of painting by Agostino Brunias (1804). Image NW0009, www.slaveryimages.org, Virginia Foundation for the Humanities and the University of Virginia Library.

(where they resided in Charlotte Amalie). In between these extremes, about 1 in 10 slaves lived in towns on most British islands, and 1 in 5 on the Spanish and Dutch islands. By the early 17th century, Havana had about 10,000 residents, half of whom were slaves; almost two centuries later, its population had grown to 41,000, but now only about one-quarter were slaves. Unlike most of their plantation counterparts, urban slaves were often outnumbered by whites and freed people, and they lived in extremely small units under the close watch of resident masters. Women usually outnumbered men, and slaves of mixed racial ancestry were often prominent. Most urban slaves worked as domestics, but hawkers, higglers, and transport workers were numerous in towns, and roughly twice as many skilled tradespeople, fishermen, and general laborers lived in urban as in rural settings. Slaves who hired their own time were a notable feature of urban life.

The internal economy of slaves varied greatly. On marginal islands such as Barbuda and Great Exuma in the Bahamas, which did not grow sugar, slaves were virtual peasants, farming extensive provision grounds, owning livestock, and spending a good deal of time hunting and fishing. Somewhat less advantaged were slaves with access to provision grounds on larger sugar islands such as Jamaica and Saint-Domingue, where they could at least sell their produce in the large urban markets. Slaves' economic opportunities were least extensive on small islands such as Antigua or Barbados, where they were permitted, at best, small garden plots.

The impact of the slaves' economy was double-edged. Drawbacks included the lack of time slaves often had to tend their provision grounds; the distance separating slave huts from outlying grounds; the pressures on aged, infirm, and young slaves; the exposure to environmental threats of hurricanes and droughts; and the poorer health, lower life expectancy, and lower fertility associated with provision ground systems (as opposed to ration systems). Benefits included the variety of the slaves' horticultural repertoires, the material advantages accruing from selling and bartering produce, and the firm foundation that independent production and marketing gave to the slaves' domestic, religious, and community life. Before long, slaves engaging in "proto-peasant" activities came to dominate the Sunday markets, and whites came to depend on them for fruits, vegetables, and meat. The trade-off was greater autonomy for greater exposure to risk.

Slave Societies and Cultural Forms

Caribbean slavery created brutal and volatile societies beset by constant tensions and power struggles. They were the first societies in the Americas to develop elaborate slave codes, which commonly prohibited and suppressed unauthorized movement, large congregations, possession of guns and other weapons, sounding of horns and drums, and secret ritual practices. French and particularly Spanish laws provided minimal protections to slaves, but control and repression were primary concerns. Terror was at the core of the institution of slavery: slave owners depended above all on local militias and imperial troops for their safety. The punishment for actual or threatened violence against whites was severe. Special slave-trial courts existed in many colonies to provide summary and expeditious "justice." Occasionally redress was possible: some colonies had an official to hear slave complaints, and legislation governing slaves tended to become somewhat less terroristic over time. The murder of a slave by a white man, for example, generally became a crime, but mandated amelioration was always limited by the sheer fact of planter power.

Everywhere custom was as important as law in shaping the slave experience. Slavery by definition involved highly personal mechanisms of coercion; the whip, rather than the law, was the institution's indispensable and ubiquitous instrument. On the plantation or in the household, the master and his delegates used various methods of physical coercion without recourse to, and usually unchecked by, external authorities. Brutality and sadism were widespread, but newly settled places and those with stark black majorities, where masters felt most isolated and insecure, gained the worst reputations. Paternalism was not a governing ideal in the Caribbean. In some colonies (most notably the British and French), many masters were absentees, distanced from their slaves. The ideals, practices, and power of white planters and their managers determined much of the context of slave life.

The masters hoped that rewards would offset punishments. Over time, allowances and privileges became entrenched in both custom and law. Granting slaves half-days or full days to tend their provision plots became commonplace, and allowing them to attend extraordinary social functions such as funerals became standard practice. Masters also generally granted slaves time off during the Christian holidays. Christmas, in particular, became a time for permissiveness and even social inversion—a black Saturnalia. Special gratuities became routine: an extra allowance of food here, some tobacco there, a ration of rum for completing the harvest, cash payments for Sunday work. Favors and indulgences were disproportionately allocated to concubines, domestics, drivers, and tradesmen.

Although masters and slaves were locked into an intimate interdependence, blacks were not just objects of white action, but subjects who regulated social relationships among themselves. Masters obviously subjected slaves' familial aspirations to enormous stress. Owners generally recognized only the mother-child tie; bought mostly men, who then had difficulty finding wives; separated slave families by sale and transfer; and committed sexual assaults on slave women. Notions of instability, promiscuity, casual mating, and inherent disorganization in slave family life are commonly overdrawn: slave families were often remarkably resilient, kinship bonds could be strong, and parent-child affection was real. Nevertheless, in slave populations dominated by Africans, family life was extremely tenuous. At least half of African slaves lived with friends or other solitaries, not with relatives. They often practiced forms of "fictive kinship," particularly toward shipmates, who looked upon one another's children as their own. When they formed families, they probably saw the unfamiliar two-parent form as an essential building block toward the extended or polygamous family types that were common in their homelands.

As populations creolized, their kinship networks grew more elaborate, and family life often centered less on the household than on networks of relationships involving various relatives and spouses. Marriage among slaves generally gained more support in Catholic than in Protestant countries, due to legal strictures, but size of estate and stage of colonial development were critical determinants of slave family life. Thus, on smaller slaveholdings the dominant unit was composed of mother and children, while on larger plantations the nuclear family was more prevalent. Similarly, the proportion of slaves living in two-parent households was always much lower in frontier regions than in long-settled areas. The notion of slaves as being stripped of kin, the mother the only recognizable family figure, is a caricature.

Language was another case in point. Although Africans for a time continued speaking their native languages, most slaves—and some masters—came to speak creole languages, each of which derived much of its vocabulary from a European language but owed much of its phonology and syntax to a prior West African creole or pidgin and, beyond that, to various West African languages. In the early modern Caribbean, scores of identifiable creole languages arose. The one exception was the Spanish Caribbean, where most slaves learned the masters' language. This trend resulted from the unusual demographic situation in the major Spanish islands, where slaves were heavily outnumbered by free peoples for so long; from the incorporative stance of the Spanish; and from the absence of Spanish-based contact languages along the West African coast.

Much as a broad spectrum of linguistic forms existed among slaves, a continuous scale of musical expression, ranging in inspiration from Europe to Africa, also unfolded. At one end of the spectrum were, for example, slaves who became integral members of military bands or street players in urban settings. At the other extreme were Africans who danced their ethnic dances to their own homeland musical accompaniments—banjos, balafos, harps, lutes, gourd rattles, or various kinds of drums. In the Caribbean some musical styles were ethnically identifiable, even if most involved some degree of syncretism. Black music developed in ways akin to the formation of creole languages. A basic musical aesthetic, which emphasized the importance of music and dance in everyday life and the role of rhythm and percussion in musical style, survived the Middle Passage. Even complex musical instruments made the crossing, although more notable is how slaves adapted traditional instruments, invented new ones, and borrowed Euro-American ones. These adaptations, inventions, and borrowings were interpreted and reinterpreted according to aesthetic principles drawn from African musical traditions. Slaves retained the inner meanings of traditional modes of behavior while adopting new outer forms. In musical terms, the key elements of the inner structure were complex rhythms, percussive qualities, syncopation, and antiphonal patterns.

Black religious expression also spanned a large continuum. Some Africans, particularly those from Upper Guinea, were Muslims; others from Kongo had been exposed to Catholicism. But overall, an extraordinary diversity of religious forms coexisted with certain widely shared basic principles. Most Africans drew no neat distinction between the sacred and the profane, shared assumptions about the nature of causality, believed in both a high god and many lesser gods, and thought the dead played an active role in the lives of the living. In the Caribbean, because of enforced coexistence with other African groups and the serious, everyday problems of dealing with harsh taskmasters, slaves turned in large measure to magical practices—the most common term for which, in the Anglophone Caribbean, became *obi* (or *obia* or *obeah*). The slaves' religious worldview featured strong beliefs concerning the power of ancestors, elaborate funeral rites, and diverse ritual practices to invoke natural or ancestral spirits—which became part of Haitian vodou, Cuban Santería, Trinidadian *Shango*, Jamaican *Myal*, and Afro-Surinamese *Winti*.

Over time, slaves began accepting Christianity on their terms. The Catholic clergy in Spanish and French territories were officially committed to converting slaves—and certainly made greater initial inroads than did Protestants—but by the 18th century other groups such as the Moravians, Baptists, and Methodists were increasingly successful in gaining members among slaves. The Moravians, for example, established the earliest Afro-Protestant congregation in the Americas (in 1736 on St. Thomas) and by the 1780s had thousands of converts in the Danish and British West Indies and in Suriname.

Slave Resistance

List all the plots and rebellions mounted by Caribbean slaves, and resistance appears structurally endemic; recall the bitter fact that the vicious system of Caribbean slavery lasted for hundreds of years and was dynamically expansive until the very end of the 19th century, and Caribbean slavery seems much less brittle. Jamaica experienced a serious slave revolt about once a decade, none more consequential than the island-wide insurrection of 1760 that resulted in the deaths of 90 whites and 400 blacks, with another 600 deported. Yet Barbadian slaves never mounted a serious slave rebellion until 1816, and even that claimed few white lives. The greatest slave revolt in history—that of Saint-Domingue in 1791—was of monumental significance, but before it, that island's slaves had no great reputation for rebelliousness. Furthermore, ambivalence marked that signal event, as it did slave resistance in general. The only successful slave rebellion in the history of the Americas served as a beacon of liberty, but 12 years of unremitting warfare destroyed this most valuable of all plantation colonies, thereby encouraging masters to launch a huge expansion of slavery in other parts of the Caribbean.

Slave rebellions and conspiracies varied over time. There were clusters of incidents: insurrections and insurrection panics peaked in the 1680s, 1730s to early 1740s, 1770s, and 1790s. Other periods saw few or no revolts. Some events seem connected to spikes in the arrivals of Africans, times of warfare, and troop movements, but mechanistic explanations will not wholly account for incidents driven by group psychology and interactions among many individuals. Shifts in composition and goals tended to occur: from events inspired primarily by Africans to events dominated by creoles, from attempts to secure freedom from slavery and restore a lost social order to attempts to overthrow slavery itself, from acts of rage to forms of industrial strife. Such neat descriptions of the transformations are too schematic, but still the revolutionary era marked an important transition. The circulation of revolutionary ideas broadened horizons: some slaves drew inspiration from Haiti while others saw the possibility of sympathy from the emerging antislavery movement. The three great slave revolts in the early 19th-century British Caribbean—Barbados in 1816, Demerara in 1823, and Jamaica in 1831–32—are most notable for their self-restraint and awareness of metropolitan debates. Rebelling against the system from within, the argument goes, caused abolition to be hastened from without.

Slave resistance was always more than collective violence. It encompassed flight, sabotage, and individual murders. Most plantations experienced a few desertions each year; arson occurred occasionally; tool-breaking, cruelty to animals, and crop destruction were everyday problems; and every now and again enraged slaves killed overseers or masters. But none of these actions threatened the economic viability of the institution. Furthermore, the cook who poisoned the master's food had first to get the job. Slaves who plotted in the marketplace had first to produce for the market. The slave who ran away was often the one who possessed a skill, had some mobility, and could perhaps pass as free in town. There was no simple unilinear gradient from accommodation to resistance.

Maroons, the ultimate symbol of resistance, were also forced to accommodate. Small groups of maroons existed in various colonies—usually ones with mountainous interiors—but only in Suriname and Jamaica were they self-sustaining. Even there, their numbers were never large—about 1,000 in Jamaica and 6,000 in Suriname during the 18th century. Maroons waged wars against colonial governments, often for decades, forcing them in some cases to recognize their free and separate existence. Post-treaty maroons, however, often proved to be effective allies, tracking down slave runaways and rebels, adopting the military hierarchy of the establishment, living in an uneasy symbiosis with their white neighbors, and seeking arms, tools, pots, and cloth as well as employment.

Figure 2.3.3 Stick fighting between English and French slaves in Dominica. Print of painting by Agostino Brunias (ca. 1779). Image Bilby-3, www.slaveryimages.org, Virginia Foundation for the Humanities and the University of Virginia Library.

Slaves were found on both sides of most disputes. In the early years of many settlements, slaves were often used as soldiers, but as their numbers grew, opposition arose to arming them. However, in emergencies—for example, local rebellions or foreign invasions—those thought to be loyal were periodically placed under arms. Moreover, slaves continued to be used as auxiliaries and pioneers, free blacks and coloreds became an important part of the militia, and the Anglo-French Wars of 1793–1815 brought an extraordinary intensification of the practice of arming slaves. Winning the allegiance of slaves became an imperative for the governments of Spain, Britain, and France during the Haitian Revolution. In 1795 the effectiveness of black troops and shortage of white manpower led the British to form black regiments. Eventually they raised 12 regiments by recruiting 30,000 slaves, but they were always careful to enlist captives from Africa, whom they thought they could more easily control.

Most resistance was not destructive of the institution. By carving out some independence for themselves and forcing whites to recognize their humanity, slaves opposed the dehumanization inherent in their status and demonstrated their autonomy. Such assertions of will eased the torments of slavery, gave slaves a reason for living, and made them less likely to sacrifice everything in what seemed like a futile, invariably suicidal attempt to overthrow the institution. For this reason, the distinction between resistance (drawing on sources outside the system) and opposition (working from within the system) is useful.

Conclusion

The history of Caribbean slave cultures abounds in paradoxes. Most slaves in the region lived short and oppressed lives, worked most of the time, grew one of the most onerous crops imaginable, formed fragile families, and suffered great brutality. Arguably, then, slave culture ought to have reached its most impoverished form here. Yet Caribbean slaves also invented creole languages, developed distinctive musical styles, created rich religious systems, and established elaborate domestic economies, thereby opposing the dehumanization involved in slavery. Similarly, African ethnicity, itself a creation of the diaspora, was a useful resource upon which many slaves could draw, yet inter-African syncretism and creolization were the dominant trends in Caribbean slave life.

Finally, in the only such occurrence in history, slaves on Saint-Domingue overthrew the institution, thereby revealing that black liberation was possible and inspiring several conspiracies, revolts, and assertions of black pride throughout the Americas. But if this massive slave insurrection was like the dropping of the atomic bomb—a nightmare for slaveholders which signified that the world would never be the same—planters in Cuba, Jamaica, Trinidad, and many other places nonetheless sought more Africans immediately. The destruction of slavery in the world's most profitable colony provided a huge boost to plantation slavery elsewhere. Furthermore, if Haiti was unforgettable, it was also unrepeatable; no other revolt could follow its model. The story of slave life in the Caribbean is depressing and uplifting in about equal measure.

Works Cited

Mintz, Sidney W. 1970. Foreword to *Afro-American Anthropology: Contemporary Perspectives,* ed. Norman E. Whitten, Jr. and John F. Szwed, 1–16. New York: Free Press.

———. 1974. *Caribbean Transformations*. Baltimore: Johns Hopkins University Press.

Price, Richard. 2006. "On the Miracle of Creolization." In *Afro-Atlantic Dialogues: Anthropology in the Diaspora,* ed. Kevin A. Yelvington, 115–47. Sante Fe: School of American Research Press.

Section II: Recommended Readings

Anderson-Córdova, K. F. (2017). *Surviving Spanish conquest: Indian fight, flight, and cultural transformation in Hispaniola and Puerto Rico.* Caribbean Archaeology and Ethnohistory Series. Tuscaloosa, AL: University Alabama Press.

Palka, J. W. (2010). *The A to Z of ancient Mesoamerica.* Lanham, MD: Scarecrow Press.

Schmidt-Nowara, C. (2011). *Slavery, freedom, and abolition in Latin America and the Atlantic world.* Diálogos Series. Albuquerque, NM: University of New Mexico Press.

Schroeder, H., Sikora, M., Gopalakrishnan, S., Cassidy, L. M., Delser, P. M., Velasco, M. S., ... Day, J. S. (2018). Origins and genetic legacies of the Caribbean Taino. *Proceedings of the National Academy of Sciences of the United States of America, 115,* 2341–2346.

Stinnesbeck, W., Becker, J., Hering, F., Frey, E., González, A. G., Fohlmeister, J., ... Deininger, M. (2017). The earliest settlers of Mesoamerica date back to the late Pleistocene. *PLoS ONE, 12*(8), 1–20.

Section II: Post-Reading Questions

1. What were the contributions of the Olmecs to Mesoamerica? Include examples in your answer.

2. What was the impact of European colonization on Hispaniola and Puerto Rico and its repercussions on the Taino?

3. Outline the major aspects of the African Diaspora to Latin America and the Caribbean. Include a brief description of the demographic impact and subsequent Creolization of both culture regions.

SECTION III

THE 19TH AND 20TH CENTURIES

Independence and Revolutions

Editor's Introduction

As we learned in the previous section, Africans' forcible migration to Latin America and the Caribbean was not without conflict, rebellion, and resistance. Colonial territories experienced a dramatic increase of their African slave population in the 18th century. Such was the case of Hispaniola, a colonial island controlled by both Spain and France that today includes the modern countries of the Dominican Republic and Haiti, where African slaves and *libertos* reached 85 to 88% of the total population. Struggling to survive the jarring colonial regime and plantation economy, Haitian slave insurgents finally succeeded in their attempts to overthrow the French colonists and end slavery. Recognized as one of the earliest successful independence and antislavery movements in the Caribbean, the Haitian revolution began in 1791. Dubois's (2011) article provides a historical background outlining the conditions and subsequent transformations that Haiti underwent after the country declared independence on January 1, 1804.

Two other political movements are explored in this selection of readings. First, Zeuske (2011) contextualizes the historical conditions leading to the rise of dictatorial regimes in Cuba and subsequent revolutionary movement in the 1950s. Outnumbered and with limited resources to engage in warfare against the American-supported Batista dictatorial regime, Fidel Castro and Ernesto "Che" Guevara's Marxist revolution succeeded in overthrowing the old regime and subsequently established the first Socialist regime in the Caribbean. The last reading in this section focuses on Colombia's FARC–EP guerrilla movement founded in 1964. Jean Batou's (2008) interview of Rodrigo Granda, a member and international spokesperson of the Marxist Revolutionary Armed Forces of Colombia—the People's Army guerrilla movement—conveys an insider's perspective on controversial practices such as civilian and political kidnappings, murders, and the revolutionary tax on coca leaf cultivation. In this interview, Granda provides a distinct overview on the effectiveness of the United States' "War on Drugs" campaign and its unexpected aftermath for Colombia's political future.

Section III: Key Terms

Abolitionists

Bay of Pigs

Bolivarian militias

cocaine

colony

Creole

dictator

Fidelista

Granma

genocidal democracy

ingenio

Iwa

Marronage

Marxism

Mulattos

Narco paramilitarism

Neoliberalism

oligarchy

socialism

sugar

terrorism

Vodou

The Haitian Revolution

Laurent Dubois

At its height, the French colony of Saint-Domingue was the most profitable of all Caribbean plantation societies, outpacing even prosperous Jamaica in its production of sugar and coffee. For many planters and officials at the time, it seemed a model of success. But in the last decade of the 18th century Saint-Domingue became a model for something very different: first the disintegration and then the destruction of a plantation world, burnt quite literally to the ground. The enslaved—those who had faced brutal work regimes, the constant threat of punishment, and a devastating disease environment to make Saint-Domingue prosper—fought back, first winning their freedom and then, when that freedom was threatened, expelling the French for good. In place of the colony they created the new nation of Haiti, which was and remains a powerful and multivalent symbol of black resistance.

The Haitian Revolution emerged from the institution that defined much of Caribbean society and economy in the 18th century: the plantation. And the plantation weighed heavily on how the revolution unfolded and on what it ultimately produced. At once a radical break with the past and an ongoing effort to erase the burden of that past, the struggle for freedom in Haiti was epochal in scale and global in its ramifications. The Haitian Revolution transformed the very meaning of freedom, not just in the Caribbean but far beyond it, ushering in a new vision of human rights. It was in Haiti that the claim that every human being, irrespective of color or status, had the right to autonomy, dignity, and freedom was first fully realized and put to the test. In confronting and overcoming the slave system that dominated the Atlantic at the time, the revolutionaries in Haiti profoundly expanded the meaning and implication of human rights, going further than the American or French revolutionaries. The

Haitian Revolution, then, is a vital part of the history of the Americas, of Europe, and indeed of global history—an event crucial to understanding the history of modern politics. A successful slave revolt that led first to general emancipation and citizenship, and then to the creation of an independent black nation-state in the Americas, it represents a signal moment in the history of ideas of universal rights.

However, the social transformation that many in Haiti dreamed of was never completed. The price of freedom was extremely high, in terms of both the carnage and devastation wrought by the war and the difficulties faced by Haiti to this day. The Haitian Revolution left a complex and in some ways paradoxical legacy. The most radical revolution of the Age of Revolution, it created a state undermined by internal conflicts and a society in which the struggle for true dignity and freedom would continue indefinitely. What happened in Haiti after 1804, of course, was only partly grounded in the revolution itself and must be explained within the larger Caribbean context of the 19th and 20th centuries. Within this context, Haiti was shaped by the same economic and political forces that shaped much of the rest of the region. At the same time, Haiti was always unique, bearing the history of a successful slave revolution—a history that powerfully shaped how Haitians perceived themselves and how they were perceived by others.

The Haitian Revolution was remarkable in its complexity. Although rarely included in histories of the French Revolution or of the history of the early American republic (at least until recently), it was deeply linked to both, shaping both and being shaped by them in return. In 1995 the Haitian scholar Michel-Rolph Trouillot famously argued that, for many in Europe and North America, the Haitian Revolution was and has long remained an "unthinkable" event, one that so deeply challenged assumptions about the nature of the world and humanity that it simply could not be assimilated into existing narratives and typologies. Since then, scholars have both built on Trouillot's claim and questioned it, pointing out, for instance, that while the Haitian Revolution was silenced in many contexts, it also echoed powerfully within many communities in the Americas as an example and inspiration for the enslaved as well as for some abolitionists, and, of course, as a source of anxiety for slave masters. True, many historians in the 20th century may have forgotten or ignored the revolution: examples abound, such as its absence (pointed out by Trouillot) from Eric Hobsbawm's classic book on the Age of Revolution, and its omission from most histories of the French Revolution. Yet few of those who lived in the Atlantic world when it took place could or did ignore it.

On the Slopes of the Volcano

At the beginning of the French Revolution, the French lawyer and representative Honoré de Mirabeau—one of several prominent proponents of abolition, many of them part of a group called the Société des Amis des Noirs—described the planters of Saint-Domingue as "sleeping at the foot of Vesuvius." His comments would soon ring prescient. Though planters would blame Mirabeau and other abolitionists for having set off the volcano's explosion—after all, sleeping at the foot of a volcano is not always deadly, just dangerous—the question of whether the planters could have escaped the destruction of their colony has occupied historians for some time. Other slaveholding societies did escape the fate of Saint-Domingue: Jamaica survived several decades longer as a plantation colony, the planters of the US South prospered for another half-century, and slavery did not end in Cuba and Brazil until 1886 and 1888 respectively.

Nonetheless, in a sense all slave societies were volcanoes, steeped in violence, strained by constant slave resistance, ready to explode. Few, however, actually did explode. Neighboring Jamaica had a demographic composition very similar to that of Saint-Domingue. There, too, a vast majority of slaves surrounded a small number of masters and free people of African descent. Jamaica, furthermore, had a much more intense history of rebellion during the 18th century, with maroon wars and Tacky's Revolt both seriously threatening the stability of its society. Saint-Domingue had also seen many rebellions, most famously during the 1750s, when a now legendary man named Makandal created a network of poisoners who terrorized the masters. Like the maroons of Jamaica in the 1730s, a small maroon community in the mountains along the border with Spanish Santo Domingo signed a peace treaty with the French colonial government of Saint-Domingue in the 1780s. But as the case of Jamaica shows, a history of resistance was not enough to create the foundation for a mass revolution of the enslaved. The eruption that took place in Haiti was not inevitable. But it was the result both of the colony's internal structure and of the larger historical conjuncture of the late 18th century.

Part of this conjuncture was demographic. During the second half of the 18th century, the pace of slave imports into the colony was remarkable. In the decade before the outbreak of the French Revolution alone, more than 30,000 people were annually brought from Africa to Saint-Domingue. Over the course of the century, the colony took in more than a million slaves from Africa. By the time the outbreak of the French and Haitian Revolutions brought the slave trade to Saint-Domingue to a halt, the enslaved population of the island stood at a mere 500,000—proof of both the horrendous death rates among the enslaved, due to disease and the brutal work regime, and the low birth rates, due mostly to the same reasons. Only a constant stream of imports sustained the laboring population, making Saint-Domingue *demographically* an African society. In 1789, not just the majority of slaves (two-thirds by contemporary accounts) but most the colony's population had been born in Africa. Although the people spoke a variety of African languages, there were forces limiting linguistic fragmentation: some of the disparate languages carried from Africa had commonalities, and by the mid-18th century a creole language had established itself so strongly that plays were written and performed in it. Likewise, African religious practices and beliefs not only survived but began to merge into a shared tradition. Many Africans also brought military experience, having served as soldiers in wars sometimes driven by the expansion of the slave trade, and having been captured in battle. Indeed, John Thornton (1991) has argued that the combat skills they learned in Africa, including the use of firearms, were put to use in a new war in the Americas.

The revolution came from the communities of the enslaved. Their thoughts, hopes, and actions made it what it was. Scholars have sometimes emphasized a cleavage between African-born and creole (that is, Caribbean-born) slaves, and there certainly were tensions and differences between the two groups. But firm distinctions between them are misleading. As Ira Berlin and others have argued, some African arrivals may have been relatively "creolized" already, having lived in cosmopolitan coastal areas or ports where cultural and social confrontations and exchanges echoed those taking place in the Caribbean. Many, especially those coming from the regions of West Central Africa, had been exposed to Catholicism, a tradition of religious practice that began with the arrival of Portuguese missionaries in the kingdom of Kongo in the late 15th century. Those born in Saint-Domingue to African parents, meanwhile, might well have maintained linkages, through practice, language, sentiment, and family histories, with the other side of the Atlantic. The religion that emerged in Saint-Domingue during the 18th century (eventually to be called vodou) represents a powerful system of thought that maintained connections with Africa and reflected on and refracted the experience of exile. Amid the brutalities of the plantation world, in the cane fields and sugar mills as well as in the thriving towns of Saint-Domingue, a remarkable process of cultural production unfolded over the course of the 18th century. It made possible the act of political imagination that became the Haitian Revolution.

Religious practices were part of a larger social world that by its very existence militated against the plantation order. Masters strove to reduce the enslaved to the status of laboring machines, their lives organized by the demands of plantation work. But the enslaved were human and they negotiated, pushed back against, and found ways to work around the insistence that they be nothing but embodied labor power. As in other slave societies, marronage (running away) was a fundamental part of daily life. What contemporaries and historians have called "petit marronage"—short-term flight from the plantation rather than permanent escape, which sometimes ended with capture and punishment and sometimes with a negotiated return—was particularly crucial in laying the foundation for revolution. For along with allowing slaves the mobility on Sundays to sell in local towns the produce grown in their garden plots, petit marronage made possible the creation of cross-plantation community and collusion. If the uprising of 1791 succeeded in Saint-Domingue, it was because its leaders were able to mobilize such cross-plantation networks in order to plan a massive, coordinated attack.

An Atlantic Revolution

The opportunity for attack came in 1791, and in an entirely unforeseen context: the French Revolution. How to understand the relationship between the French and Haitian Revolutions has intrigued and befuddled generations of historians. The most famous account, C. L. R. James's classic *The Black Jacobins* (1938), involves a rich meditation on this problem. James shows beautifully how the two revolutions shaped one another and how their histories illuminate one another. What his narrative suggests, and what subsequent historiography has urged readers to contemplate, is that ultimately it may be extremely difficult to figure out where one revolution ends and the other begins. The 1790s saw a French Atlantic revolution that played out on both sides of the ocean, and the currents of cause and effect were complex and varied but never uni-directional. In the Caribbean itself multiple revolutions were underway, for the French colonies of Martinique and Guadeloupe also saw upheaval and transformation. And the revolution that took place in Saint-Domingue really only became "Haitian" after 1802, when it aimed to create an independent nation. Before that, enslaved insurgents had actually won their freedom by arguing for, and eventually achieving, a closer legal and political connection between France and the colony of Saint-Domingue.

The revolution of 1789 in France shaped what happened in the Caribbean in many ways. First, and perhaps most important, it shook up the system of colonial governance and weakened its power, inviting protest and resistance. All social groups in Saint-Domingue saw an opportunity in the French Revolution. For many planters, who had long chafed under the commercial regulations of the *exclusif*, which required most trade in their plantation products to be with France, it was an opportunity to argue for greater economic freedom. For poorer whites in the colony, it was an opportunity to protest and fight against the social hierarchy that kept them marginalized and often landless. For free people of African descent, also called free people of color (*gens de couleur*) and often described in the literature as "mulattoes," though many were in fact not of mixed European and African ancestry, it was an opportunity to protest against decades of humiliating local legislation that constrained them politically and restricted them from practicing certain professions as well as controlling other aspects of their life, some as minute as the kind of clothes they could wear and the means of transportation they could use.

But if the French Revolution created an opening by undermining the central structure of authority and command in the colony, it also produced an outpouring of language and symbolism that could be powerfully mobilized. The 1789 Declaration of the Rights of Man thus produced a charter both immensely powerful and immensely vague in its articulation. Free people of color were particularly astute in harnessing the new language of rights to long-standing grievances about racial discrimination. Presenting themselves as wealthy, educated patriots, elite free people of color—led by figures such as Julien Raimond and Vincent Ogé, both wealthy men with substantial holdings in land and slaves—argued that they should have access to political rights alongside whites in the colonies. They allied themselves with the nascent abolitionist movement in France to take on the privilege of white planters, which they dubbed the "aristocracy of the skin." And they found that many were sympathetic to their arguments, which both drew on and buttressed the idea that a new era of equality was dawning in France.

They also ran into strenuous opposition. Despite having powerful allies—among them Mirabeau, the Marquis de Condorcet, and the Abbé Grégoire—the gens de couleur ultimately failed to make headway in the National Assembly in Paris. In 1790 an angry and disabused Ogé returned to Saint-Domingue, where he organized an armed uprising to demand political rights. Ogé and his men were defeated after a few engagements and he fled to Spanish Santo Domingo, from which he was extradited to be tortured and executed in Le Cap. His execution shocked many in France, turning the tide of opinion against French planters in the colony. It also left an impression among the enslaved, who would remember what had happened to Ogé a few years later when they negotiated with the French. Just as important, by the middle of 1790 the enslaved understood that they faced a major opportunity. Saint-Domingue's elites, including the free people of color, were divided, fighting each other openly, and lacking support or even understanding from a government in Paris that was itself in the midst of serious conflict and confrontation. In the summer of 1791, a group of enslaved organizers decided to strike.

Vodou and Revolution

The beginning of the Revolution, and the event often seen as the founding of Haiti itself, was the Bois-Caïman ceremony of August 1791. Although there has been debate about precisely when and where this event took place, the most careful study of the evidence (Geggus 2002) concludes that at least one and perhaps two religious ceremonies were organized before the great upris-ing of 1791. Plans were made, oaths taken, and inspiration gained from communication with deities, whose aid in the endeavor was seen as crucial by many. That the revolution was rooted in religious practice is no accident, for such practice enabled a diverse and fragmented slave population of disparate origins and experiences to find some common ground. Contemporary Haitian vodou carries the traces of the struggle of 18th-century slaves to retain ties to Africa and create new practices that could address the situation of plantation slavery. It also embodies the idea that diverse traditions could be incorporated into one system while retaining a certain autonomy, for the *lwa*, or gods, are organized into "nations" (in many cases into just two, Rada and Petwo, but sometimes more) that require their own rituals but still work together in a larger system of belief and practice.

Despite the oaths taken at the ceremony, a few rebels were discovered and the uprising seems to have been pushed to an earlier date. But it is hard to imagine that the insurgents could have had more success. In a simultaneous rising on the sugar plantations of Saint-Domingue's northern plain, the richest sugar-growing region in the colony, the insurgents rapidly turned cane fields and plantation houses to ash and smashed the sugar processing machinery. They killed most whites they encountered, sending the rest fleeing toward the capital in Le Cap. Soot and smoke covered the sky. At night the flames from the burning fields reached so high that according to one account a person could read by the light of the fires in the harbor of Le Cap. Had the uprising gone according to plan, the insurgents might actually have taken Le Cap, where most of the prominent planters had gathered for a meeting of the local assembly.

Nevertheless, the insurgents gained control of the plain and the mountains around Le Cap, turning plantations into military camps, recruiting new followers, finding weapons, and consoli-dating their territorial control. The French fought back, but to little avail. Despite counterattacks that anticipated characteristics of modern counterinsurgency campaigns—the French repeatedly slaughtered the old and infirm, along with women and children captured when they overran insurgent camps—the rebel army remained strong and grew steadily over the ensuing months. The insurgents also got help from the Spanish across the border in Santo Domingo, who began

Figure 3.1.1 Earliest known portrait of Toussaint Louverture, based on an oral description. Engraving by J. Barlow and Marcus Rainsford (1805).

Source: The John Carter Brown Library.

arming them in a bid to take over the valuable French colony. From among their ranks came a series of brilliant and remarkable leaders—first Boukman, Jean- François, and Biassou, and later Jean-Jacques Dessalines, Henri Christophe, the African-born Sans Souci and Macaya, and most famously Toussaint Louverture.

Louverture was born a slave in the northern plain of Saint-Domingue. (He was originally named Bréda after the plantation where he was born, and took on the name Louverture at the beginning of the revolution.) He worked as a coachman on a plantation, but gained his freedom in the 1770s. For a time, Louverture rented and managed a coffee plantation, overseeing the work of the enslaved. He also briefly owned at least one slave himself. He seems to have joined the insurrection shortly after it began and worked his way up through the ranks. By 1792 he had begun to play a crucial role, working closely with the Spanish to obtain guns and ammunition. At that time the French leadership of the colony had passed to two civil commissioners of the revolutionary state, François Polverel and Légér Félicité Sonthonax, who had been sent with the mission to quell the insurrection. They brought a decree from the National Assembly, which, hearing news of the frightening insurrection, had at last agreed to give political rights to all free people of color, hoping that this would guarantee their support against the slave insurrection. It worked, but only in part, for as rapidly as the French commissioners gained allies among free people of color, they lost them among the planters, who were increasingly convinced that the revolutionary French government was determined to destroy slavery.

Some planters began negotiating with the British in Jamaica, hoping to secure a foreign occupation of the island to preserve slavery and their position of power. In September 1792, France transformed itself from a constitutional monarchy to a republic, and in January 1793 the king was executed. Soon, France was at war with all the monarchies of Europe, and Britain was eager to strike at its enemy's most important colony. Many royalist planters deeply distrusted the radicals in France, whom they believed (with some reason) were rabid abolitionists. These planters' increasing alienation from the new leadership in France set off the remarkable transformations that took place in the summer of 1793 in Saint-Domingue, when the slave insurrection achieved a significant victory that irrevocably changed colonial and French law and politics.

By the middle of 1793 the Spanish-supported insurgents seemed unstoppable. Sonthonax and Polverel were in a desperate situation: many whites on the island were vociferously attacking their authority and, in many cases, were eagerly awaiting the arrival of the British. In June, the antirepublican planter camp found a leader in a man named Galbaud, who had been imprisoned in the Le Cap harbor by Sonthonax and Polverel and who now mobilized sailors and royalists in an attempt to overthrow their regime. The decisive intervention of militias of free people of color, and notably of an African-born officer named Jean-Baptiste Belley, saved the commissioners from being captured. Desperate for support, they made a bold move: they offered the enslaved insurgents who were camped just outside of the city to join with them. In return they offered freedom and French citizenship.

A band of insurgents under the command of an African-born man named Jeannot accepted the offer, and they rushed down into the town, defeating Galbaud and his partisans. As the fighting went on, fires were set and looting began in the city; much of Le Cap was burned to the ground. Terrified residents flooded onto ships in the harbor, leaving—in many cases permanently—for North America, where they settled in Philadelphia, Charleston, New Orleans, and New York. Sonthonax and Polverel had won, but only partially. Some insurgents were on their side now, but many more still fought with the Spanish. In the next months insurgent demands expanded, some calling for an outright abolition of slavery.

In August 1793, Sonthonax decreed slavery abolished in the Northern Province, while in subsequent months Polverel did the same in the other parts of the colony. It was a dramatic decision with profound implications. The commissioners had acted unilaterally and, with no

Figure 3.1.2 Portrait of the African-born Jean-Baptiste Belley, by French artist Anne-Louis Girodet de Roussy-Trioson (1797).

encouragement or even indication of support from the National Convention in Paris, abolished slavery in France's largest slave colony. Five hundred thousand slaves were emancipated without a period of transition and with no indemnity given to planters, as there would be in later cases of emancipation. It was the first full emancipation in the Americas, and it was improvised on the ground in the Caribbean. It also represented the victory of the slave insurrection, which was transformed from a movement of people often characterized by the French as "brigands" into one embraced by the local French administration.

Some slave insurgents, including Louverture, remained aloof from the French. Louverture seems to have been awaiting confirmation that the decision would be approved by France. That happened in 1794, when a group of three representatives from Saint-Domingue, including Belley, spoke to the National Convention and explained what had happened in Saint-Domingue, arguing that the abolition of slavery had been both politically and militarily necessary. The National Convention, with little debate, ratified the decision taken in Saint-Domingue, declaring slavery abolished and all men, of all colors, citizens of France. Emancipation, furthermore, was to be extended to other French colonies.

Liberty was won by the slaves of Saint-Domingue, then, not by attacking French metropolitan authority but by pledging allegiance to it against planters who were resisting it. Slave rebellion thus found its ally in metropolitan colonial power. In the process, republican rights were expanded to those who had been excluded from all legal rights. After 1794, France and its colonies were united, in principle, under one set of laws understood as truly universal and applicable on both sides of the Atlantic. For a time, racial hierarchies were defeated by assimilationist universalism. Racially integrated armies defended French colonies against the British and even attacked British colonies in the eastern Caribbean, playing a crucial role in the global conflict between the two imperial powers.

Independence

The decision of the National Convention helped secure Louverture's alliance to France. His military astuteness had earned him the rank of general, but it was his political brilliance as a negotiator and charismatic leader that ultimately gained him the leadership role he secured for himself by the late 1790s. Appointed governor by the French General Etienne Laveaux, his steadfast ally from the mid-1790s on, Louverture took control of the colony's military and civil affairs. By 1801, when he declared himself governor-for-life, he had already been the colony's de facto leader for several years. Throughout the 1790s, he served France's military objectives effectively, turning against his former Spanish allies, whom he drove from the colony, and expelling the British, who had occupied parts of the island since 1794.

But enemy forces were only part of the problem facing Louverture. He also had to oversee a large-scale transition from slavery to freedom, the first of its kind in the Americas, with little support from the French metropole and no examples for how to proceed. He continued the policies set in place by Sonthonax and Polverel, which required former slaves to continue working on plantations in return for a wage—paid not in money, but as a portion of the sugar or coffee produced. He also introduced some forms of democracy on the plantation, where workers could now elect their managers and could also, under some conditions, move to other plantations. As time went on, however, Louverture increasingly used coercion to keep workers on plantations, using the army of formerly enslaved men he had built to police the plantations and suppress resistance among workers. For many ex-slaves, the situation was unsatisfactory if not outright unacceptable, and there was significant and sometimes violent resistance against Louverture as many crafted an alternative vision of the future: one in which they would become small-scale landowners growing food for themselves rather than for an export-oriented plantation economy.

Louverture's service was a tremendous boon to France, for by defeating the massive British invasion of Saint-Domingue he played a central role in France's broader military campaigns in the Caribbean. Unlike the British, the French did not need to send troops across the Atlantic to fight, since so many former slaves of their colonies served as soldiers. Louverture's economic policies also were quite successful in rebuilding the coffee economy to almost prerevolutionary levels, and also in partially rebuilding the sugar economy, even though much of the machinery required for sugar production had been destroyed during the insurrection of 1791–92. But Louverture was always wary of the French government, concerned that it might ultimately reverse its support for emancipation. And he was ready for that possibility. His powerful army served France, but it was also a counterweight to French authority.

In the late 1790s, just as Louverture had feared, the French government began a retreat from policies of emancipation. This retreat accelerated with the rise to consular power of Napoleon Bonaparte and the (ultimately short-lived) peace with the British in 1801. Urged on by advisors and unchecked by the French parliament, some of whose members had in previous years eloquently supported emancipation in the Caribbean, Bonaparte decided to crush Louverture and his regime and to reverse the effects of abolition. He reacquired Louisiana from the Spanish, largely so that it could serve as a source of wood and provisions for what he hoped would be a reborn slave plantation colony in Saint-Domingue. He also ordered his brother-in-law, General Charles V. E. Leclerc, to lead a vast expeditionary force, which with later reinforcements totaled at least as many as 50,000 soldiers and sailors, to bring Saint-Domingue back under French control.

French rulers sought to hide their intention to crush the black armies that had emerged in the Caribbean, but many in Saint-Domingue understood what was happening. From their arrival, the French troops faced serious resistance, which was led by Louverture and his generals, including Christophe and Dessalines. Leclerc's troops suffered heavy losses, but ultimately Louverture surrendered, though smaller bands of fighters continued to battle against the French. Fearing that Louverture would once again join the resistance, the French imprisoned and deported him to a fortress in the Jura Mountains, where he died in 1803. Meanwhile, Dessalines and Christophe fought for the French for several months. As resistance expanded—spurred on by news that the French had reestablished slavery in Guadeloupe—these generals eventually turned against the French once again. Dessalines became the leader of the resistance and, after securing the final defeat of the French troops—only a few thousand of whom remained alive after the spirited resistance and a devastating yellow-fever epidemic—declared independence on January 1, 1804. Dessalines's fiery declaration of independence and the choice of the name Haiti—used by the island's indigenous people who had been decimated by the Spanish centuries earlier—presented the victory of the revolution as an act of vengeance against years of oppression and slavery.

Isolated by France and a fearful United States in the early 19th century, Haiti's rulers ultimately made a deal in 1825 that allowed its ports to be opened up to trade with France. In return for diplomatic recognition, however, the Haitian government granted France the payment of a massive indemnity. Former slave and plantation owners from Saint-Domingue had for decades been lobbying the French government for compensation for the economic losses they had suffered during the revolution. Much of the capital lost had, of course, been invested in the very bodies of those who had now won their freedom. Thus, the "indemnity" levied in 1825 was literally a fine for revolution, to be collected from the descendants of those men and women who had gained their freedom through rebellion a few decades before. Unable to deliver the exorbitant sum of 150 million francs demanded by the French, the Haitian government borrowed money from French banks and spent the next century contributing a good portion of its revenues to service this debt.

Independent Haiti also faced other economic challenges. The colony's very raison d'etre had been to serve the economic needs of France. By the late 18th century, its environment had already been devastated—commentators at the time complained of the problems of deforestation (which economists and development experts are only too willing to blame nowadays on the peasantry's land use practices)—and the colony had been artificially populated through a slave trade that had sustained a highly industrialized plantation system. But the economic options available to Haiti in the international system—the production of sugar and coffee—depended on labor systems that, understandably enough, were anathema to many ex-slaves. Nevertheless, 19th-century Haiti saw an impressive expansion of the increasingly profitable coffee economy, which eventually reached levels that rivaled those of the colonial past. Sugar production, however, was never restored to its previous levels. Meanwhile, throughout the country many former slaves created new lives as small-scale peasants, farming and raising livestock for local markets.

The Haitian Revolution left a complex political legacy, shaping a political culture that brings a radical egalitarianism together with traditions of militarization and authoritarianism. Outside Haiti, the nation and the struggle that produced it were regularly evoked in the battle over slavery in the Atlantic world. While many who supported slavery presented Haiti as a nation destined to fail, others held it up as an example of successful resistance. Throughout the early 19th century, debates about slavery referred—sometimes openly, sometimes obliquely—to the Haitian experience. Abolitionists evoked it regularly, though often they were not sure quite how to deal with the fact that the one successful example of large-scale emancipation had been won through massive violence. Playwrights and novelists in France—notably Alphonse de Lamartine and Victor Hugo—wrote works of literature about it. The figure of Louverture, the political and military genius of the revolution, circulated as myth, and as proof of the absurdity of white supremacist ideologies. Most important, the example of successful revolution in Haiti was a constant presence within communities of African descent throughout the Atlantic world, both enslaved and free. For them the stories and images of slaves turned generals and emperors who led the revolution were a source of fascination and hope.

What is the legacy of the Haitian Revolution? For centuries, many parties have struggled with how to tell the story. These groups include French generals and officials who wrote contemporary accounts or memoirs; Louverture himself, as he struggled in prison to produce a memoir of his military actions; early Haitian historians, like Beaubrun Ardouin and Thomas Madiou; the French abolitionist Victor Schoelcher; the Martinican poet Aimé Césaire; the Trinidadian activist and intellectual C. L. R. James; the African-American artist Jacob Lawrence; generations of 20th-century historians in the Caribbean, the United States, and France; the American novelist Madison Smartt Bell; and even the American actor Danny Glover in a promised film. If it has always been tempting to explain the revolution with recourse to social and racial categories—poor and rich whites, "mulattoes" and blacks, creole planters and French administrations, creole and African-born slaves—the history itself disrupts such attempts. If there is anything that defines the Haitian Revolution, it is the fact that its course was always unpredictable, the results always exceeding what those involved might have thought possible not long before. The revolution disrupted old categories and created new ones; it was always shadowed by the past while also bursting forth into something new, perhaps unreachable, but certainly unknown.

Of course Haiti did not make its history exactly as it chose, and in the 19th and 20th centuries it has been subjected to enormous external pressures that have contained and shaped its politics and economy. The indemnity levied by France in 1825 had a crippling effect on the state's solvency and ultimately on the coffee economy. In the 19th century Haiti was already experiencing the debilitating cycle of debt that would shape life in many other postcolonial countries in the late 20th century. Within the country the revolution itself left a complicated political legacy, for it helped create a tradition of authoritarian military rule even as it produced a radical democratic political culture. Both traditions have coexisted and clashed ever since. So, too, have different economic models: one aimed at producing agricultural products or manufactures for export in the global economy, the other focused on local production through small landholding—a radical refusal of economic relations that to some felt too much like slavery. As Haiti begins its third century as a free country, the past still lurks in present crises, such as the disrupted attempts in 2004 to commemorate a Haitian Revolution that remains in many ways unfinished.

Works Cited

Geggus, David. 2002. *Haitian Revolutionary Studies*. Bloomington: Indiana University Press.

James, C. L. R. 1963. *The Black Jacobins: Toussaint Louverture and the San Domingo Revolution*. New York: Vintage.

Thornton, John. 1991. "African Soldiers in the Haitian Revolution," *Journal of Caribbean History* 25, nos. 1 and 2: 58–80.

Trouillot, Michel-Rolph. 1995. *Silencing the Past: Power and the Production of History*. Boston: Beacon Press.

The Long Cuban Revolution

Michael Zeuske

The largest island in the Caribbean has been a site of political and economic struggles for centuries. Long before its historic 20th-century revolution, Cuba and its port city, Havana, served as an important link between the Americas, the Caribbean, and the Atlantic, as well as between the region and its dominating world powers. In fact, nearly all great empires with an interest in the region sought control over the island.

At the same time, internal pressures constantly roiled a Cuba turned wealthy and powerful, one of the most advanced, modern, and lucrative agricultural producers in the world, with a rich culture and complex African heritage. In many non-sugar-producing regions of the island, the *guajiros* (often free colored people or poor whites in alliance with local elites) formed small agricultural settlements, little influenced by the great plantations. Other such zones marginal to the plantation complex were characterized by *cimarronaje* (slave flight) and resistance against the expansion of the big sugar culture with its symptomatic institutions, like the *ingenio* (the agro-industrial complex of sugar fields and factories) and the slave barracoons of the port cities. Already in the 19th century, Cuban proponents of independence and nationalist elites, particularly in the eastern parts of the island, had formed alliances with free farmers, ex-slaves, workers, and the urban poor and middle classes against the conservative Hispano-Cuban planter class, the colonial bureaucracy, and the Catholic Church. Their most effective tool in the conflict over independence, nation, and sovereignty was the *ejército libertador cubano*, one of the largest transracial armies the Western Hemisphere had ever seen, whose traditions have lasted until the present day.

After Spain lost control over Cuba in 1898, the United States occupied the island twice (1899–1902 and 1906–9) and intervened on various occasions. Even after independence, the Cuban people had to deal with limitations on their sovereignty imposed by the US government through the Platt Amendment to the Cuban constitution of 1901. The first two Cuban presidents were imposed by the occupiers (in 1902 and 1909), and the constitutional system, only in theory fully implemented, masked harsh social and racial hierarchies.

The years between 1902 and 1925 witnessed official and unofficial conflicts among the Cuban elites, split as they were between *militares* and *doctores* (soldiers and intellectuals), liberals and conservatives, centralists and regionalists. In addition, and despite much racially inclusive rhetoric, there were hidden conflicts between "white" and "colored" elites. The first presidents were all white independence fighters. Racial conflicts were brought into the open only in one case, the Guerrita de los Negros of 1912, when the Partido Independiente de Color, an all-black political party, was suppressed with deadly force. Many protests and struggles for provincial or central power were carried out in the tradition and rhetoric of the independence wars—that is, through armed protest under the leadership of military elites (in the countryside) or civilian ones (in the cities). When the uprisings were suppressed, resistance took shape in the form of banditry and lawlessness, particularly in the *sierras* of Oriente.

In the 1920s, under Geraldo Machado's dictatorial rule, new forms of political participation and organization arose from the struggle against the alliance between a conservative military and the United States. These new forms, such as parties and cultural organizations, together with collective mass actions, a rebellion in the army, and the older forms of rural protest, played decisive roles in the socialist-inspired revolution of 1933, which was aborted under US pressure after only a few months. It is in this context—especially the attempt of rebel leader Antonio Guiteras Holmes to defend the doomed mass revolution through direct military action in rural terrains—that one can see the roots of the *fidelista* movement of the 1950s. Other former revolutionaries of military origin soon began using terrorist methods and effectively became bands of gangsters, especially in Havana. The years between 1933 and 1940 were a period of political, social, and institutional instability; within this period, Cuba had five presidents. The situation only stabilized under Fulgencio Batista, the first colored leader in highest office, initially as dictator and later (1940–44) as elected president.

One of the lasting results of the aborted revolution was the formation of a new party, the Partido Auténtico de la Revolución Cubana (the Auténticos), under Ramón Grau San Martín, the former president of the revolutionary government of 1933. During World War II, Batista formed new alliances, including with the communists of the Partido Unión Revolucionaria Comunista (PURC). The moderately radical nationalist Auténticos then won the elections of 1944 and 1948 against Batista and formed a new government that could be characterized as social democrat. Yet their leaders soon took to corrupt political maneuvers and—despite their radical and nationalistic rhetoric—assumed a pro-United States position early in the Cold War.

Struggling to maintain control of Cuba, the Auténtico government endured a series from challenges: from high-ranking military groups with contacts to Batista; from communists leading the unions; and from a new section of the Auténtico Party, called the *Ortodoxos*, under the leadership of Eduardo Chibás (1907–1951), who aimed to restore Cuban nationalism by returning to the teachings of José Martí (1853–1895), the 19th-century intellectual and champion of Cuban independence. Chibás had been one of the student leaders of 1933 and was a brilliant anticommunist speaker. But the most important goal of his "orthodox" *martianismo* was the critique of corruption under the Auténticos. The young Fidel Castro and his fellow comrades began their political career as Ortodoxos, admirers of Chibás, and members of the "generation of 1953," a designation honoring the centennial of Martí's birth.

In 1952 Batista once more took power in a coup. During the second *Batistiato*, the United States used a militarily subordinated Cuba to secure its own power over Caribbean states like Venezuela, by then one of the world's most important oil producers. But even though Batista proved less astute and skillful than during his first period in power, the older political leaders and organizations in the opposition made little headway against the *dictadura*. This was the historical moment for direct action by young politicians.

Toward the Revolution

On July 26, 1953, a group of students and workers led by Castro launched an attack on the army's Moncada Barracks in Santiago de Cuba. Although it failed, the attack demonstrated the willingness of Batista's adversaries to die for their ideal of a new nationalism embracing all social classes and groups, including the *campesinos* (both plantation workers and small farmers) and urban workers. After his imprisonment and eventual release, Castro could not stay in Cuba. Batista and the Batistianos had long used terror to repress urban resistance, political parties, parts of the unions, and civil enemies, including the Auténticos. So Castro, his brother Raúl, and their core group of supporters emigrated to Mexico, after founding the Movimiento 26 de Julio. There they began military and political training and met Ernesto "Ché" Guevara, who had participated in failed revolutions in Bolivia and Guatemala. After an adventurous return to Cuba in the yacht *Granma* in 1956, Castro's group took refuge in one of the most important regions of resistance against elite and state power, the Sierra Maestra mountains in eastern Cuba, where they transformed themselves into a guerrilla movement.

At this time, the Sierra Maestra, a small but relatively high mountain range, was still covered with primary subtropical forest, its very narrow valleys difficult to enter even with mules. The only major points of access were controlled by the cities of Manzanillo, Bayamo, and Santiago de Cuba. It was not easy for the mostly urban fidelistas to survive in this hostile environment, nor was it easy for them to form alliances with the people of the Sierra—a population of small farmers, refugees, smugglers, and bandits. The guerrilla fighters presented themselves in the tradition of the *mambises* (rebel fighters) from the anticolonial struggles of the 19th century and the rural conflicts against the oligarchic republic, combining this "invented tradition" with a strong hostility against US-owned plantation companies like the United Fruit Company.

Beginning in 1957, the Castro guerrillas succeeded in organizing local camps as institutions of a new, revolutionary power, defending the guajiros of the Sierra against state terror and taking military initiatives against the army. Thus, the struggle in the Sierra became a symbol of armed resistance against the local agents of dictatorship.

Nevertheless, until April of 1958, the leadership of the struggle against Batista remained concentrated in urban environments, controlled by leftist student organizations, parts of the Ortodoxos, the communists, and parts of the unions. Only after a failed general strike and a number of failed written *pactos* (agreements among opposition groups and organizations) did the Sierra and Castro attain undisputed leadership over nearly all opponents of Batista. The faction of the communist party (Partido Socialista Popular, or PSP) under Carlos Rafael Rodríguez, who

Figure 3.2.1   Castro in Washington, DC, 1959. Photograph by Warren K. Leffler.

Source: Library of Congress.

sympathized with the guerrillas, made contact with the Marxist wing of the fidelistas (foremost among them Guevara, but also Raúl Castro and Ramiro Valdés).

At this time Guevara viewed Castro as "the authentic leader of the leftist bourgeoisie." Cuba had strong national middle classes and powerful organizations of workers. Simultaneously faced with an economic crisis in the sugar sector, a crisis of Cuban identity, a crisis of relations with the United States (evident in conflicts between the CIA, the Pentagon, and the State Department over policy toward Cuba), and an institutional crisis, nearly all Cubans in 1958 shared the feeling that a renewed Cuban nationalism would improve their future (Pérez 1999).

That year, after an attack by Batista's army on the Sierra failed to crush Castro and his comrades, the guerrilla units took the strategic initiative and sent military columns under the commandants Guevara, Camilo Cienfuegos, Raúl Castro, and Juan Almeida to other Cuban regions, thus "invading" the whole island. In many territories, the forces of the *llanos* (anti-Batista forces from the lowlands) took power before—or, in some instances, in coalition with—the Castro guerrillas. In one of the other Cuban mountain ranges, the Escambray, Eloy Gutiérrez Menoyo created a "Second National Front." After a major defeat in the Battle of Santa Clara in December 1958, Batista fled to the Dominican Republic, handing over the army to General Eulogio Cantillo, who proposed to Castro the formation of a military junta. Castro refused. Declaring "*¡Revolución sí, golpe militar, no!*" (Revolution yes, military coup, no!), he called for a general strike, forcing the generals to retreat. The fidelistas then marched into Santiago de Cuba, and Guevara and Cienfuegos moved on Camp Columbia, the central military institution, and the Cabaña fortress in Havana.

On January 2, 1959, Castro gave a historic speech in Santiago de Cuba, remembering the 1898 occupation of the city by American troops and crying out: "This time it is a real revolution!" He declared Santiago the provisional capital of the island and proclaimed the liberal Manuel Urrutia president of the republic. The same day, Cienfuegos overtook Camp Columbia, capturing the most influential generals of the Batista army. In the following days, Castro moved in a triumphal procession across the 1,000 kilometers from Santiago to Havana. The political and military phase of the struggle thus came to an end, but it proved to be just the first chapter of the long Cuban Revolution.

The First Steps, 1959–73

The period immediately following Castro's military triumph was one of revolutionary improvisation. This was the era of major social reforms and of the destruction of capitalist forms of property and production, with assumption of control over them by the state. Linked to these changes were the expansion of political power over the whole of the island, the defense of the revolution against external threats, and a military projection of the Cuban model of guerrilla revolution to Latin America and parts of Africa. The revolutionaries regarded the internal processes in Cuba only as a first step toward a "world revolution."

The fidelistas attained national power while rapidly transcending the bourgeois national-ism (and middle-class constituencies) that had helped them win the military revolution. After extended conflicts within the Movimiento 26 de Julio, and with other nationalist forces in the government, Castro and his allies formed a revolutionary government controlled by left-wing guerrillas of the Sierra and, to a lesser degree, Communist and non-Communist activists from the Directorio Estudiantil Revolucionario.

The new government immediately implemented agrarian reform, which was overseen by the Instituto Nacional de Reforma Agraria (INRA). Private land was limited first to 400 hectares and later to 67, resulting in the nationalization of vast landholdings. Because the Cuban revolution-aries portrayed themselves as champions of the poorest Cuban farmers and sugar workers, the agrarian reform and the redistribution of land formed the core of this phase of the revolution, and the INRA became a type of parallel government in the first two years after the military victory. In the long run, however, the problem with this reform was that "modern" agrarian ideology favored large-scale, mechanized, and industrialized production, aided by large quantities of chemical fertilizers, which could not be achieved on the newly limited plots. Gradually rural landholders, urban elites, and parts of the middle classes (as well as competing military leaders, like Gutiérrez Menoyo) began to rebel against such policies of the fidelistas, using the guerillas' own methods. Other dissenters emigrated to the United States and other countries of the hemisphere.

At this point, the late Eisenhower and early Kennedy administrations began to support the diverse forms of resistance that had developed against the fidelistas, first by economic and po-litical means, then with Secret Service and military methods, using Cuban counterrevolutionary immigrants as mercenaries. Still, the US government, many political analysts, and Cuban exiles initially underestimated, neglected, or overlooked the solid alliance that had emerged between the fidelistas and the great mass of the Cuban population, primarily the urban and rural working classes but also large parts of the lower middle class. This alliance found symbolic expression in the strong position of Castro as the comandante en jefe (commander in chief) with mando único (single-handed command), and was based on revolutionary militias including all classes, genders, and institutions, which drew mass participation in the tradition of Western revolutions since 1776.

In April 1961, the Cuban revolutionary militia thus successfully repelled the invasion of Playa Girón (Bahía de Cochinos, or "Bay of Pigs") near Cienfuegos, which counterrevolutionaries had launched in the hope of activating other internal enemies of the fidelistas. The invasion was a total failure for the Cuban counterrevolution, the CIA, and the hawks in the US administration, and a great victory for Castro, his supporters, the Cuban militias, and the new Cuban army.

Such incidents also drove Cuba further into the arms of the Cold War rival of the United States. At the onset of the invasion Castro had reaffirmed the "the socialist and Marxist-Leninist character" of the Cuban revolution. Because of the hostile economic measures of the Eisenhower administration, which included a halt to sugar imports and conflicts over oil, the Cuban gov-ernment had already nationalized 37 banks and 382 international and national companies. At the same time, Cuba and the Soviet Union agreed to expand commercial relations. At the core of their agreements stood a fixed sugar quota and the delivery of oil from the Soviets. Close relations to the *rusos* or *soviéticos* expanded quickly into political and even military alliances.

In 1962 Soviet premier Nikita Khrushchev installed nuclear missiles and tactical weapons in Cuba. The Kennedy administration, which had stationed the same type of weapons in Turkey, near the Soviet border, responded with a military sea blockade of Cuba. In late October 1962, the world stood on the brink of a nuclear war. The US administration eventually gave the unwritten assurance that it would not attack or invade Cuba. The Soviets, in turn, withdrew their missiles— without the consent of the Cuban government.

In the following years, Cuba independently propagated and exported the "Cuban model" of revolution to the Caribbean, Africa, and Latin America, beginning with Venezuela. Even though the "export" effort did not immediately succeed, it had great ideological significance for those who resisted US power in the region. For its part, US diplomacy succeeded in expelling Cuba from the Organization of American States and similar groups.

Meanwhile, the revolutionaries proposed the formation of the *hombre nuevo*, or "new man," in Cuba under the doctrine of revolutionary nationalism and idealism. Between 1964 and 1973, the Cuban state subsidized the costs of transportation, telephone service, and other infrastructure as well as schools, social security, health care, and everyday needs such as bread, milk, meat, rice, potatoes, soap, cigarettes, clothes, and shoes. In return for this "historical loan," Cuba's men and women were expected to work voluntarily and transform themselves into "new" socialist citizens through labor, study, and service in the Fuerzas Armadas Revolucionarias (FAR) or other institutions to defend the revolution. The state also proposed nationwide reforms to the Cuban educational and medical systems and new infrastructure connecting the countryside and the cities. Urban reform enabled many Cubans to buy their homes, while rents on flats and apartments were fixed at a low rate. As minister of industry, Guevara strove to create a proper industrial base and to diminish the economy's dependence on sugar.

At first, the reform process was creative and open, because Cuba had not just a single revolutionary party for the whole country but rather many different national organizations (for youth, students, women, farmers, artists) and neighborhood committees for the defense of the revolution (Comités de Defensa de la Revolución). Connecting the traditionally strong regionalisms of the six provinces were the National Militia (until 1962) and later the FAR. A socialist culture that promoted national education also linked the people of Cuba.

But industrialization and the short-term formation of "new men" failed, as did such efforts as the creation of a new breed of cattle, which was supposed to improve milk and meat production. The result was a famine, alleviated only by rice purchases from China. In 1962, partly in response to the US trade embargo, Cuba began a giant distribution program, giving fixed rations of daily necessities to all households. At a time when the state needed the income from sugar exports for its ambitious social programs, the sugar harvest stood without enough workers because nobody would "voluntarily" do the extremely hard work in the cane fields. The state had to resort to drafting army personnel, prisoners, students, and members of the state bureaucracy for the harvesting, and it also relied on international volunteers who came to Cuba to help.

Between 1960 and 1968, Havana became the capital of world revolution, attracting numerous members of the international left. The question of whether the Cuban revolution was specific to the island or part of a coming world revolution against imperialism was symbolized by the figure of Guevara and a relatively small but influential group of his followers. On the one hand, Guevara was Cuba's minister of industry and director of the national bank, a core institution of the national state; on the other, he traveled the world in search for new foci of global revolution and trained guerrillas in Cuba for this purpose.

But the international politics of revolution—as expressed in Castro's Declaration of Havana (1962) and the theoretical works of Guevara, which were in line with Maoist doctrine between 1965 and 1968—proved too expensive for Cuba. After the failure of the direct export of the Cuban model of revolution to Argentina, Algeria, Somalia, Congo, Venezuela, and finally Bolivia, where Guevara died in 1967, the Cuban government decided to resolve its inner crisis by means of a "revolutionary offensive": first, the nationalization of all services, restaurants, shops, and petty commercial installations, and second, a revival of sugar agriculture planned to culminate in 1970 with a model harvest, called the *gran zafra,* with a production goal of 10 million tons of sugar. The harvest failed, however, and in a public speech Castro offered to resign. But the great performance of preparing the gran zafra had demonstrated the achievements of revolutionary nationalism and organization. In the midst of the turbulent international context of 1968–74, with its worldwide political crisis and democratic student movements, Cuba entered a new era. It began with a search for new orientations, strong repression against critics of the "mistakes" of the period of revolutionary voluntarism, and new forms of institutionalization, centralization, and bureaucratization. The state of revolutionary emergency came to its end.

Socialism in the New World, 1975–89

The second period after the military revolution was one of socialist institutionalization and international projection, linked to the building of the first New World welfare state with the highest degree of social security in the Americas. The fidelistas now saw their revolution as an original and creative part of the "real socialism" that existed in the Soviet Union and Europe. They also conceived of Cuba as the "first socialist territory in the Americas," with an important function as a model for Africa and Asia. This period witnessed Cuba's engagement with the non-aligned movement and its intense military intervention in Angola (1975–89), among other adventures in Africa.

Yet from 1968–70 (the 100th anniversary of the first anticolonial revolution) onward, the revolutionaries embarked on a "concentration on Cuba and its revolutionary traditions" that entailed increasing institutionalization, a new constitution and legal reform, the final formation of a national communist party (Partido Comunista de Cuba), and the consolidation of a social-ist economy (in reality a form of centralist state economy). The revolution of 1959 acquired a very long history. The result was a fidelista-guided process of constitution-building from the ground up (*poder popular,* "people's power," as enshrined in the socialist constitution of 1976), a political integration into the socialist network dominated by the Soviet Union, and an economic integration into the communist organization COMECON. The only remnants of formal private property were small plots called *fincas,* used in a type of socialist subsistence agriculture, which represented about 20% of Cuba's arable land. The Communist Party began to formally rule Cuban society, with Castro as head of the army, the state, the council of ministers, and the party. But he and the leading group of former guerrillas also began to develop an informal double system of power: Castro was the visible head, the spokesman, and the international strategist while his brother Raúl would become more and more the chief of personnel, the head of the armed forces and the secret services. As such, he played an extremely important role in managing the revolution.

Meanwhile, Cuba's ongoing policy of supporting revolutionary movements elsewhere—not only by military power or mere "export," but also through education of cadres within Cuba (particularly on the Isla de Pinos, also known as the Isla de la Juventud) and a combination of military, medical, educational, and organizational assistance—was successful. Sending Cubans on internationalist missions abroad was also an important element in the solution of the island's inner problems between 1970 and 1975. Castro took the initiative to support Marxist revolutionaries in Angola, declaring Cuba an "Afro-Latin country." He launched "Operation Carlota," a military, political, and cultural initiative in support of the MPLA (People's Movement of Liberation of Angola); from then until 1990, 400,000 Cubans operated in Angola.

Caribbean countries such as Jamaica under Michael Manley (1972–80) and Grenada under Maurice Bishop (1979–83) also figured prominently in Cuba's strategy of aiding other Third World nations. In the latter case, the experiment ended on a sour note with the assassination of Bishop and a subsequent US invasion. Cuba's greatest success along these lines was the Sandinista victory in Nicaragua (1979–90). Although the Sandinistas were ousted from power in 1990, events such as these quite plausibly laid the basis for the leftist turn, after the so-called lost decades of the 1970s and 1980s, of many Latin American countries including Brazil, Argentina, Venezuela, and Ecuador at the end of the 20th century and beginning of the 21st. When in 1979 the non-aligned states of the world held their summit meeting in Havana, Castro was elected president of the organization, confirming his role as a leader of the Third World.

As Cuba became firmly integrated into the communist world, it became increasingly isolated in the West but also alienated from the European left and from sympathetic Western governments. A short renewal of relations between Cuba and the United States under President Jimmy Carter (1977–81) ended with the election of Ronald Reagan as Carter's successor. Castro also feared that a reformist policy toward the United States would undermine Cuban unity, as indeed occurred in 1981 when 125,000 Cubans fled the island in a massive wave of illegal emigration to the United States, termed the "Mariel exodus."

The growth of Cuban institutions signaled a period of increasing bureaucratization and centralization of schools and universities, as well as the repression of cultural and artistic liberties during what became known as the *quinquenio gris* (the "grey half-decade") between 1971 and

1975. During the 1970s the government restructured provincial administration and privileged rural development, while inadequate housing remained a pressing social problem. But the greater centralization of society, together with the credit, goods, and oil provided by the Soviet Union, East Germany, and other socialist countries, enabled the government to maintain and extend the socialist welfare state. In Cuba nobody went hungry, and medical care and education were free. In fact, Cuba became a social, educational, and medical success story, with demographic indicators comparable to those in Western European welfare states. It is therefore not surprising that against the backdrop of the 1990s crisis, many Cubans later remembered the period between 1970 and 1990 as the "golden years" of a modest but stable "tropical socialism."

That situation, however, was not as stable as it seemed. In 1981 sugar prices fell to levels similar to those in 1920. Cuba had giant debts and was technically bankrupt. The centralist economy was inefficient and it failed to produce enough to maintain the country's expensive social and foreign policies. The government allowed semiprivate farmers' markets (*agromercados*) to soften the food problems. Cuba's survival rested on the solidarity of other socialist countries. But the Eastern bloc had its own problems, which the Soviet Union aimed to resolve with the reforms of glasnost and perestroika under leader Mikhail Gorbachev. The reaction in Cuba was the onset of conflict within the revolutionary leadership, followed by a new period of economic voluntarism (the expectation that citizens work for little or no pay to help advance socialism) and the increasing glorification of Guevara. In 1986, Castro himself decided to put an end to the remnants of a market economy in Cuba, such as farmers' markets, in what he called a "rectification of errors."

As this phase of the revolution drew to a close in 1989, Cuban troops began to retreat from Angola after military victory. However, that same year, General Arnaldo Ochoa, chief of the troops and a veteran guerrilla, was convicted of involvement in international drug trafficking and executed—an event that many analysts have interpreted as the elimination by members of Castro's inner circle of a competing leader sympathetic to Soviet perestroika and Gorbachev.

A Permanent Revolution, 1990–Present

The most recent period in Cuban history, dating from 1990, has been marked by crisis, the institutionalization of a wartime economy, retreat, reforms, and recentralization. With the breakdown of the Soviet Union (1989–91), Cuba lost its ties to a third consecutive empire. It also became the only surviving "real socialist" nation in the West (at least until 2006, when Hugo Chávez declared his brand of Bolivarian socialism in Venezuela). The Cuban revolutionaries, under the direct leadership of Castro until his resignation in February 2008, strengthened a new discourse of "permanent revolution." The term, once conceptualized by Guevara (and, even earlier, by Leon Trotsky), now included a dose of real nationalism as envisioned by Martí and was linked to new forms of economic performance as well as a new relationship with the Latin American left—Venezuela primarily, but also Bolivia and Ecuador.

The years between 1986 and 1989 had already been a time of severe problems for Cuba, but the breakdown of socialist states in the Soviet Union and Eastern Europe ushered in a period of deep crisis. While maintaining the discourse of permanent revolution, Castro declared a "special period" of wartime austerity measures in a time of peace. Informally, the centralized state had to accept local and provincial assistance in organizing economic performance and food production. The national transportation infrastructure and even the urban transport systems collapsed, while food distribution shrunk to dangerously low levels.

The black market, which at other times had been of minor significance, expanded greatly and imbued the US dollar with a new and important role, even though the possession of dollars was proscribed in Cuba. By 1993 the illegal-exchange rate had risen to 130 Cuban pesos per US dollar, which led the Cuban counterrevolution and parts of the Cuban exile community to expect the imminent breakdown of Castroism. In 1996, the US Congress passed the Cuban Liberty and Democratic Solidarity Act (known as the Helms-Burton Act after its sponsors, Senators Jesse Helms and Dan Burton), which strengthened the US trade embargo in hopes of hastening a collapse.

The Cuban state reacted by legalizing the possession of US dollars for individuals in 1993, fixing the official exchange rate at around 20 to 30 pesos per dollar, and establishing official exchange bureaus (*casas de cambio*). In the following years it also embarked on a program of economic reforms, facilitating limited international investment in certain sectors (maintaining 51% ownership by the Cuban state) as well as joint ventures, most extensively in the tourist sector but also in mining and in the marketing of Cuban cigars, pharmaceuticals, and rum. Domestically, the state reinstated farmers' markets, allowed the opening of small private restaurants (*pala-dares*), and permitted minor economic activities on a "self-employment" basis (*por cuenta propia*). Cubans who had jobs in the hotel and tourist sector, or who received remittances from relatives in the United States or other parts of the exile community, achieved special status, giving rise to new social hierarchies despite persistent rhetoric emphasizing revolutionary equality.

The state filled this growing gap between reality and rhetoric with a retreat to the core program of Cuban nationalism, *martianismo*, and permanent *revolución*. At the 1991 Party Congress it rehabilitated religious practices, including both institutionalized denominations and Afro-Cuban religions such as Santería, Palo Monte, Abakuá, and vodou. At the same time, the state sought to develop a new system of taxation, implement programs to save electricity and water, and modernize the sugar industry. All of these attempts failed to one degree or another.

Within Cuba a variety of minor opposition groups arose, largely centered on reformist programs for the future of the island. Many Cubans, especially younger people, sought to emigrate by whatever means possible—marrying foreigners or tourists, staying in other countries after an *internacionalista* mission, or fleeing to Florida aboard rickety boats and even more precarious rafts. But even during the most difficult times, when many Cubans suffered acute hunger or deficiency diseases, the Cuban state never stopped the *internacionalista* program of university education in Cuba for Latin American, Caribbean, or African students, particularly in medicine.

In 1998 Castro, who had never totally broken with the social program of the Catholic Church, invited Pope John Paul II to Cuba. Clearly, the Cuban revolution retreated but did not collapse.

One important ally with revolutionary sympathies during the later years of this period was Venezuela, where Chávez had proclaimed himself a leader of the "Bolivarian revolution." After a failed counterrevolutionary coup against Chávez in 2002 and the victory of the Chavistas in a national referendum in 2004, the relationship between Venezuela and Cuba became even closer. Chávez ramped up aid to Cuba and sent cheap oil and other goods in exchange for Cuban doctors in social missions, sports, and education.

Internal reforms in 1993, 1997, and 2003 aimed at reasserting national control over financial and economic activities, particularly private farmers' markets. These reforms ended more or less with the state's decision to grant entrepreneurial privileges to the army. Since then, the Revolutionary Armed Forces (FAR) have controlled important parts of the economy. Its members receive higher salaries, paid partly in convertible currency, which allows their families to purchase goods from dollar shops (*tiendas de la recaudación de divisas*, or TRDs). The police force has been modernized and reinforced. A group of younger politicians surrounding the civilian academic Carlos Lage formed a kind of socialist technocracy and intelligentsia, which played an important role in the making of the "reforms in socialism" during the "special period" and facilitated the creation of centers of new technologies (mainly biotechnology, but also computer programming and medical research).

Between 2002 and 2005, the neoconservative administration of George W. Bush curtailed remittances from the United States to Cuba and controlled the contacts of US citizens with Cuba. In 2004, Castro ended the era of the dollar as a legal currency in Cuba, replacing it with the convertible Cuban peso (CUC), and he levied a fee of between 8% and 20% on every foreign currency transaction, thus ending the reforms for which "dollarization" had become a symbol.

Castro's supporters in the higher army echelons reasserted power over the whole island by repressing the moderate internal opposition and continuing to cut down the possibilities for free enterprise based on the US dollar, even as industrial sugar production practically collapsed. At the same time, the state opened important spaces—literally and metaphorically—for debate (especially for the National Union of Writers and Artists, UNEAC) and made it possible for those elites regarded as "revolutionaries" to make money in new civil (medical, technical, and cultural) internationalist missions to foreign countries, particularly Venezuela. The recentralization of national power also benefited the broader population. Between 2005 and 2009 the transport infrastructure, schools, hospitals, and universities were renovated, and many Cuban households received new power-saving domestic equipment (refrigerators, stoves, lamps) at very low cost.

But nearly a half-century after their military victory, Castro and members of his circle faced the realities of their age. In 2007 Castro missed the official celebration of his 80th birthday because of an acute intestinal illness, appearing only in short television images from the hospital. This event perhaps serves as a metaphor for his place in history and the popular imagination. In Cuban public discourse he remains an undisputed iconic presence; in private conversations, however, his name may be met with silence or even jokes. Outside Cuba, he is a mythical figure—one of evil for parts of the Cuban exile community and their political allies; one of revolution, devotion to his country, and improvement of social conditions for the poor to many people in the Caribbean and the Third World in general.

Castro's younger brother Raúl, who had controlled all armed forces since 1989, took provisional power over the island in the middle of 2006 and was confirmed as president in February 2008. He started a new round of "reforms in socialism," aimed at stabilizing the economic core of Cuban society. Productivity in Cuba is still extremely low, with as much as 50% of the land uncultivated. The lack of food production in times of rising prices is opening more and more gaps between imports and local production. Ironically, many of those imported foodstuffs originate in the United States. Cuba also suffered reverberations from the global financial crisis of 2008.

In January 2009, the 50th anniversary celebrations of the Triumph of the Revolution in Santiago de Cuba featured all the elements of the present-day revolution: pride in a great tradition, sovereignty, thrift (no army parade), virtual quotations from the absent Castro, loud speeches on "revolution," and quiet discourses on new reforms, such as the possibility of buying homes, one of the greatest problems facing young Cubans. But as was made clear by the anniversary celebrations and subsequent events of 2009—the increasing presence of the army in the government, and the removal from government of the group of reformers associated with Carlos Lage and Pérez Roque—the government of Raúl Castro retains control over the nation and territory of Cuba.

Works Cited

Pérez Jr., Louis A. 1999. *On Becoming Cuban: Identity, Nationality, and Culture.* Chapel Hill: University of North Carolina Press.

Zeuske, Michael. 2004. *Insel der Extreme: Kuba im 20. Jahrhundert* (Island of Extremes: Cuba in the 20th Century). Zurich: Rotpunktverlag.

The Guerrilla in Colombia

An Interview with Rodrigo Granda, Member of the FARC–EP International Commission

Jean Batou and Rodrigo Granda

R odrigo Granda is a member of and the leading international spokesperson for the *Fuerzas Armadas Revolucionarias de Colombia-Ejército del Pueblo, the Revolutionary Armed Forces of Colombia-People's Army (FARC–EP). His name gained global prominence in December 2004 when he was kidnapped in Venezuela and handed over to Colombian authorities by a number of Venezuelan National Guard soldiers seeking a reward placed on his head by the Colombian government. At the time of his capture Granda was attending a meeting of the Bolivarian Peoples Movements in Caracas. Granda's kidnapping in Venezuela at the instigation of the Colombian government created an international dispute between Venezuela and Colombia. He was released in 2007 in response to pressures exerted on the Colombian government by French President Nicolas Sarkozy.*

The FARC–EP describes itself as a Marxist revolutionary people's movement and has been in an armed conflict with the Colombian regime since 1964. It is the largest revolutionary force in the country (the other guerilla group is the smaller ELN or National Liberation Army). At any given time it controls much of the country, although the mainly rural regions under its control vary. In 1984 the FARC–EP agreed to a truce and formed an organized political wing called the Patriotic Union (UP), which was to engage in electoral politics. The UP received such widespread support that the Colombian ruling class panicked and unleashed its death squads, assassinating thousands of UP members and drowning the truce in blood.

Today Columbia is ruled by what has been called a "genocidal democracy" (see Javier Giraldo, Columbia: The Genocidal Democracy, *Common Courage, 1996). "The richest 1 percent of the population controls 45 percent of the wealth, while half of the farmland is held by thirty-seven large landholders," The majority of the population subsists on less* than 3 percent of the arable land, while 3 percent owns more than 70 percent of that land (James J. Brittain, "The FARC–EP in Colombia," Monthly Review, September 2005). Columbia is the dominant source of cocaine in the world. Large parts of the country are dominated by drug lords with their paramilitary armies with which the government is closely associated. Columbian President Álvaro Uribe is himself linked to drug traffickers, including members of his own family.

In the 1990s under the Clinton administration "Plan Colombia" was introduced whereby the United States provided massive military aid and direct "special operations" support to Colombia aimed at the FARC–EP, under the cover of an anti-narcotics operation. During the Bush administration, Washington replaced this with "Plan Patriota," carried out in cooperation with Uribe's government, under the rubric of which the United States has intensified its war on the FARC–EP as part of the so-called War on Terrorism. In 2001–02 the United States, followed by its allies in the European Union, officially designated the FARC–EP as a "terrorist" organization. However, the dominant reality in Colombia is state/paramilitary terrorism. As part of the stepped-up repressive campaign in the Bush/Uribe period the paramilitaries in league with the Columbian military forces committed atrocities such as burning children alive and using chainsaws on others while still alive (see James J. Brittain, "Run, Fight or Die in Colombia: The Paramilitaries Burned Wayuu Children Alive and Killed Others with Chainsaws," Counterpunch, March 12–13, 2005, http://www.counterpunch.org/brittain03122005.html). Meanwhile, Bogotá and Washington continue to use chemical fumigants on large parts of the country, ostensibly aimed at coca eradication, but also as a form of chemical warfare.

An issue of growing international concern has been the humanitarian exchange of prisoners/hostages taken by the two sides in the war. In June 2007, during negotiations on the release of twelve Colombian lawmakers held by the FARC–EP, a counterinsurgency attack on the FARC–EP encampment where these prisoners were being held was carried out and eleven of the lawmakers were killed in the crossfire. The FARC–EP was accused by Bogotá and Washington of having "murdered" the captives although evidence on the ground seemed to confirm the FARC–EP's story that the death of the prisoners was unintended (see Inter Press Service News Agency, "Columbia: Pawns of War—The Hostage Crisis," November 2, 2007, http://ipsnews.net/news.asp?idnews=39902).

In fall 2007 Venezuelan President Hugo Chávez became increasingly active in negotiations for the release of FARC–EP captives, bringing in a number of important international figures to support the effort, such as U.S. filmmaker Oliver Stone. This led eventually to the release in January 2008 of two high-level prisoners held by FARC–EP. Chávez followed up his success in this regard with a demand that the FARC–EP (and also the smaller ELN) be designated as a "real army" with political objectives and not a "terrorist" organization; that it be accorded "belligerent status" in international law. This would then facilitate further releases of prisoners on both sides. His call was supported by the Venezuelan Assembly and Ecuador but rejected by the United States, the Colombian government, and the European Union. The according of belligerent status to the FARC–EP would mean that both the Colombian military and the FARC–EP would have to conform to the Geneva Conventions on warfare and the treatment of prisoners. It would also result in increased pressure for peace negotiations on both sides. Both Washington and Bogotá are therefore adamantly opposed to any such change in the international designation of the FARC–EP as a "terrorist" organization.—Ed.

JEAN BATOU: The Fuerzas Armadas Revolucionarias de Colombia–Ejército del Pueblo, the Revolutionary Armed Forces of Colombia–People's Army (FARC–EP) looks upon itself as a politico-military movement waging a social/insurrectional war against the Colombian state. As such, the FARC–EP takes prisoner police officers, soldiers, officials, and mercenaries. The FARC–EP has also decided to kidnap civilians representing the Colombian state apparatus. In short, it also kidnaps civilians, the release of whom depends upon payment of a ransom. While no one can argue with an army taking its armed adversaries prisoner, how can the FARC–EP justify taking civilians captive? Does the FARC–EP not realize that such practices tend to isolate it from broad swathes of antigovernment public opinion in Colombia?

RODRIGO GRANDA: The FARC–EP is indeed a politico-military movement making use of the inalienable right to rebel against a state that practices paper democracy. What we are doing is responding to a war imposed on us from the highest echelons of power in Colombia. *State terrorism* has been wielded against us and our people as a method of extermination for decades.

Of course, it is common knowledge, that war of this kind needs funding. This war was forced on us by Colombia's rich, so they are the ones that have to finance the war they unleashed. That's why the FARC–EP holds people for whom a monetary payment is collected, which is really a tax. This money is set aside to maintain the apparatus of the people's war.

As you may know, we talk about *constructing a new power,* a new state. If in Switzerland, France, or the United States someone ducks out of their duty of paying taxes, then that person has to go to jail. The new state we are shaping has fixed the payment of a *peace tax*. That means that any individual or corporate body, and any foreign companies operating in Colombia and making profits of over a million dollars a year, have to pay a peace tax equivalent to 10 percent of these profits. Debtors are told they have to enter into dialogue with those who manage the FARC–EP's finances to pay this sum. If they fail to do so, of course, these people will be arrested and taken to prison until they pay and fulfill their obligations toward those of us who are shouldering the responsibility of the *new state,* constructed and led by the FARC–EP, acting as the People's Army.

Now, within the context of military operations some officers, noncommissioned officers, policemen, and soldiers do fall into the hands of the FARC–EP and some are currently being held as prisoners of war. Likewise, during our confrontations with the Colombian state some prisoners from our side have fallen into enemy hands and, following summary rigged trials, they are now serving extremely long sentences in different jails across the country. Unfortunately, this is par for the course during a war. At any rate, amid the extremely acute conflict taking place in Colombia it is possible that some detentions might not, on the whole, be looked upon by the population in a favorable light. But we believe that, by making Law 002 public, according to which certain economically powerful individuals and entities have to pay a peace tax, we have already given them warning and they also have the option to discuss and resolve their situation and to settle up within the time period set. If we can ensure this is complied with then the number of detentions will certainly tail off as a result.

As for whether this divides us from the civil population ... it may have some effect on that, but it probably is not crucial, because large sectors of the Colombian population are fully aware that, in general, the FARC–EP only arrests people whose economic situation is pretty comfortable. There is no way this is about arresting people for the sake of arresting them.

Prisoners of war are kept for the purposes of humanitarian tradeoffs, which we are hoping to carry out very soon. Let's not forget that in Colombia the public prosecutor's office and the specialist judges impose heavy sentences on many guerrilla fighters (who are lucky enough not to have been killed during their capture), sentences that will keep them in prison practically for life, because justice in Colombia is class justice and is applied as such. And, obviously, those of us who make use of the inalienable right of rebellion are labeled "terrorists" or "kidnappers." You should know that the sentences dished out to revolutionaries range between forty and eighty years.

So you can see that this matter of the tax is a need determined by the current war situation affecting Colombia. We would like it if we did not have to detain anyone, no civilians or oligarchs, not to mention the military. ... But the confrontation, the daily reality in Colombia, means that this is how things happen—not the way we'd like them to.

JB: The armed struggle is largely funded by the collection of the revolutionary tax on coca leaf cultivation and cocaine base production—and also, to some extent, on ransom payments from kidnappings. If a peace process is initiated, could the guerrilla movement stop using these sources of funding without jeopardizing its politico-organizational autonomy? In other words, are there not certain forces within your movement that are attempting to defend the status quo for fear that demobilization might deprive the FARC–EP of these decisive sources of funding and that this might lead to its isolation?

RG: The first thing that has to be said is that the FARC–EP has always been an autarkic movement, that is to say, it has always operated using its own means and has never depended, either in the past or at present, and will never depend, on any funding of a foreign nature. As the FARC–EP, we were able to develop a subsistence economy initially and then factors of production that have enabled us to keep the movement going.

The FARC–EP existed long before either drug trafficking in Colombia developed or a logistical policy for the systematic detention of persons was implemented. These were by-products of the general situation in the country.

Over the years the FARC–EP has diversified its financing through all kinds of investments: in high finance at home and abroad, and in agricultural production, cattle raising, mining, transport, construction, and many other productive investments.

Now, there is no doubt that the face of Colombia was transformed by the neoliberal policies imposed through terror that ruined the countryside forcing thousands of poor peasant families to survive by producing for this economy so as not to starve to death as a result of the devastation caused to their traditional crops of coffee, corn, banana, sorghum, cotton, and so on.

The FARC–EP is chiefly a rural movement and we are in direct contact with that reality, but we have no authority to force people to abandon so-called illicit crops without giving them an alternative.

At the talks in the Cagúan region (1999–2002) during the government of President Pastrana, the First International Public Audience on the replacement of so-called illicit crops and protection of the environment was held under the initiative of our guerrilla organization. The meeting was attended by the EU, Japan, Canada, the UN, and the International Group of Friends of the Peace Process in Colombia. The United States was invited but did not take part.

At these talks, the FARC–EP presented a viable project for eradicating coca leaf plantations in the municipality of Cartagena del Chairá in the Caquetá Department, of which there were around 8,000 hectares at that time.

We wanted the international community to commit to an alternative to repression and to promote social investment in the area so as to create an "experimental laboratory" there, in the search for ways to eradicate those crops, and then extend the experiment to other regions of Colombia and possibly the continent: Ecuador, Peru, and Bolivia. This proposal is still valid.

At the same time, we believe that legalization of the drug will help to solve the problem. Economists such as [Milton] Friedman and reputable journals like the *Economist* acknowledge that this is the case. There is a reason for this: as it is a clandestine business, profitability due to capital turnover is staggering. It is currently estimated that there are $680 billion circulating in the world as a result of drug trafficking and there is no crime people would not commit to get their hands on such an enormous sum of money.

First and foremost it is an economic problem, then a political, and of course, an ethical and moral one, but if the huge profits are eliminated, then the fundamental incentive, which is the return on investment, will be cancelled out and the states will be able to control the market. This would be something like what happened, allowing for differences, with the legalization of whisky ... in the United States.

What must be made clear, and we have demonstrated this to the national and international community, is that there is no way the FARC–EP is a drug trafficker, not by any stretch of the imagination. We are not involved in the production, transport, commercialization, or exportation of narcotics. On the contrary, the FARC–EP is willing to work with the international community and with the U.S. government itself to solve this serious problem plaguing the world.

Our organization has implemented the collection of a tax on coca paste buyers who have to enter the areas where these crops are grown and we operate. This payment is collected as a way of controlling the abuses committed against the peasant growers. Of course, we act as policemen. It is the Colombian state that must control this area, but, up until now, it has been incapable of doing so, in spite of the billions of dollars poured in by the U.S. government to put an end to this business.

It is also important to bear in mind that the money provided by this tax is a tiny quantity in relation to the costs of the FARC–EP military apparatus. As for the arrests, it has to be said that this income also helps with the economic maintenance of the FARC–EP, but it is not the most crucial part.

The FARC–EP's ultimate aim is not to "line the pockets" of its directive personnel, its hierarchy, or its combatants. For us money is a means, something that can help us attain the strategic political end of the FARC–EP, which is to take power in order to bring about political, economic, social, and ecological changes of all kinds that Colombia needs and is demanding. So, the financing is just a means to achieve these ends. Nobody in the FARC–EP aspires to become a millionaire. This is the big difference between us and the drug barons and paramilitaries who are seeking personal gain and want to live "the high life."

With respect to what you say about a possible demobilization, that is not in the FARC–EP's immediate plans. I mean, there is not even any contact with Uribe's government. In the hypothetical case that the war was stopped and other action embarked upon, the FARC–EP has its "plan B." But we're talking about hypotheses; the reality is quite different.

However, the FARC–EP is not at war just for the sake of it. We have said that if the political environment changes and the conditions exist for engaging in open, legal politics without fear of reprisals or of being killed; if the door to real democracy is opened, then we could think about changing the form of military confrontation in response to whatever situation was instituted. It has fallen to the FARC–EP throughout the period of Uribe, and before, to act as the political opposition and the armed opposition to the regime because there has been no other way we could express our thinking. The Colombian bourgeoisie is a bloodthirsty, reactionary bourgeoisie that only understands the language of arms. If we had not responded to the aggression, they would already have branded us with red hot iron, and chained us up, like in the age of slavery.

JB: The recent mass mobilizations against the violence and kidnappings have pointed the finger of blame at both the government and the insurgents. Don't these mobilizations represent a setback for the left in that Álvaro Uribe has been able to use them to his advantage to divert public attention from his involvement in parapolitical scandals?

RG: The mobilizations, as you yourself say, express a repudiation of violence and particularly official and paramilitary violence. The Colombian people are certainly showing signs of fatigue over the military-type confrontation, but what people wouldn't after forty years of war imposed by the regime?

Álvaro Uribe tried to capitalize on a movement that incorporated popular sectors very close to the FARC–EP, and even members of our guerrilla organization. There, at these mobilizations, you could see the banners demanding a humanitarian exchange, in the search for dialogue toward a political solution to the social and armed conflict in Colombia. If you analyze the press releases, and radio and television reports, you will find that Colombia's most prestigious commentators criticized the government's political opportunism. You have to remember that there was even a public confrontation between the interior minister and one of the relatives of the eleven congressional representatives killed in the failed military rescue attempt ordered by the government on June 18 this year. And then the claim that President Uribe has capitalized on the mobilizations is untrue. On the contrary, in the latest opinion polls following those events Uribe's image is shown to have been tarnished and his popularity is in "free fall" for the first time since he took office.

As for the problem of parapolitics, this is something that has been denounced for over twenty years by the newspaper *Voz*, the organ of the Communist Party of Colombia, by the FARC–EP, and by democratic friends throughout the country. However the Colombian state has always ignored these denunciations.

A year and a half ago I had the opportunity to talk to the peace commissioner of Uribe's government, Dr. Luis Carlos Restrepo, at the Cómbita high-security prison, where I was being held hostage. During our conversation, we touched on various topics and I was able to demonstrate to him that the policy of "democratic security" imposed by the president and the "Plan Colombia" had failed. He said to me, "Look, Señor Granda, the Colombian state has certainly used unorthodox methods to fight you. ..." Those methods Restrepo was referring to are none other than parapolitics and paramilitarism: that was a project that was cold-bloodedly calculated for Colombia. It is an expression of fascism, through which mainly the financial monopolies, the industrial sector, and the landowners have benefited from all the economic restructuring resulting from globalization and privatizations in Colombia. The deals and profits these sectors have made are phenomenal. At the same time, what there is left to privatize in the country is at present minimal, which tells us that the most acute period of pushing forward the neoliberal project in Colombia is over to an extent, as there are no state companies of any size left to sell to the transnationals.

That is why the state is now trying to dismantle all the killing mechanisms they created as a military support for their fascist project to impose neoliberalism and, in this sense, we could draw a comparison with General Pinochet's Chile. Remember that it was right when the military coup took place in Chile in 1973 that they started to implement neoliberal policies for the continent. The military coup practically wiped out the popular resistance, the working class, the middle classes of the population, the peasantry, and imposed the social discipline of the monopolies: fascism in the service of neoliberalism that used terror in our America as a basis for implementing its economic project and its ideological politics.

Now in Colombia the establishment has egg on its face: it is the institutions, along with the men that constitute them, that are implicated in the crisis they have led the nation into. Colombia is a country with one of the highest corruption rates in the world. It was said that Colombian institutions were created as a protection from all forms of corruption. That is why, in order to implement its neoliberal policies, the establishment threw overboard any sense of ethics in politics and now it is paying the price for its "unholy alliance" with narcoparamilitarism created with the intention of eliminating the revolutionary left whatever the cost. That model and that fascist project for Colombia have failed them. When the tidal wave of denouncements comes, the president tries, obviously, to avoid any kind of public debate, and creates smokescreens: the reelection, the referendum, the Soccer World Cup, etc., aiming to distract Colombian public opinion. The scandals and the corruption prevailing in Colombia are of such magnitude that none of these publicity "shows" can manage to distract attention away from one fundamental aspect: the corruption imposed by the "mafia," paramilitarism, and narcotrafficking (which are the same thing) for a government that is a government of "mafiosi" exercising narcodemocracy.

JB: The ELN (National Liberation Army) recently decided to lay down its arms. To what extent does this weaken the armed struggle of the FARC–EP, given that from now on the Colombian state, the paramilitaries, and the United States will be able to concentrate all their efforts to fight it?

RG: The question of whether at present the whole counterinsurgent struggle orchestrated by the Colombian government and the United States can be focused against the FARC–EP is relative. Practically from the outset of Plan Colombia, the FARC–EP has withstood these operations [of the Colombian military and the United States] alone. There is no doubt that the Colombian state has never fought paramilitarism militarily. While military operations in areas where ELN comrades are active have been minimal, so, to some extent, the responsibility of combatting the bulk of operations by the Colombian army and the "gringos" have fallen on our armed organization. You must remember that at present Colombia is the third largest recipient of U.S. military aid, after Israel and Egypt. During the first stage of Plan Colombia, the United States provided $7.5 billion and the Colombian state imposed a war tax of 12 percent, which was increased this year by a further 8 percent. Even so, Plan Colombia and all subsequent operations have failed against the FARC–EP resistance and counteroffensive.

So it's highly debatable whether the enemy can defeat us even if it trains its entire arsenal on us. Our history has shown this ever since our birth in Marquetalia (1964). Remember that sixteen thousand troops were moved into the region against the founding group of the FARC–EP made up of forty-eight peasants, two of them women. Besides, at that time, there was no other insurgent movement in the country either. The bulk of that offensive against the rural self-defense zones, known as "Operation LASO [Latin American Security Operation]," naturally hit the FARC–EP.

We believe, in this new period, that as far as military action by "gringo" troops, mercenaries, and the Colombian army are concerned, the limit has already been reached. What we're talking about now is a decline. It must be said that in high circles of the Colombian government and the corridors of the Pentagon there is talk of the complete failure of "Plan Colombia," "Plan Patriot," "Plan Colombia Consolidation," and "Plan Victory" (2002–07).

In other words, a military victory by the "gringos" and the Colombian state is impossible over an armed movement like ours that has been fighting for forty-three years and has extensive experience at the level of both its leadership and its combatants. It has to be said that this experience is almost unique in Latin America and the world. Just look at the fact that there's currently no other great "plan" or "military operation" in the western hemisphere that has the scope and detail of the one being performed in central and southern Colombia, and throughout most of Colombia's national territory.

We have truly had to fight a war alone. In the past there was the socialist camp, there was international solidarity, we had to "dance with the ugliest girl at the party," as we say in Colombia. But we've shown we can confront and beat the enemy alone. For us, this is an obligation and it is our contribution of solidarity with the oppressed peoples of the world. The combination of all the forms of mass struggle is going to assure us victory in the near future.

The Colombian state has no alternative other than to accept that it has been incapable of defeating the insurgency and that its fascist project, which uses state terror and the chainsaw as an offensive weapon, has failed. The only thing left for this state to do is to seek a rapprochement with the insurgency so that we can sit down and talk to find a negotiated political solution to this long social and armed conflict affecting Colombia.

What you say about the ELN, well, that is the first I have heard about it. … As far as I know the ELN has not laid down its arms. I cannot give an opinion on the ELN's decisions. They are a sovereign organization, a guerrilla organization that has been fighting for years and, to my knowledge, have not so far handed over a single weapon.

JB: The FARC–EP was born from a peasant movement which continues to be its main social base. To what extent has the FARC–EP been able since then to implement a strategic reorientation in the light of extremely rapid urbanization in Colombia? In other words, how does the FARC–EP address the pauperized urban masses suffering constant attacks from the paramilitaries and the repression exercised by the Colombian state?

RG: I have been telling you that the FARC–EP is a politico-military organization, the struggle of the FARC–EP is not one of confrontation between apparatuses, i.e., between the military apparatus of the Colombian state and the FARC–EP's military apparatus proper.

In general, if we analyze the behavior of bourgeois states over time, we observe that they have various ways of applying what they call "representative democracy" and that they combine practically all forms of struggle to exploit the people. The "gringos" call it the "carrot and stick approach," which they practice in the following way: if they consider that the masses are meek, they can let them develop certain forms of restricted democracy for a time; if they consider that those masses are becoming radicalized, then they take troops into the streets and impose repression. But if they notice that those mass movements have already become radicalized, then they employ state terrorism, and wage genocide against their opponents and the extermination of the mass organizations. It is this terror at its most horrifying that was experienced by nearly all countries here in our America in the recent past and still persists in Colombia.

From this viewpoint, it is legitimate for the revolutionary movements of Colombia and the world to employ every form of mass struggle to achieve the revolutionary changes that society needs at a given moment in its development.

We have not declared armed struggle by decree, nor can it be declared by decree, or by the will of person or party X or Y. Armed struggle is born of the overriding need to defend class interests at a particular moment in time, when the bourgeoisie close every door of democracy and expression the masses may have.

Unfortunately, Colombia's history has shown what I've just said to be true: seeking national reconciliation in 1982, the FARC–EP entered into dialogue with then-president Belisario Bétancourt and the Uribe Accords were signed. As a corollary of these accords the broad movement called the Patriotic Union (UP) was founded.

This movement erupted into national political life with enormous support among the inhabitants of town and country, the middle classes, students, etc. In other words, it was a movement that brought together very wide-ranging sectors. When the UP began to develop, the bourgeoisie panicked and commenced the planned systematic extermination—first of its leaders, then they massacred its members. This all ended in the most abhorrent political genocide ever seen in Latin America. The FARC–EP learned from this experiment, which was curtailed by state terrorism, and will not let history repeat itself.

We have been making an enormous effort with the creation and development of popular and political movements and organizations at the national level.

We are making an enormous effort with the formation of the Clandestine Colombian Communist Party, which has to be clandestine because we have already had over five thousand members of the UP killed.

We are also working on the formation of the Bolivarian Movement for the New Colombia, in which anyone can take part. This movement has no statutes, people can get together in small groups to avoid enemy strikes, nobody must allude to their political militancy, and its forms of expression are clandestine.

Through such forms of organization, we participate in the student movement, the workers' movement, the peasant movement, the popular movement ... but the FARC–EP is also setting up the Bolivarian Militias, which operate in the countryside, on the outskirts of big cities and within them.

The FARC–EP believe that the revolution in Colombia must, in part, lead to urban insurrectional expressions, perhaps very much like those that took place in Nicaragua at the time (let's remind ourselves of the battles in Managua, Masaya, Estelí, and León, to name a few), which were guerrilla-type actions combined with popular insurrection, and which together brought down the Somoza dictatorship.

We are making a really big effort with regard to the union movement, the student movement, the urban middle classes, informal workers, the cooperative, and communal movement of family heads. In other words, we are trying to direct everything through simple forms of organization so as steadily to create from the inside-out a politico-practical consciousness of the need for change in Colombia, all the more so when the disastrous consequences of neoliberal policies not only radicalize the urban and rural masses but also, paradoxically, bring them together and ally them in their struggle.

In Colombia, the FARC–EP wishes to build a new government of national reconciliation and reconstruction, one that is broad and democratic, not exclusive in the slightest, in which all sectors of national political life can participate that are concerned about dragging Colombia out of the abyss it finds itself in and establishing it as a country that can face up to the challenges of the twenty-first century with a good deal of hope and optimism, putting us at the vanguard of the democratic and revolutionary nations of the world.

JB: Which social urban movements does the FARC–EP believe require strategic development in this process?

RG: In the cities we work fundamentally with the industrial workers sector. We are also active in the cooperative movement, with neighborhood communal action committees, with associations from the informal economy, which have grown in number in recent years due to neoliberal policies. In addition, we pay a lot of attention to the problems of women and young people in general. So we are represented in all those sectors. We are working conscientiously to give them an organizational character and steer them toward the political struggle. At the same time, this political work, with the experiences it provides of ways of fighting repression, nourishes our own political action. Although the FARC–EP was born essentially as a peasant movement, and this base is maintained in its current make-up, it is also true that there are other sectors of Colombian society that are accompanying us in the struggle. There are middle classes and professional, technical, and upper-class sectors, as well as liberal professionals, clergy, and people from the world of popular culture and art in all its forms linked to the FARC–EP. This has been changing over recent years. We must emphasize the participation of women in our ranks, who now represent 43 percent of the guerrilla force.

JB: It is claimed that, in the regions under its control, the FARC–EP has not always shown itself to be capable of fully allowing the development of a civil society organized autonomously around the different interests it is made up of (cooperatives, unions, various associations, indigenous minorities, etc.). Doesn't this situation reveal a rather authoritarian project for society based exclusively on the capabilities and competencies of a kind of party-state?

RG: [laughing] I don't know where you're going with that question or where we have had control over any part of the national territory. That has not happened yet. We are not waging a war of positions in Colombia. We are a nomadic guerrilla force. When we are in certain areas for a time, we develop direct democracy as it has never been seen in any other type of organization promoted by the state or the oligarchic parties. As a matter of fact, I think that internally the FARC–EP is far more democratic than certain states and democracies; our maximum organ of leadership in the FARC–EP is the National Conference of Guerrilla Fighters, which meets every four years (or more, depending on the war situation). The leaders, without exception, are elected by the votes of all the guerrilla fighters. In other words, there are no appointments.

It is by popular vote, by the votes of FARC–EP members, that democracy (and the question of hierarchies) is managed within the guerrilla movement. In conjunction with the communities. The most significant case was that of San Vicente del Caguán, in south central Colombia during the period of clarity and dialogue from 1999 to 2002. We were there for three years and worked with the communities on civic-military activities. Between them, the civilian population and the "guerrillerada" built bridges, roads, schools, hospitals, local footpaths, and reclaimed certain rivers, creeks, and streams that were heavily polluted. In addition to this, the FARC–EP laid down regulations regarding ecology issues (hunting, fishing, tree felling, and forestry, and protection for native trees), all with the participation of the community. For example, for the construction of a highway, 100 or 200 community action committees from the entire region were brought together and there, by popular vote, it was decided who was going to work, in what way, and how much they would contribute economically and logistically. Then the sums were done and these were handed over to the masses so they could work out for themselves how each of the contributions had been invested. This is open, participative democracy and true mass democracy such as Colombia has never seen before. That is our experience.

There is no place for authoritarianism in the principles of the FARC–EP. The thing is we defend principles. And when it comes to principles we are unwavering. We have our own vision of what democracy should be. Democracy should be open and as direct as possible. In other words, mass democracy as a way of defining and discussing major problems. It's very simple, if there are a hundred people in a community, why should ten of them decide for everyone? For us those hundred people have the power to make decisions. In Colombia they talk to us about representative democracy because there are elections, but in reality these crooks, all these bums who go to the Senate or the Chamber of Representatives, are not real representatives of the communities. They are mostly individuals who get there with the help of their wealth, through clientelism and by means of the threats they subject our people to. So, my dear journalist, it's essential to be clear about what kind of democracy we're talking about, what we the FARC–EP understand by democracy and what you in Europe understand by democracy. I consider the FARC–EP to be a democratic organization practicing democracy in the areas where it works. Our option is a direct democracy that is as broad and participative as possible. Democracy exercised by and for majorities. Not paper democracy. Not democracy for a privileged few. We do not like that type of "democracy" and we are not going to practice it. I was saying that in the FARC–EP we like to organize the masses into all kinds of collectives so that they can defend their own interests. That is the secret of the FARC–EP's existence in the midst of so complicated a conflict as Colombia's.

JB: The FARC–EP is often criticized, even by leftist forces, for its internal use of "expedient" methods: as in the cases of deserters being executed, "demoralized" militants being sent on suicide missions, pregnant militants being forced to have abortions, and so on. There is no doubt that the FARC–EP is involved in an extremely tough armed struggle, but don't such methods or practices strike at the individual rights of combatants or freedom of discussion at the heart of the guerrilla movement, thereby revealing an extremely vertical form of political organization in the purest Stalinist tradition?

RG: Your question shows how little is known about the FARC–EP and how, perhaps subconsciously, you are echoing all the enemy propaganda (the oligarchic Colombian regime and its ally the United States). It is the enemy who has claimed we are vertical, that we solve all problems in the expedient way you refer to in your question.

We use political methods to solve any type of problem within the FARC–EP. Initially new combatants attend a six-month training school where the materials studied are fundamentally the statutes, rules of command, and disciplinary regime. If applicants realize they cannot, for physical or moral reasons, obey those rules, they can return home no problem, because until that point they know nothing and nobody other than the people with whom, clandestinely, they have taken the initial training course. Once that level has been passed, the person makes a commitment and joins the FARC–EP for life, in other words, until the triumph of the revolution and in the subsequent construction of the new society.

We do not have obligatory military service or voluntary military service either. Admittance to the FARC–EP involves thorough development in political and military training, in terms of conscious training. … Let's not forget that anyone can use a weapon, but handling politics, the class struggle and social changes, in a society like ours, is much more complicated. This, which is what we are concerned with, calls for permanent long-term training.

It is not true then that we use firing squads or executions without trial, for instance. We have no need to because our statutes contain many ways of penalizing any violation of the organization's discipline.

Execution by firing squad is only envisaged for traitors or infiltrators who are consciously working for the enemy. That is the most serious measure taken in the FARC–EP. Other than that, any situation can be dealt with using criticism and self-criticism based on Marxist-Leninist principles, which are an integral part of our revolutionary concept.

The other issue, reflected in your question's content, is a defamatory campaign seeking to reduce the FARC–EP to an undisciplined movement, without a hierarchy and without recognized leaders. A military organization simply cannot survive in those conditions. There is a saying that goes "the discipline is complied with or the militia is washed up."

It would be absurd to think we could send people on missions who are demoralized, have psychological problems, or lack the sufficient politico-military qualifications. (In a war situation, who could possibly make such a miscalculation?) Quite the contrary, within the FARC–EP participation in missions constitutes a recognition of good work, and is an incentive and an honor for combatants. The FARC–EP employs conscious participation, which is why, prior to action, the leaders make a detailed study of the qualities of the combatants who are to participate in each of the war activities or on special missions determined by the FARC–EP.

As for the conditions of women in the guerrilla force, they are free. In other words, for the first time a left-wing organization and revolutionary movement has defined women as people who are absolutely free and enjoy full equality with men, taking on the same responsibilities and the same jobs, and having the same rights. Ever since the matriarchal era, it's perhaps only now, in the guerrilla struggle, that women are beginning to play the part they lost in the past, which was the greatest defeat the female gender has suffered in the history of humanity.

As for the issue of pregnancy in the FARC–EP, the female fighters know from the outset that in the war situation they have to go through they cannot get pregnant. Within our organization, we do a lot of educational work on diffusion of information and prevention so that women are well informed about this matter and about how to avoid pregnancy and/or sexually transmitted diseases.

Sometimes, by mistake or by accident, there are cases of involuntary pregnancy. Taking into consideration the objective rules and living conditions in the midst of combat, they are generally interrupted at the request of the combatants themselves. In these cases the interruption is carried out in hygienic, sterile conditions, by qualified doctors with all the necessary measures taken to prevent any risk to their lives.

The interruption of pregnancy has been legalized in many countries and is part of certain constitutions around the world, but we have always been accused of arbitrariness on this matter and we have been demonized. What is going on here? Double standards, that's what.

We want you to know that, for the FARC–EP, family values and the family unit are the basis for the conception of the new society we want to build. But we're at a stage that doesn't facilitate the development of this important aspect of life in any way.

It is telling that, in spite of all the propaganda waged against our organization, the female presence in the ranks of the FARC–EP accounts for 40 percent of combatants at present. The FARC–EP's women fighters are real Amazons on the battlefield, or as Simon Bolivar said, in reference to those brave Roman women warriors, they are real "Bellonas." When they are away from the war situation, the behavior of our female comrades is very feminine. In combat, they are every bit as tough as the men. They teach us about honesty, dedication, sacrifice, fraternity, and heroism ... we could hardly mistreat our female comrades, they are a fundamental part of the struggle for the triumph of our revolution.

JB: Señor Granda, who was responsible for the deaths of the eleven congressional representatives detained by the FARC–EP? How is it possible that those eleven hostages were all together in the same place? Do you think it was a deliberate operation by the Colombian state to launch a vast political campaign against the FARC–EP guerrilla movement?

RG: The FARC–EP had been warning public opinion at home and abroad that operations to rescue prisoners by force posed an exaggerated threat to the lives of the hostages it was holding.

This is why the FARC–EP has pointed out that responsibility for the deaths of the eleven representatives from the Valle del Cauca on June 18, 2007, lies mainly with those who gave the order and aided the rescue attempt by force—Uribe, first and foremost.

To explain why they were together would be to indulge in speculation because on that date you remember I had just left prison in La Dorada.

What has to be said about the deaths of the eleven congressmen is that it was undoubtedly a meticulously prepared plan, both politically and militarily, and also in terms of propaganda.

Uribe's government began its plan by talking about the possibility of releasing a number of FARC–EP prisoners for whom no one had made any request, because we had sought a bilateral humanitarian exchange of prisoners between the FARC–EP and the government. But then, Uribe took the completely unilateral decision to free some of the FARC–EP combatants. This, in my view, had to do with the preparations for action on a larger scale in the Colombian mountains.

That covertly planned action was none other than the rescue of the twelve congressional representatives by a special force of CIA agents, British and Israeli mercenaries, and Colombian army commandos.

The intended blow was that, if this special force appeared to have successfully freed the twelve congressional representatives, Uribe would have kept in prison those he was supposedly attempting to free and embarked on a political campaign at home and abroad claiming that ransoms would henceforth be the most appropriate way to secure the release of those being held by the FARC–EP, thereby ruling out the feasibility of humanitarian exchange or any possibility of dialogue.

The result of this and other similar events have led us to believe that Lima- or Entebbe-style rescue operations cannot be repeated in the Colombian rainforests. What is unequivocally required in Colombia is a humanitarian exchange between the government and the FARC–EP as a preamble to dialogue that might open the way to peace with social justice. Let us hope that many of your readers, the international community, and social, religious, humanist, and left-wing states, governments, peoples, parties, and organizations can contribute toward this search for a solution to the social and armed conflict taking place in Colombia.

Jean Batou directs the Institute of Economic and Social History at the University of Lausanne in Switzerland and teaches international history there. He has published numerous books and articles on uneven development and is most recently coeditor with S. Prezioso and A. J. Rapin of *Tant pis si la lutte cruelle. Volontaires internationaux contre Franco* (Paris: Syllepse, 2008). This interview was conducted on July 24, 2007, in Havana, Cuba and was originally published in French by the Swiss biweekly *Solidarités*, September 5, 2007, http://www.solidarites.ch. It was translated from the original Spanish by Ian Barnett of Parole Translations & Literary Agency.

Section III: Recommended Readings

Girard, P. R. (2011). *The slaves who defeated Napoleon: Toussaint Louverture and the Haitian war of independence,* 1801–1804. Atlantic Crossings Series. Tuscaloosa, AL: University of Alabama Press.

Kapcia, A. (2014). *Leadership in the Cuban revolution: The unseen story.* London, UK: Zed Books.

Leech, G. M. (2011). *The FARC: The longest insurgency.* Rebels Series. London, UK: Zed Books.

Popkin, J. D. (2007). *Facing racial revolution: Eyewitness accounts of the Haitian insurrection.* Chicago, IL: University of Chicago Press.

Section III: Post-Reading Questions

1   Discuss the following contributing factors to the Haitian revolution: *petit marronage*, the French Revolution, *gens de couleur*, and Vodou.

2   Outline the long-lasting political and economic transformations resulting from the Cuban revolution. Be sure to mention specific examples and relevant historical figures.

3   Who is Rodrigo Granda? Why is Colombia perceived as a "genocidal democracy" by the ARC-EP?

SECTION IV

POPULATION, MIGRATION, AND URBANISM

Editor's Introduction

The readings in this section focus on two relevant topics to the regions of Latin America and the Caribbean: migration and urbanization. Historically, migrations, particularly the regional and international movement of locals and foreigners, contributed to shape the current population makeup with the arrival of Europeans, Africans, and Asians to these regions. Nevertheless, the nature and impact of such population movements continues to be the subject of debate and controversy. In modern times, the nature of push-and-pull factors has intensified as a response to environmental, economic, and political changes leading to an increase in the wave of migrants moving out from underdeveloped and developing areas to developed nations such as the United States and Canada, searching for jobs, freedom, and a safe future. The article by Aguila, Akhmedonoj, Basurto-Davila, et al. (2012) discusses the historical context and push factors particular to Mexico, a country relevant to the topics of this chapter for supplying large numbers of undocumented migrants, including those traveling from Central America aiming to come across into the United States.

The process of globalization continues to play a vital economic and social role by fostering migration and urban development. Latin America as a region has some of the largest urban areas worldwide, with Mexico City as an example of a 16th-century settlement suffering the consequences of unplanned growth and massive rural-to-urban migration. The reading by Janoschka and Borsdorf (2006) discusses the case of Nordelta, a gated community located in the city of Buenos Aires, Argentina. As one of the largest gated developments of Latin America, Nordelta illustrates the role that an "imagined" urban insecurity and economic-based segregation are playing in redesigning urban landscapes. Latin American cities, characterized by a polarized geography, are being modernized with the inclusion of gated residential islands, which, by segregating the urban poor, aim to provide an idealized and secure environment to their wealthier residents.

Section IV: Key Terms

Agglomeration

favelas

gated community

insecurity

micro-neighborhoods

migration

networks

polarization

poverty

pull factors

push factors

rural

segregation

supply

transnational

unemployment

urban planning

vecindades

wages

Causes of Migration from Mexico to the United States

Emma Aguila, Alisher Akhmedjonov, Ricardo Basurto-Davila, Krishna B. Kumar, and Sarah Kups

We determined three categories for the main factors that cause migratory flows:

- *Demand-pull* includes recruitment by U.S. employers or significant job availability in the United States, in addition to significant wage differentials between the two countries.

- *Supply-push* includes poor performance of the Mexican economy and strong regional socioeconomic inequalities in Mexico.

- *Networks* include family members and friends who already live in the United States or other channels that facilitate Mexican migration (P. Martin, 2002).

Demand-Pull: U.S. Economic Factors

U.S. Economic Conditions Are Critical to Decisions to Immigrate

Job availability in the United States is generally considered the main determinant of short-term immigration flows (Escobar Latapí and Martin, 2008; Passel and Suro, 2005). Immigrant flows usually follow U.S. economic conditions, such as the sustained growth in the 1990s, and the economic cycles during the 2000s (see Figure 4.1.1).

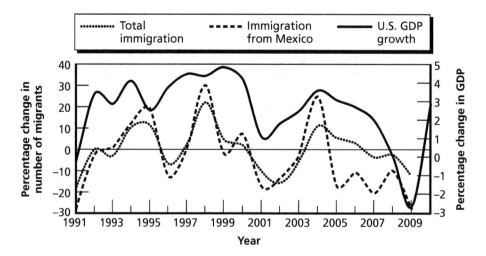

Figure 4.1.1 Annual Change in Immigrant Flows to the United States and U.S. Gross Domestic Product, 1991–2010

Sources: Passel and Suro, 2005; Pew Hispanic Center, 2007; BEA, 2010.
RAND *MG985/1-6.1*

Wage Differences Between the Two Countries Also Play a Role

In Figure 4.1.1, we observe a high correlation between U.S. gross domestic product (GDP) growth and the change in immigrant flows from Mexico, particularly since 2000. Demand-pull factors also include the significant wage differentials between the two countries, shown in Table 4.1.1. For example, a Mexican between 23 and 27 years old with four years of education is likely to make almost six times as much in the United States as he or she would in Mexico. Those differentials decline with education and age.

Table 4.1.1 Ratio of U.S. Wages to Mexican Wages for Mexican-Born Workers, 2000

AGE	YEARS OF SCHOOLING COMPLETED					
	4	5–8	9–11	12	13–15	16+
18–22	5.8	4.9	4.2	3.9	3.4	2.2
23–27	5.9	4.6	3.9	3.2	2.5	2.5
28–32	5.3	4.4	3.6	3.0	2.0	2.4
33–37	5.7	4.4	3.6	2.9	2.2	2.4
38–42	5.6	4.4	3.2	2.9	2.2	2.2
43–47	5.8	3.9	3.1	2.4	2.2	2.0
48–52	5.8	4.1	3.0	2.2	1.9	2.0

Source: Hanson, 2006.
Note: Mexican wages are rescaled to adjust for cost-of-living differences between Mexico and the United States, using the 2000 purchasing power parity (PPP) adjustment factor for Mexico, as listed in Hanson (2006).

It is worth mentioning that the wage differential is very similar for all age groups that have the lowest levels of education. According to the wage-differential hypothesis, the least skilled have more incentives to migrate to the United States.

Supply-Push: Performance of the Mexican Economy

Mexican Economic Conditions Are Critical to the Decision to Migrate

Immigration to the United States from Mexico has risen following economic problems in Mexico, such as the debt crisis in 1982 and the exchange-rate collapse in 1994 (Massey and Singer, 1995; Passel and Suro, 2005). Economic instability leads to unemployment and low real wages. Figure 4.1.2 presents the real minimum wage from 1986 to 2010. In this figure, we observe that economic crises have eroded real wages in Mexico. Although the real minimum wage has been stable since 2000, the lack of job opportunities in Mexico has led to high migrant flows.

Unemployment in Mexico Is Relatively Low but Still Stimulates Migration

According to employment statistics, unemployment in Mexico is low when compared with other countries with similar development levels. However, these numbers can be misleading because Mexican unemployment statistics do not include some individuals who would be counted as unemployed under U.S. measurement standards. For instance, due to a weak unemployment-compensation scheme, persons without work in Mexico are often forced into marginal activities (e.g., street vending, moving, repairing), which results in their classification as employed

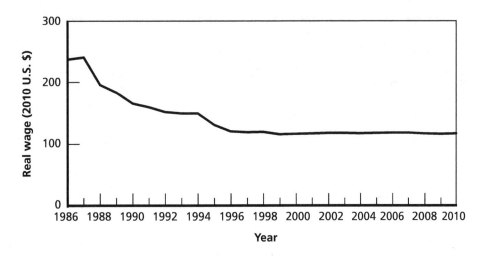

Figure 4.1.2   Real Minimum Wage in Mexico, 1986–2010

Sources: CONASAMI, 2009; BANXICO, undated.
RAND *MG985/1-6.2*

rather than unemployed even if they work as little as one hour per week. According to Fleck and Sorrentino (1994), the reported rate would still be relatively low after its adjustment to the U.S. concept.

The last time the unemployment rate in Mexico was at a level considered high relative to rates in other countries (around 8 percent) was following the December 1994 peso devaluation. After achieving macroeconomic and financial stability, the private sector and temporary government public works programs absorbed a sizable fraction of the Mexican active population, which led to a boost in employment (Lustig, 1998).

Figure 4.1.3 shows a clear inverse relationship between migratory flows from Mexico to the United States and Mexican GDP growth during the 1990s. After 1999, however, Mexican GDP growth and migration flows appear to move in the same direction, an indication that both factors were following the U.S. GDP decline and recovery during those years (as observed in Figure 4.1.3). Figure 4.1.3 also shows the unemployment rate in Mexico, which fluctuates significantly less than migration flows except for the spike during the 1995 crisis but still appears to be related to them: Higher unemployment is associated with more migration to the United States.

The 2007 U.S. Recession Increased Unemployment in Mexico

Given that the Mexican economy grew more slowly in 2008 and contracted severely in 2009 due to the economic recession in the United States (and elsewhere), there was another rise in unemployment in Mexico. According to INEGI, Mexican annual real GDP grew 3.3 percent in

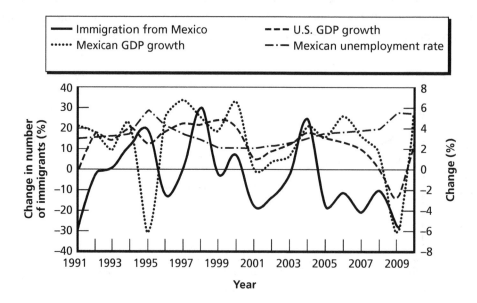

Figure 4.1.3 Annual Change in Immigrant Flows from Mexico to the United States, Mexican Unemployment Rate, and Mexican and U.S. Gross Domestic Product, 1991–2010

Sources: Passel and Suro, 2005; BANXICO, undated.
RAND *MG985/1-6.3*

2007 and by an additional 1.5 percent in 2008 but fell by 6.1 percent in 2009. It rebounded to 5.5 percent in 2010. Unemployment rose until the third quarter of 2009, when it peaked at 6.2 percent, still lower than in the 1995 economic crisis. It had fallen to 5.3 percent as of the fourth quarter of 2010. The actual performance of the unemployment level depends on just how sluggishly the economy performs because economic stagnation naturally leads to less hiring and the loss of jobs. As explained earlier, the impact that higher unemployment has on migration flows is not entirely clear because U.S. economic growth appears to dominate the supply-push effects of Mexican unemployment. The Pew Hispanic Center estimates that the number of unauthorized immigrants from Mexico living in the United States did not increase from 2007 to 2008 (Passel and Cohn, 2008b).

Poverty and Economic Performance in Mexico

In 2010, Mexico was ranked 56th in the United Nations' Human Development Index, falling within the classification of high human development (UNDP, 2010). According to this measure, Mexico's main deficiencies are in the proportion of population that is illiterate, malnutrition, scarcity of physicians, and high income inequality (UNDP, 2007). Mexico's purchasing power–adjusted GDP per capita in 2010 was US$14,566.

We analyze poverty using two official measures reported by Mexico's government: (1) *capability poverty*, which refers to a person's inability to satisfy his or her minimum requirements of food, health, and education, and (b) *food poverty*, which is a person's incapacity to purchase the minimum necessary food basket, even if all his or her income were allocated to it. The 1994 economic crisis brought a significant increase in the incidence of poverty in Mexico, with capability poverty growing from 30 percent in 1994 to 46 percent in 1996 and food poverty increasing from 21 percent to 37 percent in the same period. However, as economic recovery began in 1996 and continued throughout the rest of the decade, poverty rates declined steadily, so that, by 2002, capability and food poverty had reached levels of 27 and 20 percent, respectively (see Figure 4.1.4). It took five years to observe a recovery from the 1995 economic crisis.

The economic crisis of the late 2000s reversed the decline in poverty at least temporarily. Between 2004 and 2005, there were no statistically significant changes in poverty rates then important reductions in poverty between 2005 and 2006 such that, by 2006, the rate of capability poverty had reached a value of 21 percent and only 14 percent of the population was living in food poverty, compared with their peak values of 46 and 37 percent, respectively. The 2010 figures reported by the National Council for Evaluation of Social Development Policy (Consejo Nacional de Evaluación de la Política de Desarrollo Social, or CONEVAL) (undated [b]), a Mexican government agency that evaluates social policies and measures poverty levels, show that food and capability poverty increased to 19 and 27 percent, respectively, effectively reversing the gains in the fight against poverty that had occurred from 2005 to 2006. Lower poverty rates do not seem necessarily to translate into reductions in migratory flows, however, as can be seen by comparing the migratory flow shown in Figure 4.1.3 and the poverty rate in Figure 4.1.4: The decreases in poverty that started in 1996 precede reductions in migratory flows from 1998 to

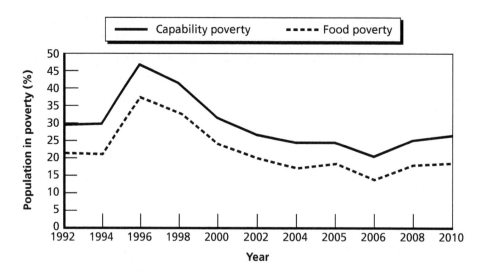

Figure 4.1.4   Poverty Rates in Mexico, 1992–2010

Source: CONEVAL, undated (b).
RAND *MG985/1-6.4*

2001, but poverty continued to decrease up to 2004, and migration rose again between 2002 and 2004. Migratory flows declined substantially in 2005, and poverty slightly increased. From 2006 to 2007, migratory flows and poverty followed a negative correlation; in 2008, poverty and migratory flows both increased. In summary, we cannot observe a clear correlation between migratory flows and poverty.

Poverty Rates Differ According to Region

Average poverty figures might disguise the underlying differences between urban and rural communities. Poverty rates are significantly higher in *rural and small-town* communities—defined as those with fewer than 15,000 inhabitants. As of 2010, 29 percent of rural households lived in food poverty, but merely 13 percent of urban households were in that condition. Similarly, 38 percent of rural but only 20 percent of urban households lived in capability poverty in that year (CONEVAL, undated [a]).

Despite the larger incidence of poverty in rural communities than in urban ones, the first decade of the 21st century saw reductions in poverty levels only in rural, not urban, communities: The percentage of households in rural food poverty decreased by 12 percent, going from 50 to 38 percent in that period, and urban food poverty remained at 20 percent (after first dropping significantly to 14 percent in 2006). The declines in the percentage of households in capability poverty between 2000 and 2010 are similar to those in food poverty: 13-percent decline for rural communities and no decline for urban communities.[1]

---

1   These figures vary, but only slightly, when persons instead of households are considered, since rural households are typically larger than urban households.

In the past six decades, Mexico has undergone a rapid process of population movement toward urban areas. Between 1950 and 2010, the population living in rural areas decreased from 57 percent to only 22 percent of Mexico's total population. Despite this rural-urban population shift, rural regions still constitute more than 80 percent of the Mexican territory; thus, the bulk of Mexico's population concentrates in a few urban centers, and the rest is dispersed in a large number of small localities. Individuals from rural areas, though no longer constituting the majority of emigrants, are still overrepresented among the migrant flows (Riosmena and Massey, 2010).

The states with the highest levels of rural population also have the highest levels of poverty. The top panel in Figure 4.1.5 shows poverty levels for every municipality in the country, using a poverty index based on the 2005 Mexican census developed by CONAPO. Poverty is higher in the middle and southern regions of the country. The map also shows that regional inequality is extreme: We can see that most municipalities have either high/very high or low/very low poverty, while only a small number of municipalities are in the category of medium poverty.

The bottom panel in Figure 4.1.5 adds, for each municipality, the number of migrants counted by the Survey of Migration in Mexico's Northern Border (Encuesta sobre Migración en la Frontera Norte de México, or EMIF) between 1993 and 2004.[2] Clearly, most migrants come not from the most-disadvantaged areas of Mexico but from those with either low or medium poverty levels; international migration is costly, and those living in poverty might not be able to afford to migrate (McKenzie and Rapoport, 2007). It can also be seen in the figure that the traditional sending regions in central and western Mexico still account for a large proportion of total migration to the United States. However, states that contributed very little to migratory flows just a couple of decades ago have experienced a significant increase in their number of migrants. In particular, the southwest region (Oaxaca, Guerrero, and Chiapas) has increased its contribution considerably. Even the indigenous population from the south of the country has started to show migration patterns to the United States. If this trend continues, the distribution of characteristics of migrants to the United States might change because these states contain some of the most-disadvantaged areas in the country.

It is clear from this discussion that lack of regional development is one of the main problems in Mexico. Pastor (2001) suggests that reducing regional disparities by improving road networks from the north to the center and south of the country and thereby increasing foreign investment in these regions could contribute to reducing migration from Mexico to the United States. The government has implemented policies aimed at channeling remittances, which now constitute one of Mexico's main foreign sources of income […], toward regional development. However, it has been pointed out that remittances cannot be considered a reliable source of funds because they are subject to several factors that can be affected even in the short term. Studies on remittances indicate that permanent migrants send back a lower percentage of their earnings than temporary migrants

---

2   Only individuals who were planning to cross into the United States to work or who planned to stay in the United States for at least one year were classified as migrants.

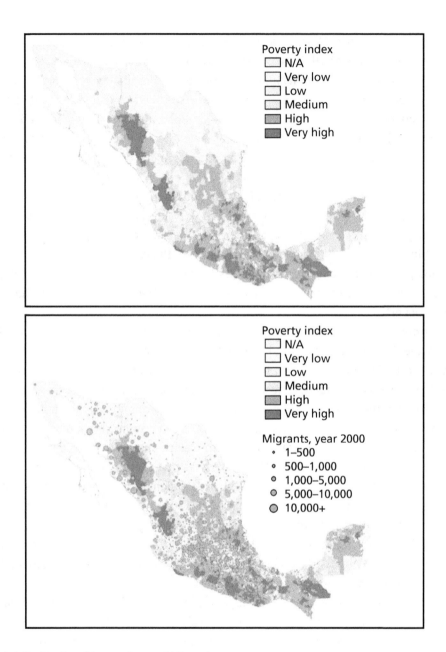

Figure 4.1.5 Regional Inequality and Migration

Source: CONAPO, 2005a.
RAND *MG985/1-6.5*

(Zárate-Hoyos, 2005). This might be a cause for concern regarding future remittance flows to Mexico because permanent migration has grown relative to temporary migration in recent years (García Zamora, 2005a). The recent increase in deportations and legal measures against illegal immigration at both the federal and local levels in the United States might also result in reduced migration or increased returning migrant flows, which would also reduce remittance flows to Mexico. In fact, both the number and dollar amount of remittances grew minimally between 2006 and 2007, and estimates by the Mexican Central Bank (Banco de México, or BANXICO) indicate that remittances in 2008 were nearly 4 percent lower than in 2007 and then dropped by 16 percent from 2008 to 2009 (BANXICO, undated). When we compare the first nine months of 2010 with the same period in 2009, however, it seems that the dollar amount of remittances has stabilized. Therefore, even if effective mechanisms are developed to maximize the positive impact of remittances on the regions that receive them, both families and governments need to develop strategies to prepare for the potential volatility in remittance flows.

Networks

In addition to demand-pull and supply-push factors, existing migrant networks can contribute to additional migration flows. For example, U.S. employers can use current employees to get word back to Mexico about job availability, and the presence of family members or people from the same village or neighborhood can help ease transition costs for the new migrants by providing them with financial assistance, lodging, food, or help finding employment.

As discussed in the previous section, most migration from Mexico to the United States has been from the central and western portions of the country. The importance of migration networks is evidenced by the persistence of these source regions: The correlation between sending states in the periods 1955–1959 and 1995–2000 is 0.73 (Hanson, 2006). In fact, Massey and García España (1987) argue that social networks help explain the surge of migration between 1970 and 1980, a period when real wages were falling and unemployment was high in the United States while wages were increasing and unemployment was low in Mexico.

Zuñiga Herrera, Leite, and Rosa Nava (2004) report that 80 percent of temporary migrants with family or friends in the United States have received some type of assistance. Amuedo-Dorantes and Mundra (2007) find that family and friendship ties raise unauthorized immigrant wages by an average of 2.6 and 5.4 percent, respectively, and those of legal immigrants by 8 and 3.6 percent. Higher wages might effectively increase the returns to migration, therefore providing a stimulus to continued emigration.

Munshi (2003), using data from well-established migrant-sending communities, finds that preexisting social ties of migrants ensure that those migrants receive various forms of assistance during their trips to the United States. These ties have an effect not only on location patterns of Mexican migrants but also on the occupations they choose, so they could explain the persistence of low-skill occupations among Mexican migrants.

References

Amuedo-Dorantes, Catalina, and Kusum Mundra, "Social Networks and Their Impact on the Earnings of Mexican Migrants," *Demography*, Vol. 44, No. 4, November 2007, pp. 849–863.

Banco de México, "Estadísticas," undated web page, referenced December 14, 2008. As of January 30, 2012: http://www.banxico.org.mx/estadisticas/index.html

____, *Addendum to the Inflation Report July–September 2009*, quarterly inflation report, December 2, 2009. As of October 5, 2010: http://www.banxico.org.mx/publicaciones-y-discursos/publicaciones/informes-periodicos/trimestral-inflacion/%7BC915D461-0A6C-70CE-DCB1-425E415B0979%7D.pdf

BANXICO—*See* Banco de México.

BEA—*See* Bureau of Economic Analysis.

Bureau of Economic Analysis, "Table D. Cross-Border Services Exports and Imports by Type and Country, 2005," June 2007b. As of June 1, 2010: http://www.bea.gov/international/xls/tabD.xls

Colegio de la Frontera Norte, "Encuestas sobre Migración en las Fronteras Norte y Sur de México," undated web page. As of June 1, 2010: http://www.colef.mx/emif/

Comisión Nacional de los Salarios Mínimos, "Salarios mínimos," last modified December 21, 2009.

CONAPO—*See* Consejo Nacional de Población.

CONASAMI—*See* Comisión Nacional de los Salarios Mínimos.

CONEVAL—*See* Consejo Nacional de Evaluación de la Política de Desarrollo Social.

Consejo Nacional de Evaluación de la Política de Desarrollo Social, "Pobreza por ingresos," undated (a).

____, "Evolución de las dimensiones de la pobreza 1990–2010: Anexo," undated (b), referenced September 12, 2011. As of January 30, 2012: http://www.coneval.gob.mx/cmsconeval/rw/pages/medicion/evolucion_de_las_dimensiones_pobreza_1990_2010.en.do

Consejo Nacional de Población, *2005, Municipales y estatales*, c. 2005a.

Escobar Latapí, Agustín, and Susan Forbes Martin, eds., *La gestión de la migración México–Estados Unidos: Un enfoque binacional*, México: SEGOB, Instituto Nacional de Migración, Centro de Estudios Migratorios, 2008.

Fleck, Susan, and Constance Sorrentino, "Employment and Unemployment in Mexico's Labor Force," *Monthly Labor Review*, Vol. 117, No. 11, November 1994.

García Zamora, Rodolfo, "Mexico: International Migration, Remittances and Development," in Organisation for Economic Co-Operation and Development, *Migration, Remittances and Development*, Paris, 2005a, pp. 81–87.

Hanson, Gordon H., "Illegal Migration from Mexico to the United States," *Journal of Economic Literature*, Vol. 44, No. 4, December 2006, pp. 869–924.

INEGI—*See* Instituto Nacional de Estadística y Geografía.

Instituto Nacional de Estadística y Geografía, *Los extranjeros en México*, Aguascalientes, México, 2007a.

____, *National Survey of Occupation and Employment*, 2007b.

____, *Información sobre el flujo migratorio internacional de México*, Aguascalientes, México, 2009.

____, *Anuario estadístico de los Estados Unidos Mexicanos 2010*, Aguascalientes, México, 2010.

Lustig, Nora, *Mexico: The Remaking of an Economy*, 2nd ed., Washington, D.C.: Brookings Institution Press, 1998.

Martin, Philip, "Economic Integration and Migration: The Mexico–US Case," in United Nations University World Institute for Development Economics Research Conference on Poverty, *International Migration, and Asylum*, September 19, 2002.

Massey, Douglas S., and Felipe García España, "The Social Process of International Migration," *Science*, Vol. 237, No. 4816, August 14, 1987, pp. 733–738.

Massey, Douglas S., and Audrey Singer, "New Estimates of Undocumented Mexican Migration and the Probability of Apprehension," *Demography*, Vol. 32, No. 2, May 1995, pp. 203–213.

McKenzie, David J., and Hillel Rapoport, "Network Effects and the Dynamics of Migration and Inequality: Theory and Evidence from Mexico," *Journal of Development Economics*, Vol. 84, No. 1, September 2007, pp. 1–24.

Munshi, Kaivan, "Networks in the Modern Economy: Mexican Migrants in the U.S. Labor Market," *Quarterly Journal of Economics*, Vol. 118, No. 2, May 2003, pp. 549–597.

Passel, Jeffrey S., and D'Vera Cohn, *Trends in Unauthorized Immigration: Undocumented Inflow Now Trails Legal Inflow*, Washington, D.C.: Pew Hispanic Center, October 2, 2008b. As of May 3, 2010: http://pewhispanic.org/files/reports/94.pdf

Passel, Jeffrey S., and Roberto Suro, *Rise, Peak and Decline: Trends in U.S. Immigration 1992–2004*, Washington, D.C.: Pew Hispanic Center, September 27, 2005. As of January 31, 2012: http://www.pewhispanic.org/2005/08/16/attitudes-toward-immigrants-and-immigration-policy/

Pastor, Robert A., *Toward a North American Community: Lessons from the Old World for the New*, Washington, D.C.: Institute for International Economics, 2001.

Pew Hispanic Center, "Indicators of Recent Migration Flows from Mexico," fact sheet, May 30, 2007. As of September 22, 2007: http://pewhispanic.org/files/factsheets/33.pdf

_____, "Mexican Immigrants in the United States, 2008," fact sheet, April 15, 2009. As of June 10, 2009: http://pewhispanic.org/files/factsheets/47.pdf

Riosmena, Fernando, and Douglas S. Massey, *Pathways to El Norte: Origins, Destinations, and Characteristics of Mexican Migrants to the United States*, University of Colorado at Boulder, Institute of Behavioral Science, Population Program, June 2010. As of August 9, 2011: http://www.colorado.edu/ibs/pubs/pop/pop2010-0002.pdf

UNDP—*See* United Nations Development Programme.

United Nations Development Programme, *Informe Sobre Desarrollo Humano México 2006–2007*, 2007.

Zárate-Hoyos, Germán, "The Development Impact of Migrant Remittances in México," in Donald F. Terry and Steven R. Wilson, eds., *Beyond Small Change: Making Migrant Remittances Count*, Washington, D.C.: Inter-American Development Bank, 2005.

Zúñiga Herrera, Elena, Paula Leite, and Alma Rosa Nava, *La nueva era de las migraciones: Características de la migración internacional en México*, México, D.F.: Consejo Nacional de Población, 2004.

Condominios Fechados and Barrios Privados

The Rise of Private Residential Neighbourhoods in Latin America

Michael Janoschka and Axel Borsdorf

Abstract

Private and gate-guarded residential neighbourhoods have sprawled in all major Latin American city regions during the last two decades. The aim of this text is an analysis of the spatial and social implications of the 'condominisation' of the urban landscape within a theoretical and empirical frame. Starting from a historical background, the actual patterns and consequences associated with the distribution of gated communities are discussed and presented in a model of the current Latin American city structure. Further attention will be focused on the relation between urban insecurity and the spread of the private neighbourhoods based on empirical data gathered via narrative and biographical interviews with inhabitants. From our results we conclude that insecurity and crime rates are not the driving forces motivating life behind gates but rather the achievement of an ideal lifestyle.

Introduction

Buenos Aires' inhabitants proudly introduce their city to visitors by enumerating records. Taking a taxi from the international airport to the city centre, everyone will learn that the Plate River is the broadest river crossing an agglomeration in the southern hemisphere or that 9th of July Avenue is the widest urban avenue crossing the densest central business district (CBD) in South America. By the late 1990s the Argentinian capital had notched up two more records: the widest metropolitan motorway on the subcontinent (16 lanes) links the dense city centre with Nordelta, Latin America's largest gated development. As we shall indicate, the so-called town-village *(CiudadPueblo)* of Nordelta contrasts with the rest of the 14-million-inhabitant mega-city, in which approximately 60 per cent of the population live on a daily income less than one euro.

> An avenue surrounded by palms. Great green areas and parks. Lime trees, spruces, willow-trees and magnolias. An enormous and silent water surface. And everything that design and comfort can nowadays introduce to achieve a better life. A place like this does exist. And it is not at the end of the world. It is exactly in the geographical centre of Nordelta. Its name is the Island. (Nordelta 2002)

Although Nordelta is far from being an isolated island, the marketing target is based on selling an image of a grand, self-sufficient garden city completely detached from the local and national economic and social setting. The 1,600-hectare development for about 80,000 inhabitants contains, among other facilities, a huge sports complex, its own private schools, a technical school and a private university. Despite the proximity to commercial and leisure facilities in nearby suburbs, Nordelta has its own mall and urban entertainment centre and also a Civic Centre (figure 4.2.1). These spaces have a pseudo-public character. Common spaces are available to Nordelta residents and help create a sense of local citizenship and social interactions, which is otherwise inhibited by the access controls at each of the 30 or so planned neighbourhoods inside Nordelta (eight of which are functional as of 2001). Public life in this sprawling urban club is well controlled, however, distinguishing it from equivalent spaces outside. Surveillance cameras monitor the use of public space and the unusual has a strong chance of being detected. Every point of the development can be reached by security or service vehicles within a 90-second response time.

Analysing the wish to attain distinction and the citizenship-building processes occurring in Nordelta, it is easy to conclude that this is not only an official strategy of the real-estate companies to improve the sale of the properties. Individuals living inside also follow a personal strategy that stresses the change in personal lifestyle that took place after moving to Nordelta. Many inhabitants refer to themselves as *Nordelteños,* in contrast to the local characterisation of Buenos Aires' inhabitants as *Porteños* (Janoschka 2002a: 90). Education institutions pick up the

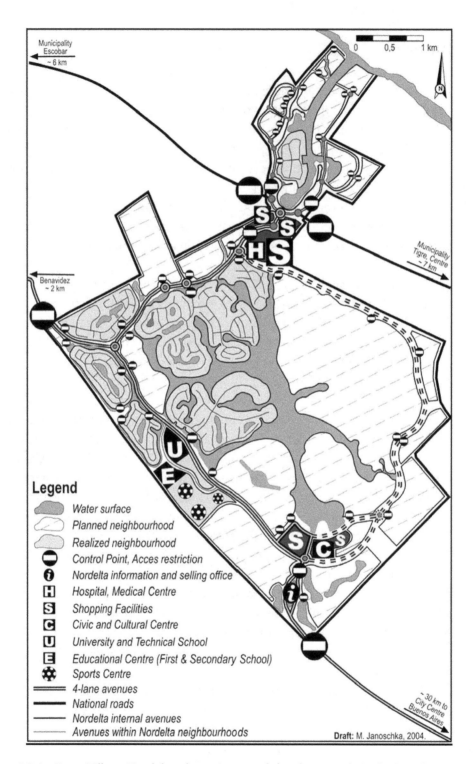

Legend

- Water surface
- Planned neighbourhood
- Realized neighbourhood
- Control Point, Acces restriction
- Nordelta information and selling office
- H Hospital, Medical Centre
- S Shopping Facilities
- C Civic and Cultural Centre
- U University and Technical School
- E Educational Centre (First & Secondary School)
- Sports Centre
- 4-lane avenues
- National roads
- Nordelta internal avenues
- Avenues within Nordelta neighbourhoods

Draft: M. Janoschka, 2004.

Figure 4.2.1   Town-Village Nordelta, the major gated development in Latin America.

Source: based on Janoschka 2002a, Janoschka 2004 and Nordelta 2002

same nuance, such as the Catholic Cardinal Pironio College's promise of a 'new education for a new civilization'.

Nordelta is still the biggest and most complex private urban development in Latin America, but it is not alone. With the exception of Cuba, gated and access-restricted neighbourhoods have become a key part of the real-estate market throughout the whole continent. [...] we comment on the historical evolution and contemporary importance of gated communities for Latin American city regions. The discussion focuses on the reasons for the proliferation of access-restricted neighbourhoods and the controversial question concerning urban insecurity. A comparative analysis based on empirical evidence from the authors' case studies in different cities and countries is used to characterise common aspects and differences in the phenomenon. We use a lifestyle-based analysis derived from our empirical work with inhabitants of gated communities. The likely political consequences for local administration and social contract between different classes are addressed in the conclusion. We begin with a short introduction to the socio-political and urban transformation processes in Latin America.

From Polarised City to Fragmented Agglomeration

Massive changes have been taking place in Latin American societies since the early 1980s, when re-democratisation processes started to replace the military regimes of the previous decade. Regardless of the ideological orientation of the new democratic governments, capitalist and neo-liberal politics were implemented. That time marked the end of the development strategies employed since the start of the post-war period, strategies that were based on the substitution of imports by domestic industrialisation. This industrialisation was accompanied by import restrictions and active economic intervention by the public sector. From the 1980s this development strategy began to change towards one of integration into world markets, with subsequent lowering of tax barriers. Privatisation of state-owned companies and former state-organised services and a new pro-market ethos led to a complete reorientation of Latin American economic activity. Foreign direct investment and subjugation to open market laws led to a reduction of the importance of the public sector and in many countries induced a deindustrialisation process due to the greater competitiveness of imported products. In the social sphere, the results of the neo-liberal economic trend included a substantial increase in social polarisation (cf. Ciccolella 1999) and the rise of unemployment, despite high economic growth rates experienced by most Latin American countries in the 1990s.

Following the finance market crisis of the late 1990s, Latin America's economic panorama notoriously changed. With the exception of Chile and Mexico, the latter country profiting from NAFTA integration with the USA and Canada, the dynamics of Latin American economies became negative. Reverse capital flows were experienced from 1998 and still continue. Economic growth has been low and the income per capita has been slowly decreasing. Some countries, such as Argentina, Uruguay or Venezuela, suffered strong economic depressions accompanied by internal political problems. Under such conditions, social polarisation has accelerated (Ocampo 2003; Ruiz 2003).

In South American cities over the last 15 years, there has been a rapid modernisation of the urban infrastructure, driven in many cases by foreign investment. This investment was concentrated partly on basic urban services such as telephone and water provision, which are now owned by international companies providing an international standard of service for the middle and upper classes. However, investment also took place in the trappings of modern globalised cities: tolled motorways, private industrial parks, international hotel chains with integrated business facilities, shopping malls and hypermarkets, urban entertainment centres, multiplex cinemas and gated and access-restricted residential quarters in the city and the suburbs (Janoschka 2002b). The absence of state intervention in urban planning led to most new private investment being directed towards an exclusive urban form, based on private transport. A new car-based lifestyle flourished, encouraging fragmentation and spatial segregation. While earlier decades of urban growth were driven primarily by lower-income migration from rural areas, the pattern has changed since the 1980s, with migration strongly declining. In the last two decades urban expansion has been substantially a result of the greater use of space per capita, chiefly driven by changes in residential areas of the upper and middle classes.

A Model of Fragmented Agglomeration

During the period of development strategies led by import reduction, ending in the 1980s, one of the distinctive features of Latin American cities was the strong polarisation of urban spaces. Differentiation in social status was heavily bound to location within the city. Urban space was divided into polarised sectors creating a strongly differentiated rich city and poor city (Gilbert 1998). This has changed during the last two decades. Settlements of poor and rich people moved closer to one another due to the occupation of suburban and formerly poor areas by high-income populations. Poor families also installed themselves in abandoned, formerly homogeneous, middle- and upper-class districts. This process has been accompanied by a stronger delimitation of small areas (microneighbourhoods) often accompanied by private security services. This helps explain the function of gated communities in Latin American cities. They are homogeneous, highly segregated and protected areas allowing the middle and upper classes to cohabit increasingly scarce space. They are reshaping the physical and social ecology of urban space (Sabatini, Cáceres and Cerda 2001; Parnreiter 2004; Borsdorf and Hildalgo 2005; see figure 4.2.2). They have become the new model of Latin American urban agglomeration.

In 1976 German geographers Bähr and Borsdorf published two independent models of Latin American city structure which were the starting point for an intense discussion in Europe and North America (Griffin and Ford 1980; Gormsen 1981; Deler 1992; Crowley 1995; Bähr and Mertins 1981; Borsdorf 1982). Following this, the dramatic transformations which occurred in Latin American city regions from the 1980s, were related to new theoretical insights in the work

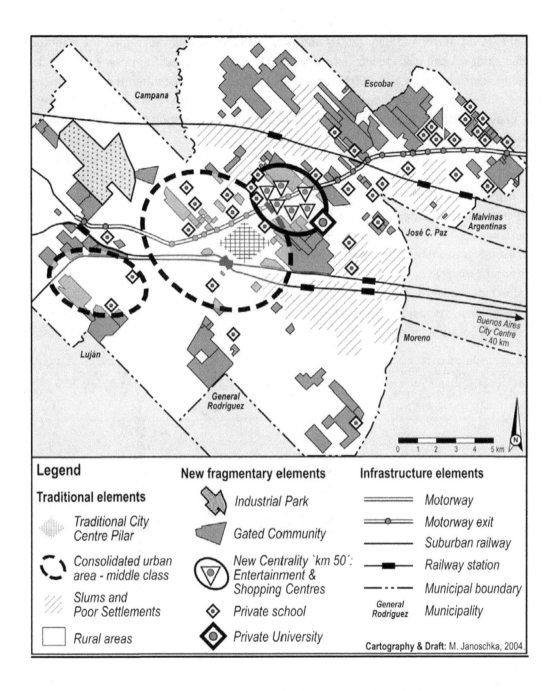

Figure 4.2.2 Fragmented urban space in the suburban municipality of Pilar in Buenos Aires, 2004.

Source: Janoschka 2004

of Ford (1996), Meyer and Bähr (2001) and Borsdorf (2002a), who redesigned the traditional models or developed new models (Janoschka 2002b, 2002c), derived from new empirical data. Borsdorf, Bähr and Janoschka (2002) suggested a model which integrated the different arguments of the other authors (figure 4.2.3). City development in Latin America is characterised in four phases, which correspond to different modes of state intervention (urban planning) in the real-estate market.

In the early phase, the colonial time, the dominant planning principle was compactness of the urban body and a social gradient according to distance from the central plaza. Social status was higher close to the plaza due to the central social and political functions concentrated there and the high cost and the time of travel under available technology. This pattern gained importance due to royal instructions for the foundation of cities, the subsequent location of the higher-order urban functions in and around the central plaza and the settlement of the colonial elite around the plaza.

After independence, linear structures began to gain in importance. The upper classes moved to new houses extending along the main street—the *prado*. The most important streets then became the location for market gardening and artisan activities and, later on, early industrial

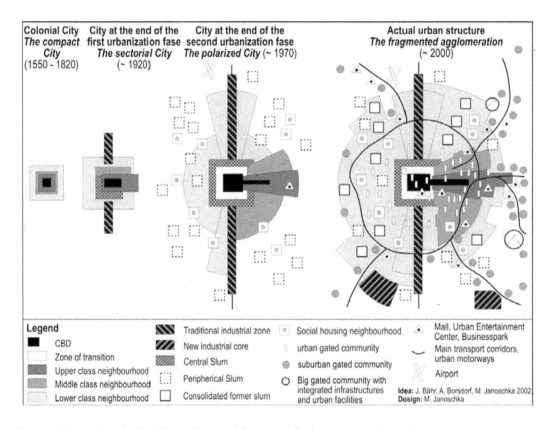

Figure 4.2.3   Borsdorf, Bähr and Janoschka's model of Latin American city structure.

Source: Borsdorf, Bähr and Janoschka 2002; adapted

activity. These sectoral patterns did not completely change the older ring structure, but strongly transformed the urban format.

From the 1930s onwards movement from rural areas to urban centres caused a massive population increase, and the agglomeration process began to display intense polarisation between rich and poor areas, implying a development pattern typical of the modern industrial city (Marcuse 1989). The upper-class areas transferred from the centre towards the suburbs, but the main feature was the expansion of poor neighbourhoods. Formal urban political institutions became less and less able to set the guidelines for urban development, not only due to high growth rates, but also because of corrupt and polemic policies which alternated with authoritarian regimes during phases of dictatorship. The sectoral principle of urban growth remained broadly intact but was overlaid by the polarisation principle. Only some time later in this period did a process of cell-type growth begin in the peripheries. In suburban or outer urban areas there began to emerge neighbourhoods of low-income housing such those in illegal marginal areas *(favelas, villas miserias)*, creating a cellular pattern, which started to gain importance.

During the last two decades, as we have indicated, urban expansion took a different direction. To be more specific, contemporary development can be characterised along the following lines (Janoschka 2002c: 65f):

- Gated communities for the upper and middle classes are appearing throughout the whole metropolitan area, breaking with the sectoral concentration of upper-class areas.

- The dispersion of malls, shopping centres and urban entertainment centres is taking place across the whole agglomeration, no longer concentrated in the upper-class sectors.

- Gated communities occupying a larger area and integrating more and more urban functions are becoming more common. Complexity and size of major gated communities are passing the level of small cities, particularly in São Paulo and Buenos Aires, but also in smaller cities such as Córdoba in Argentina.

- New transport infrastructure is helping shape this dispersal, with proximity to a motorway entrance being the most important influence shaping the spatial pattern of demand for detached housing areas.

- Industrial production is becoming suburbanised and logistical activities located in peripheral industrial or business parks.

- Lower social groups and marginal areas are increasingly segregated through walls or more informal barriers to access.

The crucial spatial influence on the new fragmentary and nodal urban structure is the transformation of the transport system, especially the motorways. These have been transformed from insufficient and saturated low-capacity highways to modern and effective ones. This has chiefly been made possible by private investment and so the stimulus for widespread private-led urban development under the neo-liberal political and economic governance regimes has been private-led modernisation of the transport infrastructure. Strong reduction in commuting times made suburban locations newly interesting to the middle and upper classes, whose valuation of time is that much greater.

As a result of the increased accessibility of the urban periphery, the cellular developments there, which in former times were predominantly in marginal areas, are becoming more integrated into the market sphere and increasingly interesting investment areas for real-estate enterprises. Another feature of the fragmentation process relates to the location of different urban functions. This is especially notable in the retail sector. Although the urban centres have gained new importance due to renovation programmes and other upgrading intervention, they cannot compete with suburban malls, which represent a North American lifestyle of rising popularity. Social exclusion works here not through the construction of walls but by accessibility. These islands of consumption and leisure are generally accessible only to those who have access to a car. However, while the first malls were clearly oriented to the upper-class market in the urban upper-class sector, such facilities are now found in the whole urban area due to the dispersion of the upper and middle class. This implies a degree of improvement in the access of the poor. Poorer areas also have been transformed during the last two decades. Marginal areas have been integrated into the city and in some cases have been upgraded. On the other hand, there are numerous cases of marginal areas which have resisted any integration and are now almost inaccessible nodes of criminality.

This discussion of the transformation of Latin American city structure shows that urban enclosure of the environment and the resulting fragmentation of accessibility is not only the preference of the high-income population, but a more general societal principle. In order to understand the specific case of Latin America better, a historical analysis of the rise and diffusion of gated residential neighbourhoods is presented in the next section.

The History of Gated Residential Neighbourhoods in Latin America

Discussion about gated communities in Latin America is dominated by characterisation of the new aspects of urban dynamics (Meyer and Bähr 2001; Coy and Pöhler 2002), the growing importance of a North American-dominated lifestyle and the impacts of global real-estate firms and a globalised elite labour force and consumption sector. Globalisation and the fear of criminality are two central arguments used to explain the proliferation of gated communities. These aspects should not be neglected, but analysing the appearance of gates from a historical point of view tempers the macro-explanations with local specificity. It is possible to find important lines of explanation in the typical behaviour of the Latin American elites through decades if not centuries.

The Spanish colonial cities of Latin America were open and without city walls. But this openness was accompanied by strong internal closure. The residential buildings—atrium houses with internal patios—were closed towards the street with heavy wooden doors, and until the mid-19th century windows were small and located to guarantee privacy. Even inside the build-ings, different grades of segregation and privacy were established; guests never had access to the second or third patio, which was reserved for women or for garden activities (cf. Borsdorf 2002b). Also in the colonial epoch, enclosed neighbourhoods for multiple households, notably widows, orphans or priests, are reported in cities such as Santa Catalina in Arequipa or the Hospitolio Cabañas in Guadalajara (cf. Borsdorf 2002b: 239). During the 19th century, another form of access-restricted neighbourhood emerged—company towns for the workers and em-ployees of mining companies. These were highly segregated and in many cases walled or with other public-access restrictions. These examples show that the principle of gating has occurred in Latin American cities throughout history, but this does not differ so much from what is known about European cities.

The more significant precursor to the modern closed neighbourhood was the presence of poor households in the atrium houses of central areas. This occurred from the late 19th century, when the owners of such houses moved towards the latest fashionable areas of the expanding city. Single-family atrium houses were subdivided, and each room rented to a low-income family. This transformation occurred in all bigger Latin American cities. The housing areas were called *tugurios* in Peru or *vecindades* in Mexico. In Chile and Argentina the term *conventillo* semantically connotes the concept of the walled sacred communities already referred to. The wooden entry gates of the former patio houses were transformed into 24-hour, guarded entrances to prevent the entry of new neighbours who did not pay rent. When the historical building stock was filled, this kind of structure was also reproduced in new lower-income areas, for example in Chile during the 1920s and 1930s or in Mexico until the early 1950s. Hidalgo (1999) and Rovira (2002) point out the similarity of these neighbourhoods to the gated communities of lower-income groups in the late 20th century. In a context of political instability, military regimes and the loss of state control, the gated communities of these groups become comprehensible presently and historically.

A parallel exists with many Latin American slum areas on city outskirts, *called favelas* in Brazil and *villas miserias* in Argentina. In most cases, the origins of these settlements, which sprawled in Latin America from the 1950s, are irregular if not outright illegal. The lack of legality led to a series of hardline state interventions including mass evacuations and demolition in the 1960s and 1970s. This followed and exacerbated a rising criminalisation of these areas (headquarters of drug dealing, organised criminality) and it induced the creation of internal organisation struc-tures to prevent the access of persons living outside. These were not created in the same way as modern entrepreneurial gated communities but the effect is very similar. The public cannot enter and a part of the city has become enclosed and locally governed.

There are also historical precursors to gated communities for the upper classes. Some au-thors have suggested that the origin of the 'wealthy' gated communities can be traced to the country clubs or golf club model. Borsdorf (2002b) describes the case of Mexico City, where, at the beginning of the 20th century, golf was imported by wealthy English immigrants and became rapidly popular among the European upper class. In the case of Buenos Aires, the first country clubs were built in the early 1930s, also emulating the lifestyle of the English-oriented bourgeoisie (Janoschka 2002d). At the time of their foundation, such clubs were still far away from the city, but the rapid growth of the agglomeration brought them within the urban core during the second half of the 20th century. Clubs found it necessary to guard their territories and secure the entrance due to low occupation during the week and the close proximity of potential trespassers. Up to the early 1970s the number of these clubs was low and they were still mostly used for vacation and weekend activities. From that time, however, a first wave of diffusion of such clubs was observable. As an example, about 70 country clubs for the upper and upper middle classes were founded in Buenos Aires in the mid-1980s, mainly for sports activities in a quasi-natural environment.

Gated Neighbourhoods in the Last Two Decades

Linking today's wealthy gated communities with their historical antecedents, advertisement remains focused on connecting gated housing with an elitist lifestyle, as the quotation from a Nordelta publicity leaflet shows clearly at the beginning [...]. Until the mid-20th century, European elites provided the reference points; now it is North America. Many advertisements, especially in Colombia and Brazil, offer a recipe for achieving this target lifestyle. Photos and remarks about lifestyle in Miami accompany the discourse of fear and insecurity which is especially strong in those two countries. The result is the construction of exotic habitats, including a range of temperate-zone plant species not naturally occurring in Latin America.

Constructing a typology of these developments begins with a problem of definition. Throughout Latin America, a range of terms are in common use. The meaning of the same word may substantially vary in different countries. *Condomínio fechado* (Brazil), *barrio privado* (Argentina) or *fraccionamiento cerrado* (Mexico) stand for different products of the real-estate market in the different countries, and even the term *barrio cerrado* (closed neighbourhood), used in various countries such as Chile, Ecuador and Bolivia, has a wide range of meanings. Therefore we adopt a consistent language using English terms.

Three main types of gated neighbourhood can be differentiated by structure, location and size. The three groups are defined as follows:

- Urban gated communities, which can be defined as groups of attached houses or tower blocks with few common facilities. The target of these developments may be middle- or lower middle-class families in intermediate locations (even social housing projects) or upper middle- to upper-class families in central areas where land shortage limits the development of common facilities. This category also includes the enclosure of existing areas, in most cases upper-class single-family housing areas in central or intermediate locations.

- Suburban gated communities, predominantly for the middle and upper classes with single detached houses. These developments share a wide range of common facilities including sports and community facilities and landscaped gardens. There are also sub-urban gated communities without common facilities and these may be oriented to lower middle-income groups.

- Mega-projects with integrated cultural and educational facilities. Although there are still only a few of these projects, the dynamics and the internationalisation of the real-estate market make this the most rapidly growing segment.

All three types have boomed throughout Latin America. Between 1990 and 2001, in Mexico City, around 750 new gated neighbourhoods with almost 50,000 housing units were launched on the market (Parnreiter 2004). In the Argentinian capital Buenos Aires more than 450 suburban gated communities currently exist, 80 per cent of them were started between 1995 and 2001. A dozen of these reach a size of more than 5,000 inhabitants (Janoschka 2002a). To this figure an unknown number of urban gated communities known as garden-towers (*torre jardín,* cf. Welch 2002) must be added in Argentina. In 2002 more than 130 of these garden-towers were listed in the local newspapers as offering new apartments. The quantity of pre-existing stock is unknown. Estimation of the total population ranges between 300,000 and 600,000 persons. In another example, Pöhler (1999) estimates that more than 100,000 people live in *condomínios fechados* in Rio de Janeiro's upper-class and beach-oriented city expansion area called Barra da Tijuca. Brazil's financial centre and megacity São Paulo also has a mega-project, Alphaville, with around 35,000 inhabitants and more than 100,000 people working inside the gates. Gated communities have also diffused to secondary cities such as Córdoba, Argentina (1.3 million inhabitants). Within the metropolitan area there are more then 50 gated residential developments; one of them, Valle Escondido (Hidden Valley), promoted with the slogan 'the new city', offers a cluster of different gated communities for a total population of approximately 25,000 inhabitants (Roca 2001; ECIPSA 2003). Data for Curitiba in Brazil estimate the number of gated communities at about 300. This pattern is repeated in most big Latin American cities. In medium-size cities (less than 500,000 inhabitants) and in some cases even in small towns (for example Gualeguaychú, Entre Rios, Argentina), gated communities are also becoming more and more common.

The market share of gated housing complexes is extremely difficult to estimate. There are poor statistical data for the construction sector and in most cases differentiation between the products is not clearly specified. For the case of Buenos Aires, our own calculation is that there are about 100,000 units in the city's suburban gated communities. In relation to the whole housing stock, which is about 3 million, the market share represents not more than 3 per cent. But considering only the proportion of suburban housing, the market share has already risen to 10 per cent. If the calculation is based on the demand group (the upper 15–20 per cent of the population in terms of income, equivalent to 450,000 households), these 100,000 units repre-sent between 20 and 25 per cent of the market share. The market for single detached houses or lots for construction of detached houses in suburban locations is more or less synonymous with gated communities. During the period of macro-economic stability from 1991 to 2001, between 80 and 90 per cent of urban expansion was related to the expansion of gated communities.

To these figures should be added the 'quasi' gated communities; streets and neighbourhoods with strong vigilance and closure of access during the night or retrospectively enclosed neighbourhoods, which do not appear as gated developments in the open real-estate market. Also, social housing projects from the 1970s, which are nowadays walled and gate-guarded, add to the contemporary stock of enclosed neighbourhoods. The same happens with a whole range of areas which are inaccessible due to internal governance and the predominance of criminal structures.

Urban Insecurity

Our earlier discussion showed that the proliferation of gated communities started in Latin America long before political decisions led to internationalisation of the region's economy. Neither globalisation nor Americanisation of society can adequately on their own explain the peculiar rise in gated housing areas in Latin American cities.

Explanations focussing on security seem at first sight rather convincing. Superficially there seems to be a temporal correlation between the socioeconomic transformation of most Latin American societies, which led to a substantial rise of urban insecurity, and the proliferation of enclosed neighbourhoods (Caldeira 2000; Dammert 2001). The development of gated housing complexes seems to be a rational solution not only for the richest parts of the population, but also for everyone else. It is an obvious consequence of rising criminality. Empirical data from several studies in Latin America show, however, that concern about criminality cannot fully explain why people move to a gated neighbourhood. The exception is Colombia, where about 40,000 murders per year are committed due to haphazard and organised violence and internal political conflict. However, in all other cases there are more important reasons than violence in itself. Between different countries and cities, the significance of the fear of violence varies. Caldeira (2000) showed that for the Brazilian city of São Paulo, urban violence reached such high levels that most inhabitants of gated communities had direct experience of some kind of criminality before making the decision to move inside the gates. This experience is also found in several big Brazilian cities and also in Mexico City. But this may not be a representative picture for the rest of the cities in the hemisphere. Biographical interviews with inhabitants of Nordelta in Buenos Aires, for example, show that despite media discourse and marketing emphasis, which stress fear of crime, inhabitants of the private city do not mention these factors as key influences on their decision to move there (Janoschka 2002a). There are several aspects which are more important for the new inhabitants of Nordelta. These include:

- Political and economic insecurity in the wider city, accompanied by the incapacity of the state to organise urban services and social infrastructure.

- The enhanced urban and suburban environment in the gated city, created by high levels of private investment. On the one hand, suburban spaces were viewed as more attractive because of the better standard of infrastructure (motorways, private schools, shopping and entertainment facilities). On the other hand, the urban environment outside was viewed as being degraded due to increasing density, rising motorisation and state retreat from maintenance of public spaces.

- The desire for a change of personal lifestyle and the search for a more socially homogeneous environment. Nordelta inhabitants are mainly between 35 and 40 years old and have one or more children. The location gives them space and time with the family and outdoor activities for the children. The decision to move into the private city is an option to change lifestyle and guarantee a secure and predictable quality of life for the family. The package purchased is not only the immediate benefits within the gates but also the chance of a high standard of education and future networks for the children, to help secure the long-term social standard of the family.

- Last, but not least, the wish to achieve a new lifestyle is motivated by face-to-face propaganda, personal knowledge and group behaviour. Most people moving to Nordelta know from relatives and friends how life is organised in the gated neighbourhood. Some people even commented on friend-group pressure as a determinant for their decision. In certain social groups you are 'out' if you do not move to the suburban gated neighbourhood.

Empirical data collected by the authors from other Latin American cities, such as Santiago de Chile, Mexico City or Quito, show similar patterns (Janoschka 2002e). Despite the huge differences in urban settings, social behaviour and socio-economic development between different countries in Latin America, the importance of criminality is much lower than expected and in many cases irrelevant.

Conclusion

[...] Inhabitants of Latin American gated communities rapidly change their lifestyle and fully adapt their daily habits to life within an access-restricted area. Local public spaces lose their basic role as points of interaction between different classes as each class organises its own homogeneous space 'inside'. This tendency rises with the growing complexity of urban functions within the new private cities, as shown in the example of Nordelta. Inhabitants are increasingly living live in bubbles which are detached from the surrounding local political and social environments. The central difference compared to former times is the fact that today all social classes show signs of wanting to escape from the wider public sphere.

Latin American elites never strongly oriented themselves towards their own society but followed lifestyles imported from Europe and later from the US. A life behind walls may lead gated neighbourhood inhabitants even further away from the social reality of their 'home' society, which for the great majority of the population consists of a struggle for daily survival. From this point of view, the proliferation of gated neighbourhoods must surely inevitably lead to a decrease in solidarity between different social groups. The historical behaviour of the elites in

Latin America today dominates also the middle and lower middle-class populations. During the gating boom of the last two decades, neither Latin American media nor urbanists, architects or politicians have recognised it as a long-term problem for society. This is not surprising since all these groups, which are helping lead economic progress, directly or indirectly benefit from the gated communities. With the exception of Brazil and Colombia, gated neighbourhoods are partly a product of an imagined insecurity promoted by the media and real-estate companies, both gaining from exaggerating fears. On the other hand, as we have argued, residents may respond not so much to the security on offer as to the provision of neighbourhood services and facilities. Real-estate agents, developers, the media and an army of willing consumers have wielded sufficient economic power to prevent local and regional governments from attempting to regulate gated communities. Politics in Latin America are not driven so much by the implementation of citizens' desires as by the pressure of particular interests, and gated communities represent the perfection of Latin American traditions applied by the regional elite. Only recently and in the light of economic crisis is a rethink process starting, in which the negative consequences of urban disintegration through gated neighbourhoods have been raised. The announcement from the urban government in La Paz, Bolivia to open by force a dozen gated neighbourhoods to the public in March of 2003 shows that changes in urban policies may be possible in the future. Credible politicians and active civic participation are required to increase public awareness of urban social problems. And the problems being stored up by a fragmented urban form have not yet had the political debate in Latin America that they deserve.

Bibliography

Bähr, J. (1976) 'Neuere Entwicklungstendenzen lateinamerikanischer Großstädte', *Geographische Rundschau*, 28:125–33.

Bähr, J. and Mertins, G. (1981) 'Idealschema der sozialräumlichen Differenzierung lateinamerikanischer Großstädte', *Geographische Zeitschrift*, 69 (1): 1–33.

Beckett, K. (1997) *Making Crime Pay: Law and Order in Contemporary American Politics*, New York: Oxford University Press.

Borsdorf, A. (1976) *Valdivia und Osorno. Strukturelle Disparitäten in chilenischen Mittelstädte*, Tübingen: Universität Tübingen (Tübinger Geographische Studien 69).

_____(1982) 'Die lateinamerikanische Großstadt. Zwischenbericht zur Diskussion um ein Modell', *Geographische Rundschau*, 34 (11): 498–501.

_____(1999) *Geographisch denken und wissenschaftlich arbeiten*, Gotha and Stuttgart: Klett.

_____(2002a) 'Barrios cerrados in Santiago de Chile, Quito y Lima: tendencias de la segregación socio-espacial', in L.F.Cabrales (ed.) *Latinoamérica:países abiertos, ciudades cerradas*, Guadalajara and Paris: Pandora: 581–610.

_____(2002b) 'Vor verschlossenen Türen—Wie neu sind die Tore und Mauern in lateinamerikanischen Städten? Eine Einführung', *Geographica Helvetica*, 57 (4): 238–44.

Borsdorf, A. and Hidalgo, R. (2005) 'Barrios cerrados y fragmentation social en America Latina. Estudio de las transformaciones socio-espaciales en Santiago de Chile 1990–2000', in R.Hidalgo, R.Trumper and

A.Borsdorf (eds) *Transformaciones urbanas y procesos territorial. Lecturas del nuevo dibujo de la ciudad latinoamericana.* Santiago de Chile: Geo-Libros: 105–22.

Borsdorf, A., Bähr, J. and Janoschka, M. (2002) 'Die Dynamik stadtstrukturellen Wandels in Lateinamerika im Modell der lateinamerikanischen Stadt', *Geographica Helvetica*, 57 (4): 300–10.

Burgess, E.W. (1925) 'The growth of the city: An introduction to a research project', in R.Park, E.W.Burgess and R.McKenzie (eds) *The City*, Chicago, IL: University of Chicago Press.

Caldeira, T. (2000) *City of Walls: Crime, Segregation and Citizenship in São Paulo*, Berkeley, CA, Los Angeles, CA, London: University of California Press.

Ciccolella, P. (1999) 'Globalización y dualizacion en la Region Metropolitana de Buenos Aires. Grandes inversiones y reestructuración socioterritorial en los años noventa', *eure (Estudios urbano regionales)*, 21 (76): 5–28.

Coy, M. and Pöhler, M. (2002) 'Condomínios fechados und die Fragmentierung der Stadt. Typen—Akteure—Folgewirkungen', *Geographica Helvetica*, 57 (4): 264–77.

Crowley, W.K. (1995) 'Modelling the Latin American city', *Geographical Review*, 88 (1): 127–30.

Dammert, L. (2001) 'Construyendo ciudades inseguras: temor y violencia en Argentina', *eure (Estudios urbano regionales)*, 27 (82): 5–20.

Dear, M. (2000) *The Postmodern Urban Condition*, Oxford and Maiden, MA: Blackwell.

Deler, J.P. (1992) 'Ciudades andinos: viejos y nuevos modelos', in E.Kringman Garcés (ed.) *Ciudades de los Andes: vision histórica y contemporánea*, Quito: Institut français d'études andines: 351–74.

ECIPSA (2003) *Valle Escondido News—La ciudad nueva*, Cordoba (publicity leaflet of Valle Escondido developers).

Ford, L.R. (1996) 'A new and improved model of Latin American city structure', *Geographical Review*, 86 (3): 437–40.

Gilbert, A. (1998) *The Latin American City*, 2nd edn, London: Latin American Bureau.

Gormsen, E. (1981) 'Die Städte in spanisch-Amerika. Ein zeit-räumliches Entwicklungsmodell der letzten hundert Jahre', *Erdkunde*, 35 (4): 290–303.

Griffin, E. and Ford, L. (1980) 'A model of Latin American city structure', *Geographical Review*, 70 (4): 397–422.

Harris, C.D. and Ullman, E.L. (1945) 'The nature of cities', *Annals of the American Academy for Political Science*, 242:7–17.

Hidalgo, R. (1999) 'Continuidad y cambio en un siglo de vivienda social en Chile (1892–1998). Reflexiones a partir del caso de la ciudad de Santiago', *Revista Geográ-fica Norte Grande*, 26:69–77.

Hoyt, H. (1939) *The Structure and Growth of Residential Neighborhoods in American Cities*, Washington, DC: Federal Housing Administration.

Janoschka, M. (2002a) *Wohlstand hinter Mauern. Private Urbanisierungen in Buenos Aires*, Vienna: Verlag der Österreichischen Akademie der Wissenschaften (Forschungsberichte des Instituts für Stadt- und Regionalforschung 28).

_____(2002b) 'El nuevo modelo de la ciudad latinoamericana: fragmentation y privatizatión', *eure (Estudios urbano regionales)*, 28 (85): 11–30.

_____(2002c) '"Stadt der Inseln". Buenos Aires: Abschottung und Fragmentierung als Zeichen eines neuen Stadtmodells', *RaumPlanung*, 101:65–70.

_____(2002d) 'Urbanizaciones privadas en Buenos Aires: Hacia un nuevo modelo de ciudad latinoamer-icana?', in L.F.Cabrales (ed.) *Latinoamérica: países abiertos, ciudades cerradas*, Guadalajara and Paris: Pandora: 287–318.

_____(2002e) 'Die Flucht vor Gewalt? Stereotype und Motivationen beim Andrang auf *barrios privados* in Buenos Aires', *Geographica Helvetica,* 57 (4): 290–9.

(2004) 'El modelo de ciudad latinoamericana. Privatización y fragmentation del espacio urbano de Buenos Aires: el caso Nordelta', in M.Welch (ed.) *La ciudad en cuestión. Nuevos lugares, viejos espacios,* Buenos Aires: Biblos (forthcoming).

Janoschka, M. and Glasze, G. (2003) 'Urbanizaciones cerradas: un modelo analítico', *Ciudades,* 59:9–20.

Marcuse, P. (1989) '"Dual city": A muddy metaphor for a quartered city', *International Journal of Urban and Regional Research,* 13 (4): 697–708.

Meyer, K. and Bähr, J. (2001) 'Condominios in Greater Santiago de Chile and their impact on the urban structure', *Die Erde,* 132 (3): 293–321.

Nordelta (2002) *Nordelta CiudadPueblo—El camino para vivir mejor, Información,* Buenos Aires (publicity leaflet of Nordelta S.A., developer of Nordelta).

Ocampo, J. (2003) 'Las políticas económicas en America Latina y el Caribe', in Real Instituto Elcano (ed.) *Anuario Elcano: America Latina 2002–03,* Madrid: Real Institute Elcano de Estudios Internacionales y Estratégicos: 260–75.

Parnreiter, C. (2004) 'Entwicklungstendenzen lateinamerikanischer Metropolen im Zeitalter der Globalisierung', *Mitteilungen der Österreichischen Geographischen Gesellschaft,* 146:1–28.

Pöhler, M. (1999) *Zwischen Luxus-Ghettos und Favelas. Stadterweiterungsprozesse und sozialräumliche Segregation in Rio de Janeiro: Das Fallbeispiel Barra da Tijuca,* Tübingen: Universitätsverlag Tübingen (Kleinere Arbeiten aus dem Geographischen Institut der Universität Tübingen 21).

Reuband, K.-H. (1999) 'Kriminalitätsfurcht—Stabilität und Wandel', *Neue Kriminalpolitik,* 2:15–20.

Roca, J. (2001) *Los Barrios Cerrados en Córdoba,* Córdoba: Universidad Nacional de Córdoba.

Rovira, A. (2002) 'Los barrios cerrados de Santiago de Chile: En busca de la seguridad y la privacidad perdida', in L.F.Cabrales (ed.) *Latinoamérica: países abiertos, ciudades cerradas,* Guadalajara and Paris: Pandora: 351–69.

Ruiz, J. (2003) 'Los siete pecados capitales de Iberoamérica: mito, realidad y consecuencias', in Real Instituto Elcano (ed.) *Anuario Elcano: America Latina 2002–03,* Madrid: Real Instituto Elcano de Estudios Internacionales y Estratégicos: 276–307.

Sabatini, F., Caceres, G. and Cerda, J. (2001) 'Segregation residencial en las principales ciudades chilenas: Tendencias de las tres últimas décadas y posibles cursos de action', *eure (Estudios urbano regionales),* 27 (82): 21–42.

Soja, E. (2000) *Postmetropolis: Critical Studies of Cities and Regions,* Oxford and Maiden, MA: Blackwell.

Welch, M. (2002) 'Gartentürme des Wohlstands. Buenos Aires: Projektionen einer Wohnhaustypologie', *RaumPlanung,* 101:71–6.

Section IV: Recommended Readings

Anton, D. J. (1993). *Thirsty cities: Urban environments and water supply in Latin America.* Ottawa, Canada: International Development Research Centre.

Cervantes-Rodriguez, M., Grosfoguel, R., and Mielants, E. H. (Eds.). (2008). *Caribbean migration to Western Europe and the United States: Essays on incorporation, identity, and citizenship.* Philadelphia, PA: Temple University Press.

Davids, R. (2016). *Shaping terrain: City building in Latin America.* Gainesville, FL: University Press of Florida.

Foote, N., & Goebel, M. (2014). *Immigration and national identities in Latin America.* Gainesville, FL: University Press of Florida.

Wade, P. (2017). *Degrees of mixture, degrees of freedom: Genomics, multiculturalism, and race in Latin America.* Durham, NC: Duke University Press.

Section IV: Post-Reading Questions

1   Briefly describe each of the three categories of factors that cause migratory flows.

2   Are gated communities the ideal urban structure for Latin American cities? Is segregation the solution to prevent urban insecurity?

SECTION V

CULTURE, GENDER, AND RELIGION

Editor's Introduction

Historically framed on hybridity, *mestizaje*, and Creolization, the nature and diversity of the cultures and societies inhabiting Latin America and the Caribbean, continues to be largely misunderstood and stereotyped by outsiders. The Day of the Dead, machismo, and religiosity are three topics explored in the readings of this section in an attempt to demystify some relevant aspects of Latin American and Caribbean cultures.

Congdon's (2003) reading explores Mexico's perception of death as inevitable, worthy of humor and celebration. For outsiders, Day of the Dead yearly celebrations are usually confused with Halloween, a modern interpretation of the ancient Celtic festival *Samhain*. Sadly, the commercial nature of Halloween is having a profound impact on Mexicans who choose to celebrate it instead of the traditional Day of the Dead. In the United States, movies such as *Coco* and *The Book of Life* offer a Hollywood interpretation—not culturally or socially relevant to the meaning of the Day of the Dead. Ironically, these media depictions may change the future outlook of this celebration in Mexico.

Another cultural trait associated to Latin American and Caribbean populations is that of *machismo*. Gutmann's (2006) excerpt clarifies that machismo, as a cultural position, should not be perceived solely as a term defining male chauvinism. This reading historically frames the contradictions, current interpretation, and relevance to social relationships that the terms *macho* and *machismo* have to modern Latin American and Caribbean societies.

The last reading in this section addresses another stereotype common to Latin America and the Caribbean: Catholicism as the dominant religion in both regions. Lopez (2015) offers a succinct analysis of the historical conditions that led to the demise of the religious monopoly that Catholicism had enjoyed since the 15th century. The impact of an individualized and customized practice of Christianity welcomed competing versions, allowing for the exponential growth of a myriad of Protestant denominations. As such, the religious character of Latin America and the Caribbean has changed, reducing the scope of the Catholic Church and enabling the growth of alternative ideologies such as "Liberation Theology."

Section V: Key Terms

Atheism	homosexuality
Aztecs	humor
calaveras	Liberation Theology
cartoneros	*macho, mandilon*
charros	manliness
cheating	missionaries
Comunidades Eclesiales de Base	*ofrendas, piñatas*
corridos	Roman Catholicism
domestic violence	stereotype
Evangelicals	

Making Merry with Death

Iconic Humor in Mexico's Day of the Dead

Kristin Congdon

C hildren eat sugar skulls with their names printed on the candied foreheads, public figures endure attacks with predictions of their impending demise, and papier-mâché skeletons appear, inviting the dead to live amongst us. These *calaveras* (literally "skulls," but also used in reference to whole skeletons) walk the dog, play musical instruments, and perform other day-to-day activities. Mexico's Day of the Dead festival, also celebrated in many parts of the United States (Beardsley 1987, 64), is a time to honor death while mocking it with great abandon.

It would be difficult to point to another culture that celebrates with so much amusement and gaiety what many other people feel is the most difficult rite of passage. In Mexico, the more hilarious the confrontation of the dead with the living, perhaps the greater the pleasure and engagement with the celebration. Death is unavoidable, and the response of many Mexicans and Mexican-Americans is to accept it as a permanent companion. This relationship is friendly, comical, ironic, and full of mockery. Octavio Paz described it this way:

> To the inhabitant of New York, Paris, or London death is a word that is never used because it burns the lips. The Mexican, on the other hand, frequents it, mocks it, caresses it, sleeps with it, entertains it; it is one of his favourite playthings and his most enduring love.[1] (1961, 10)

This essay will explore how humor is used in Day of the Dead rituals with special attention to the function of the iconic *calavera* or skeleton [...]. I will analyze how humor is an inseparable part of the aesthetic process of the Day of the Dead celebration, allowing for a breakdown of opposing forces, opposites that are somehow overcome and conquered in the popular Mexican and Mexican-American worldview. The two pairs of opposing forces, which I will analyze, are life and death and the upper and lower economic classes. In Day of the Dead rituals, the boundaries between these entities, typically seen by most Europeans as opposites, are broken down through the aesthetic process of reversal. In a reversal, something that is thought to be ugly becomes pleasurable, or even beautiful. If the aesthetic is not inverted or reversed, it is at least blurred (Lippard 1990, 200–201). As this aesthetic reversal takes place in ritual space, the boundary between the artist and the participant is also deconstructed during the fiesta experience. Humor is the catalyst for this aesthetic process. Were it not for the success of the humor, the reversal would perhaps not be accepted, and the power of the ideas about death would be diminished. These ideas will first be explored and then further grounded in the widely celebrated *calavera* prints of José Guadalupe Posada and the Linares family's papier-mâché *calaveras*.

Ideas about Death

There are wide differences between the way Europeans and Mexicans approach death (Brandes 1998a, 364; Garciagodoy 1998a, 192–193). For Europeans, death is an omen that has nothing to do with social issues, but can have a symbolic sense to it, or a moral teaching. In contrast, according to Héctor Grimrac, Mexicans view death as a "splitting of the personality" (Garciagodoy 1998:192). Whatever they cannot do themselves in regard to their social situation, they can impute that limit to death. It is death, represented in the skeleton, which, with the use of humor, can make the daring kind of social statements with which it would be too risky and certainly improper for the living to involve themselves (Garciagodoy 1998, 192–193).

This explanation, though, makes a complex topic seem too simplistic. Mexico's indigenous people had strong ideas about death in pre-Hispanic times that involved a melding of life and death. These ideas have changed over time, as they have incorporated practices and ideology of Spanish origin. For example, Spain also has a tradition of using humor with an anthropomorphized character, Death, which exposes social wrongs on an allegorical level (Garciagodoy 1998, 192). However, the Aztecs held the strong belief of life coming from death—and therefore the view that life and death are co-dependent. In fact, in this way of thinking, death feeds life. It was this belief that allowed for the sacrificial spilling of blood, and the offering of beating hearts to the gods. These ritualistic acts ensured ritual participants that the world would continue to exist as it should. The sun would shine in the sky, and the maize would grow tall to feed the people (Scalora 1997, 65).

For Mexicans, then, death is simply a part of life. It is not separate from life, as an entity from somewhere else, a force that somehow comes to you at a certain time. Rather, it constantly lives within you, in the form of a skeleton, a *calavera*. María Antonieta Sánchez de Escamilla, from

Puebla City, teaches her nursery school children not to fear death. She tells them that "our loved ones never really die while we remember them." When her children feel uncomfortable about death, she tells them to touch themselves, and explain why they are afraid when each of them "owns a skull and a skeleton." She further says that "We all carry death within us," and when they [the children] understand that we are all made of bones, death makes more sense (Carmichael and Sayer 1991, 119).[2]

At a young age, children are taught to respect the dead and that if they do not do so, it could result in severe danger (Scalora 1997, 76). Having an understanding that the dead do not go away forever, that they can return to visit, and that death can be welcoming, permits both children and adults to have a feeling of security. It makes that which might be foreboding and terrifying more welcome in everyday life. In a country where health care and sanitary conditions are poor, death and dying are all too prevalent. The fact that death returns in a humorous manner makes it easier to approach. The living are able to take part in the joke.

The connection between life and death is explained and heightened in several ways. Many believe that the dead remember the living in the same manner that the living remember the dead (Carmichael and Sayer 1991, 105). The living make *ofrendas* (literally "offerings," but also altar-like constructions for the dead, usually placed on a tabletop), and it is believed that the dead respond by leaving signs of their presence for the living (see figure 5.1.1). It could be the unexplained snuffing of a candle, a strange shadow, a tipping over of a glass, a soft whisper, or the sensation that you have been touched by a presence you cannot see (Scalora 1997, 79). Before the dead reach their final destination, they visit places important to them when they were alive. They may be able to make these visits in various forms,

Figure 5.1.1 *Ofrenda* by Catalina Delgado Trunk, set up at the Florida Folk Festival in White Springs in 1996. Photo by Kristin G. Congdon.

perhaps as a hummingbird or a cloud. It is believed that the Toltecs handed down these ideas to the Aztecs and that, in some manner, the idea of the dead surrounding us in various forms exists today (Carmichael and Sayer 1991, 55).

Ancient beliefs of the Totonac, who today reside in the state of Veracruz, maintained that living relatives were expected to help the dead in their journey on to the next life, at *Kalinin*, the world of the dead. It was believed that the immortal part of the being is what travels—the spirit-soul or that which is the seed of life. When it gets to its destiny, it is guided by the gods (Carmichael and Sayer 1991, 62). Both the living and the gods, therefore, assist the dead on their journey in the afterlife.

Death is embraced by the Mexicans for other reasons besides having the responsibility to as-sist relatives on their journey to a better place. Life is often seen to be so difficult that, relatively speaking, death may not be so bad. Suffering, therefore, is a part of life, and death releases you from the pain. In support of this idea is a common Mexican proverb that asks, "Why should I fear death when life has cured me of frights?" (Garciagodoy 1998, 175). Another formulaic expression with similar sentiment reflects the view of a bereaving mother: "I loved the little angel; but I am glad that he is happy, without having to experience the bitterness of life" (Carmichael and Sayer 1991, 54).

Partly because Mexicans understand that death is imminent, they embrace it in a manner unlike Europeans and Anglos. Instead of expressing angst about death, as Camus did,[3] Mexicans face it with humor (Garciagodoy 1998, 186). And it is with this sense of humor that the living welcome the dead into their homes during the Day of the Dead. This is a time for reunion, connections, celebration, and constructing meaning in one's life. Humor is used to find a comfort zone in which to express a respect for death, by making it a part of living. Humor is also used to mock death, as it mocks the living, especially those from the upper economic classes who, like everyone else, cannot escape it.

Mexicans on the lower economic rungs of life understand that the plans they make and the dreams they have are only possible if they have life to see them through. Unlike the upper eco-nomic classes of people, they do not have access to the kinds of lifestyles and medical facilities that, to some degree, might ensure a healthier life. Nonetheless, they also know that a stable economic life will not necessarily grant anyone a long and healthy life. In this regard, the rich and poor are the same; they both face death. Neither group has control over it, a fact which can be empowering to people who struggle every day to have their basic needs met. Death is an equalizer. Consequently, all the pomp and circumstance, the fancy clothes, and the daily activities of the rich become somehow trivialized, even ludicrous. These are key lessons presented by the ever-smiling *calaveras* (Garciagodoy 1998, 186).

There is another reason why the *calaveras* are so merry. They are festive because they are the dead welcoming the living when they die. As Arsacio Benegas Arroyo explained, "When I die I want there to be music, I want people to dance, to get drunk and to feel no sadness" (qtd. in Carmichael and Sayer 1991, 130). It only makes sense, then, that Mexicans would embrace the *calaveras* who are involved in these merrymaking activities.

Day of the Dead

The Day (or Days) of the Dead is one of the most significant yearly celebrations for Mexicans. It is not necessarily a celebration unique to Mexico, but "it is now and has long been a symbol of Mexico" (Brandes 1998a, 362). While Day of the Dead celebrations clearly make connections to the Catholic Church, the Day of the Dead has aspects of ritual which go beyond church doctrine. Although the Catholic Church does not embrace all aspects of the fiesta, Day of the Dead celebrations are generally tolerated.

Ofrendas

During Day of the Dead celebrations, graves are decorated and family vigils occur, special foods are made, a form of ritualized begging or solicitation occur, and *ofrendas* are created, usually in a spiritual site within the home of the deceased relative (Brandes 1998a, 363). *Ofrendas* differ from place to place. In Veracruz, for example, sugar cane, banana leaves, palm leaves, and coconuts are often used to make an arch around the altar space. In Puebla, *papel picado* (cut paper) is placed around the altar.[4]

Usually, an *ofrenda* is placed on a table that serves not only as an altar, but also as a place for food to be served, specially baked for the deceased. Also arranged as part of the *ofrenda* are rosaries, pictures of saints, *milagros* (charms), and statuettes. Bright and colorful flower arrangements combine *cempitsuchil* (marigolds), *terciopelo* (cockscomb), gladiolas, and *nube* (a gypsophilia-type flower). These flowers are placed around the altar, along with items that the deceased person would enjoy; often these relate to his or her life's work or hobbies. The scent from the flowers, mixed with *copal* (incense), is unmistakable, and said to entice spirits into the house. Sometimes, in order to make the invitation even more clearly marked, the flowers are extended from the doorway of the home to the street (Congdon, Delgado-Trunk, and López 1999, 313–314).

According to Chicana artist Amalia Mesa-Bains, there is symbolic significance in the way an *ofrenda* is constructed. The canopy or arch may be expressive of celestial imagery, and the repeated use of aged surfaces is reflective of time and erosion. She notes the continuous placement of memorial objects on the *ofrenda* as important in that they focus the work on the deceased. Mesa-Bains also observes the formalist aesthetic dimensions of *ofrendas,* in that there is often a striking balance between scale and volume and a serialization of objects placed in a pleasing formal arrangement (1997, 126). Catalina Delgado-Trunk makes several *ofrendas* for Day of the Dead celebrations every year. Often they are placed in public spaces for the purposes of educating the community (see figures 5.1.2–5.1.6.).

In some respects, *ofrendas*, like other Mexican home altars, can be read as if they were family albums complete with deities and "an iconic portrait of negotiations between family members and the divine in which requests and promises are traded" (Beezley 1997, 100–101). This is a site where the secular and the sacred worlds come together. All kinds of relationships are negotiated in this altarspace (Beezley 1997, 93). As it is made, the creator is mindful that the purpose of every object placed on the *ofrenda* is meant to entice the absent spirit(s) to visit (Gutiérrez 1997, 46).

Figure 5.1.2 Day of the Dead *ofrenda* by Catalina Delgado-Trunk, 1996. This *ofrenda* was installed in Orlando, Florida's City Hall in an effort to educate the public about the Day of the Dead. Photo by Kristin G. Congdon.

Figure 5.1.3 Detail of figure 5.1.2.

Figure 5.1.4 Detail of figure 5.1.2.

Figure 5.1.5   Detail of figure 5.1.2.

Figure 5.1.6   Detail of figure 5.1.2.

It is traditional for people to purchase new objects for the Day of the Dead celebration, such as new cooking dishes, jugs, kitchen utensils, small and big cups, and incense burners. Creative crafts are also purchased, such as candlesticks, trees of life, candied skulls, and *calaveras* (Pomar 1987, 24). New toys are purchased for both living and deceased children to play with (Pomar 1987, 28). Although it is often not economically feasible, even the clothes people wear are supposed to be new (Carmichael and Sayer 1991, 18). The demand for new purchases creates a vibrant marketplace where the activity of making and selling goods is heightened. The marked increase in activity, in both public and private spaces, marks these special celebratory days in a way that cannot be ignored (Garciagodoy 1998, 202).

All-night vigils of praying and feasting take place in cemeteries across Mexico. Flowers are placed on the graves along with other decorations such as crosses. Graves are swept and head-stones repaired. Tomás Ybarra-Frausto reports that often, along with drinking coffee or stronger libations, groups will tell stories about the living and dead. Often strange happenings will be reported, including tales of the *levantada del muerto* (folktales of the dead sitting up in the coffin at the wake).[5] There is always talk about the afterlife (1991a, 24).

During the festival, Fredy Méndez from the State of Veracruz said, "we all treat all living beings with kindness. This includes dogs, cats, even flies or mosquitos" (qtd. in Carmichael and Sayer 1991, 80). He further explained that if people are not pleasant to each other, the dead know it, and will become unhappy, perhaps even sick (Carmichael and Sayer 1991, 80). This belief enhances the sense of connectedness that is pervasive in Day of the Dead celebrations. The dead and the living are intertwined to such a degree that what the living do directly affects the dead. A decreasing number of people set their dinner tables with place settings for the dead, but it does still happen. Some of the deceased's favorite possessions are placed on the chairs (Carmichael and Sayer 1991, 21).

In Mixquic, four people carry a coffin with a cardboard skeleton in it. They mourn the dead by pretending to cry, but they do so in such a way that it is humorous and people laugh (Carmichael and Sayer 1991, 140). Happiness and pleasure are mixed with mourning and sadness. They become hard to distinguish, just as it becomes more difficult to clearly define the difference between the living and the dead, for on these days, the dead are thought to intermingle with the living. They come to joke, celebrate, and feast with family and friends. These activities bring great comfort to the living. And as the festivities take place, everyone is reminded of the democratic spirit of death. No one is immune to it, regardless of economic privilege. Elena Poniatowska explained it this way: "We are here only on loan, only passing through. The earth tries to catch us, that's why we shouldn't hold on so hard to life. Dying is good, but it is a matter of luck" (1991, 56).

Skeleton as Aesthetic Reversal

Death's presence is visualized in many areas by the skull and skeleton, or *calavera*, which dates back to pre-Columbian times. Mexicans dance with skeletons, children eat sugar skulls with their names printed on the foreheads, and the famous painter Frida Kahlo painted herself sleeping under a papier-mâché skeleton which rested on the canopy over her bed (Congdon, Delgado-Trunk, and López 1999, 315).

The practice of eating sugar skulls with one's name on it may be interpreted in several ways. It may be a reminder that death resides inside every person, and that the skull (read as death) is part of us. Garciagodoy suggests one possibility of meaning associated with eating the skulls, as she reflects on the practice as cannibalistic:

> The eater wants magically to appropriate characteristics of the morsel as when an Aztec runner ate a bit of the calf muscle of a sacrificed warrior who was a good runner. During Days of the Dead, by consuming a sweet skull the eater is inoculated against fear of death because she or he has taken in the peace of death or the dead. Another desire can be to dominate or destroy what is eaten, in which case the ingestion leaves the eater alone in the field. If one consumes a skull, one pronounces one's immortality. (1997, 138)

The eating of sugar skulls may also be likened to eating the sweet Day of the Dead bread, sometimes made in the shape of bones. While it gives the consumer pleasure to eat the tasty bread or sugar skull, there is clearly more to it than pure taste enjoyment. Garciagodoy points out that philosophers since Aristotle and psychologists since Freud have noted the seriousness of both play and humor (1998, 137). These activities, playful and lively as they are, carry more meaning than satisfying a sweet tooth or hunger.

Another way of looking at the act of eating skulls and death bread is to liken it to the Holy Feast. In this sense, to eat is a powerful act and a powerful verb. It has to do with consuming, assimilating, and becoming God (or as in the Catholic faith, to become nearer to God as in receiving grace). As God saved the world, he fed a people who were in their agony (Garciagoday 1998, 137). This interpretation is one that demonstrates that God cares about all His people, especially those who have little in this life. To "take him in," therefore, is to be redeemed. To eat of the dead, then, is seen as an empowering act. It is to risk, to believe, and to live again in the next life with those who have died before. To have this knowledge is to be able to rise above life's difficult circumstances. It is better than being rich and privileged in this life, because life is so short. To eat of the dead, knowing this, is certainly cause for celebration, a kind of reversal where the poor and disenfranchised become equal to the ruling class—on a level beyond the one experienced in this life.

Just as the bread signifies life in death, so too does the presence of the skeleton. If one dances with the skeleton, makes it and eats of it in this life, the continuity of life after one dies is ensured. There is humor in the celebration and the accompanying equalizing knowledge, which is continuously represented by the lipless grin of the *calavera*. The smirk is a sign of "resistance to the usual order of things" (Garciagodoy 1998, 204).

During the Day of the Dead, instead of the living looking after themselves, they take care of the dead, making sure they are fed, honored, and remembered. But in doing this, the living are also cared for in a way that goes beyond day-to-day mundane concerns. The humble classes have not only gained the power to live forever, but they have spoken, in a bold and visible, but humorous way, to the ruling class. Garciagodoy suggests that if the *calaveras* spoke in words to the dominant culture, they would mock the upper classes by saying:

> You think us quaint? You think us colorful? You think us chronologically anterior and therefore inferior to you? Here is what our stereotypes look like, what they feel like, and they are as dead as the reductionist minds from which they originally came. And as alive. Here they are, stripped down to the bones, having come back to haunt you and bite you back. (1998, 201)

These are skeletons that do not sit still in their coffins. They do not decay. They take up the activities of the living and denounce the power of politics, science, position in society, and any kind of logic the upper classes take as truth. They turn the world upside down, and they laugh out loud while doing so. The dead are not placed on the fringes, the outskirts of town. They are not forgotten, and they are not out of sight. They have managed to tip the world to its side, making that which is often seen as marginal—the dead and the underprivileged—the focus of attention (Garciagodoy 1998, 198).

Images like the *calavera* in Day of the Dead celebrations have the power to tease certain emotional responses from us, such as desire, faith, laughter, hatred, and empathy. These emotions commingle with other firmly established cultural ideas, and they produce meaning (Doss 1999, 29). For Mexicans, the meaning, in large part, comes from being on the lower rung of the economic ladder and being able to transcend it. It is this recognition, deeply imbedded in their sense of identity, that helps to define the aesthetic attraction.

In Chicano culture[6] this aesthetic, associated with an economic and political positioning, takes the form of what is called *rasquachismo*. Recognizing that the codes set by the established community to keep up appropriate appearances can never be met, *rasquachismo* acts to shatter the attitude. If you live in an environment that is always on the verge of coming apart, things must be held together with whatever can be found or tapped into, both physically and emotionally. If the job is tenuous, the car is old and rusted, and the toilet is always breaking, a sense of humor is needed for survival. *Movida* is the word used to represent a coping strategy; it is to buy time, to make options, and to find a way to keep a hopeful outlook. Resilience comes from resourcefulness. As Tomás Ybarra-Frausto explains, this process of making use of available resources that results in *rasquachismo* "engenders hybridization, juxtaposition, and integration" (1991b, 156). It results in an aesthetic that flies in the face of the dominant culture. It is the ability to re-invent in an irreverent kind of way, placing unlikely objects and ideas together. It is a kind of survival, both physical and emotional. Ybarra-Frausto further observes:

> To be *rasquache* is to posit a bawdy, spunky consciousness, to seem to subvert and turn ruling paradigms upside down. It is a witty, irreverent, and impertinent posture that records and moves outside established

boundaries. ... *Rasquachismo* is a sensibility that is not elevated and serious, but playful and elemental. It finds delight and refinement in what many consider banal and projects an alternative aesthetic—a sort of good taste of bad taste. It is witty and ironic, but not mean-spirited (there is sincerity in its artifice). (1991b, 155)

In this tradition, the lower economic class transforms things that are considered to be garbage by the cultural elite. Automobile tires become plant containers and old coffee tins become flowerpots (Ybarra-Frausto 1991b, 157). For Texas Mexicans, this act of recycling is an artistic practice that not only connects makers with their homeland, but also demonstrates their differences with the dominant Anglo culture (Turner 1996, 62). Like the aesthetic of *rasquachismo*, the appeal of the low-rider tradition can also be said to be a reversal. Unlike a luxury car, valued by a wealthy jet set, the low-rider is "low and slow" (Sandoval and Polk 2000, 12).[7]

The same aesthetic sensibility and worldview described as *rasquachismo* is seen in the Mexican *calavera* and Day of the Dead celebrations. That which might been seen as bad taste is somehow played with and reversed into good taste.[8] While in some company it might be rude or inappropriate to flaunt or laugh at death, or to conspire with the dead, an aesthetic reversal, especially in a ritual space,[9] can make the unacceptable acceptable. Additionally, those who might be set aside or forgotten, like the dead, are remade, enjoyed, and visible.

Calaveras are created for reversal; they offer the realization that it is absurd to perceive things as opposites, like life and death (Garciagodoy 1998, 199). *Calaveras* represent the dead in living form. Opposites collapse. The construction of opposites or dualisms is a way of seeing the world that has been constructed by Europeans. To see opposites, we must view things from the outside. In this manner, the viewer, as subject, sees the world as object. This approach further divides the body and the mind, and the conscious from the unconscious (Turner 1982, 100), but the *calavera* mocks that way of seeing and thinking, and reconstructs the world as a continuum. Dualisms (life/death, the haves/the have-nots) disappear, and a more connected, integrated world takes its place.

The same reversal takes place in art. For example, the classical body of the privileged elite is typically fleshed, even in the rare occasions when artists represent the figure in death. The figures are often posed at rest, or enjoying their leisure, whereas the *calavera* is skeletal, active and working, unless it is a member of the upper class who is, nonetheless, still de-fleshed. Seeing the humorous depictions of all *calaveras* in bare-bone form trivializes what they do, whether they engage in work or play (Garciagodoy 1998, 203). The mockery and inversion of the reversal deconstructs the rules of the upper classes as it equalizes relationships. For the underdogs, there is clearly great pleasure in this process.

To an outsider, the Day of the Dead might seem crass, ugly, disrespectful, and perhaps even nonsensical. But to understand the way the ritual functions is to understand how the reversal works in the aesthetic worldview of the participants. Garciagodoy explains:

> The grotesque is transgressive in and of itself, uniting life and death, dis-
> playing the nonbeautiful, nonclassical, unglamorous practices of the sub-
> ordinated in, no less, the form of nonbeautiful, nonclassical, unglamorous,
> living skeletons. In addition, making death the center of attention turns
> the usual order of things upside down and inside out, for the privileged
> classes prefer to pretend that death is too far in the future to be relevant,
> feeling protected by their wealth, their access to medical resources, and
> their generally low-risk lifestyles. (1998, 203)

The aesthetic, then, is based on social defiance and humor. It is glitzy, unsubtle, and raucous fun.

The idea of a "quality" art experience is mocked, as it is recognized to be class-bound. Lippard suggests that the word "quality" is used simply to describe what the ruling class values, as they lay claim to the aesthetic turf in the structured world they have created. However, she further notes, what constitutes "quality" substantially differs among classes, cultures, and even genders (1995, 301).[10] For those who embrace the Day of the Dead celebrations, quality means dramatically changing the rules. It means embracing many artistic characteristics that define the identity of the everyday lives of the lower classes, including welcoming the dead.

The fact that Day of the Dead activities are performed in sacred time allows for the coming together of the living and the dead. As a Yaquis Indian commented, "There are certain days when the wall between worlds becomes so porous that the living and the dead can pass through without being subject to the laws of space or time" (qtd. in Garciagodoy 1998, 40). Just as in abstract form the living and dead become more indistinguishable, so too do the performers and the participants in Day of the Dead celebrations. Everyone shares equally in the ritual group's belief systems and practices. Any customary isolation is removed and camaraderie is reinforced (Turner 1982, 112).

Many Mexican and Mexican-American artists, rooting their work in Day of the Dead and other Mexican rituals, have successfully utilized the aesthetic of reversal. Their work embodies the humor and mocking necessary to promote the Day of the Dead *calaveras*' message about death. José Guadalupe Posada, for example, made prints of *calaveras* that are widely recognized today, and the Linares family continues to make papier-mâché *calaveras* that are appreciated throughout the world. Understanding the artistic process and the life history of these artists is useful in further assessing how humor is used to reverse ruling class belief structures, while making peace with the inevitability of death.

José Guadalupe Posada

Generations of printmakers have been inspired by the Mexican artist José Guadalupe Posada. An extremely prolific artist, he created about 15,000 prints in thirty years (Traba 1994, 15). Born in 1852, Posada lived through and illustrated two violent revolutions. He died (1913) before the end of the second revolution, the mass uprising of 1910–1921 (Brenner 1967, 185).[11] Posada came into the world at a time when the inventive tradition of satirical newspapers was well underway in Mexico. *El Calavera*, founded in 1847, used the skeleton in modern dress as a symbol of the moral, critical voice of the newspaper. Visual content was stressed, yet artists preferred to remain anonymous; the editors and news writers were continuously being arrested for their revolutionary words, and the disrespect they repeatedly showed to the ruling class and the clergy. They made fun of physical defects and private foibles, and satirized those they believed to be engaged in wrongdoing. Names of newspapers changed, and editors, like the artists before them, attempted anonymity in order to remain safe from reprisals.

In 1871 Posada worked as head lithographer for a weekly periodical called *El Jicote* in Aguascalientes, the town where he was born. It folded after eleven issues, and Posada moved, with his employer, to León, where a new press was started. His early work shows his familiarity with earlier caricaturists from Mexico City (Ades 1989, 111–113).

By the early 1890s the number of cheaply illustrated papers increased dramatically, with Posada greatly associated with their popularity (Ades 1989, 114). His work was aimed at various kinds of popular culture forms such as songbooks, children's stories, and parlor games, including playing cards (Carmichael and Sayer 1991, 11, 126).

Posada's images were varied. Most of his work in Mexico City was done for publisher Antonio Vanegas Arroyo, who requested broadsides of sensational news items such as a mining disaster, a collision of a tram and a hearse, and a woman who gave birth to three babies and four iguanas. He created images of Robin Hood-style bandits, and terrifying deaths by firing squads that were repeatedly used by Vanegas Arroyo, with new names of new victims. Broadsides of *calaveras* would be used in various publications and later sold on street corners (Ades 1989, 117).

Don Blas, a middle son of Antonio Vanegas Arroyo, described Posada when he knew him as a likable man, bald with a fringe of white hair, and diligent with his work.

> He was very industrious. He began to work at eight o'clock in the morning and worked until seven at night. My father would enter the shop (we set up a shop for him after he had worked a while with us) with whatever he wanted to print, and say, 'Señor Posada, let's illustrate this', and Posada would read it and while he was reading would pick up his pen and say, 'What do you think about this little paragraph', and he would dip his pen into the special ink he used and then give the plate an acid bath and it was finished. He got three pesos a day whatever he did, and in that time it was a lot because whoever had as much as seventy-five pesos a month was at least a general. Posada was very good-humored and peace loving. He hated quarrels, and treated everyone well. He was no snob. (Qtd. in Brenner 1967, 188–9)

Posada scanned the workings of society in much the same manner that he visually probed skeletal features. Often what he saw was corruption, pain, poverty, and disaster, which he exposed with wit, irony, insight, and courage. Just as the bones of humans provided the structure and framework for their existence, the skeletal figures of the ruling class composed the structure of society, with all its flaws and misgivings. What Posada saw was so damaging, and so cruel, that, reflecting on the traditions of his people, and utilizing the popular culture of his day, he ingeniously mocked it with lipless creatures from the dead.

Posada's interpretation of events greatly pleased the revolutionary public. The rulers were often depicted as puppets; Posada made them bow and smile, appear all too plump, or somehow foolish looking. The revolutionary figures, however, along with the working class, were depicted as heroes, in somber grandeur. Brenner noted how he used this twisting of viewpoint, complete with humor, to help along revolutionary activities:

> By implication not evident in the text he was illustrating; by interpretation grown of conviction; because of his shafted laughter; because of enormous pity and tranquil clairvoyance, Posada is the prophet of the sudden shift in the national scene that comes with the revolution. There is a different reliance on miracles. Hope walks out of its mystic garments and girdles itself with bullets. (1967, 193–4)

With the use of the laughing, mocking skeleton, he made political statements that spoke clearly to the public. He commented on the abrupt transition of power to a new president, and he did a series of *calavera* images that directly related to the Revolution. Another series depicted the human cost of the civil war. In dialogue with photographs of the Revolution, he replaced the fleshy soldier, boy recruit, and firing squad with skeletal figures (Ades 1989, 122). In *Metamorphosis of Madero*, he showed the division between the classes—the poor in wide-brimmed hats and the rich in distinguished top hats (Ades 1987, 123). The Mexican muralists picked up on his class distinctions and his biting political criticism, and continued, to some degree, in the tradition he had made so popular.

Posada's images of the *calaveras* inspired many Latin artists who came after him. For example, Diego Rivera's mural *Dream of a Sunday Afternoon in Alameda Park* depicts Posada's famous skeleton *La Catrina*, the upper-class woman *calavera,* in a wide-brimmed hat, beside him as a child. Many artists continue to use Posada's images, especially *La Catrina*, in their *ofrendas* (See figure 5.1.7). José Clemente Orozco claimed that Posada was like the greatest artists in that he understood the "admirable lesson of simplicity, humbleness, balance, and dignity" (Poniatowska 1991, 57, 62).

Like the muralists, Posada drew on traditions that came before him. The Aztecs had carved partially skeletal figures in earthenware and stone (Garciagodoy 1998, 101), and skeleton figures were prevalent in eighteenth-century funerary catalogues. Before that, they were traditionally used in medieval art. Skeletons had been animated as if they were living long before Posada made it so popular in Mexico (Carmichael and Sayer 1991, 58). But Posada seemed to have the gift to take the skeletal sweets that were prevalent in his youth and build on their characteristics and purpose. His genius was that he was able to make the *calavera* work so effectively as a statement of his people and his time (Garciagodoy 1998, 101–102). Creating scenes from traditional ballads, revolutionary statements, and popular songs, he communicated to everyday people. His *calavera* Day of the Dead riddles, though, gave him his universal standing. One such popular riddle explains the Mexican's approach to death:

> This brilliant general
> Won a thousand battles
> The only one he lost
> Was with death's rattle
> Now you can't tell
> Whether he's a genius or a nut
> Today on a skull
> His general's hat does sit
> And despite his medals
> He's changed quite a bit.
> (Qtd. in Poniatowska 1991, 62)

While Posada is now internationally known, his beginnings were relatively humble. Born to nonliterate parents in central Mexico, even in his adolescence he performed professional work as an engraver and drafts-man. Despite his artistic success, he died in poverty in

Figure 5.1.7 *Ofrenda* for art teacher Jouita Idar by Catalina Delgado-Trunk, 1997. Note paper cut of *calavera* in the large hat, making reference to Posada's important work, *La Catrina*. Photo by Kristin G. Congdon.

1913. His skeletal remains were tossed into a common grave with other penniless individuals (Garciagodoy 1998, 96–98). This ironic, yet perhaps fitting, "ending" to his life is somehow poetic. It seemed to be Posada's choice to remain relatively unknown during his lifetime, by doing work for the mass public rather than the elite few (Brenner 1967, 192).

Arroyo went on publishing Posada's works after his death, yet no one seemed interested in the identity of the artist. In the 1920s, muralist Jean Charot, who had recently come to Mexico from France, rediscovered him, as later did the famous painters Diego Rivera and Clemente Orozco. In 1943 there was an extensive exhibition of Posada's work at the Palacio de Bellas Artes in Mexcio City, and his fame grew from there (Carmichael and Sayer 1991, 126).

In a manner fitting Posada's legacy, the muralists who were inspired by him also sought to democratize art, by making their art public with the intent to speak to the masses, including those who were illiterate. While they drew inspiration from his political zeal, his use of the laughing *calavera*, and his devotion to Mexico's poor, some also worked to overturn the exclusive power of the galleries and museums that controlled "good art" and "good taste." Yet it is one family of artists, the Linares family, who have most clearly followed in the footsteps of José Guadalupe Posada.

The Linares Family

Diego Rivera introduced the Linares family to Posada. When he was studying at the Academy of San Carlos in Mexico City, Rivera said he frequently visited Posada in his studio, which was close by the school. In the 1950s, Rivera commissioned the Linares, also of Mexico City, to make him a papier-mâché Judas,[12] and indirectly, during this transaction, he showed them Posada's art (Masuoka 1994, 86). This influence was to have a long-term effect on the artwork of the Linares family. Many of the figures they now make are three-dimensional interpretations of Posada's drawings (Carmichael and Sayer 1991, 127).

The Linares family has created papier-mâché objects for over a hundred years (Masuoka 1994, 121).[13] They are known as *cartoneros*, makers of *cartonería* objects, traditionally used as props during fiesta celebrations. Constructed from paper, cardboard, and papier-mâché, which is made of a wheat-flour paste and paper, they are formed and painted for specific celebrations.[14] A *cartonero's* work follows the fiesta calendar: Mardi Gras, Holy Week, Independence Day, Day of the Dead, and Christmas. There are also fiestas for local saints which a *cartonero* works on all year long (Masuoka 1994, 1–2).

The most well-known member of the Linares family was Pedro Linares, who lived from 1906 to 1992. As a child he recalled surrounding clay pots with papier-mâché to make *piñatas*. His family made papier-mâché Judases for Easter celebrations (Masuoka 1994, 9). Pedro was seen as the head of the family business. Three sons, Enrique, Felipe, and Miguel, and three grandsons, Leonardo,[15] Ricardo, and David, are considered the key members of the artistic Linares family business. Don Pedro was the family's central figure until his death in 1992 (Masuoka 1994, 17–18). Women in the Linares family also work on the *cartonería*, but their domain is mostly the home, and the papier-mâché work they do is mostly routine work to help out with orders when the men need assistance (Masuoka 1994, 27–33).

Typically, Day of the Dead papier-mâché figures are *calaveras* and skulls, mimicking the sugar skulls with names on them (Pomar 1987, 41). While this celebration and the Linares objects most clearly focus on the dead, all the work of the Linares family is deeply rooted in traditional beliefs about death. Perhaps this is why they were so easily drawn to the work of Posada.[16] It makes sense that Posada's two-dimensional renderings would successfully translate into sculptural form, since they were inspired by Day of the Dead papier-mâché figures and candied skulls

(Masuoka 1994, 90). There are many successful examples of Felipe Linares' interpretation of Posada's works, which he usually quite literally translated. Posada's *La Calavera Don Quijote*, for example, depicts a *calavera* in armor with lance in hand, riding a skeletal horse while skulls fly all about. Although Felipe Linares did not capture the fast movement of Posada's horse, he certainly captured the action of the skeletons flying about, grinning widely as they go. In *"Panteon" de Diablito Rojo*, Posada (and, in turn, Filipe Linares) depicted a devil with wings who throws the police into a burning pot. While the *calaveras* boil *en mass*, other mocking figures both look and flee.

Not only do members of the Linares family reproduce Posada's illustrations in papier-mâché form, but they also make many other *calaveras* engaged in familiar day-to-day activities. Just as Posada did before them, members of the Linares family satirize the flaws of Mexican society. In Day of the Dead celebrations, the Linares' *calaveras* represent living friends and political figures depicted as if they were dead. By creating key figures in Mexican politics, especially those who have violated the trust of the working class, a mythology is created and transmitted to the public. The choice of subjects they make demonstrates concern for their community, and represents their ability to participate in the political dialogue of their times.

The Linares family also depicts natural disasters that have occurred in Mexico City. Their *Earthquake Scene*, for example, represents varied perspectives on the 1986 catastrophe. Large-scale unfleshed skeletons are depicted as trapped under fallen bricks, while another figure attempts a rescue. A coffin is carried, medical staff look on, and soldiers attempt to prevent looting as a *calavera* walks off with a television. One woman carries water in a bucket due to the destroyed plumbing. All *calaveras* carry out their activities with wide grins and a full set of teeth.

Popular culture inspires all members of the Linares family. They create scenes for places like a local discotheque, where a jazz band leans out the windows of a Volkswagen bug while a couple dressed in 1940s clothing dances on a car's top. They watch Mexican films on the studio televisions as they work. The wall where Felipe Linares works is full of images that come from newspapers. There are photos of a mushroom cloud from an atomic bomb, tanks and WWII Japanese airplanes, boxing scenes, cartoon illustrations, and logos from canned foods. He even saves interesting small matchbook covers with different dinosaurs depicted on them (Masuoka 1994, 68–69, 103). The family is clearly engaged with the world around them, and they use their art to make a humorous statement about it. That statement is deeply rooted in politics, popular culture, folklore, and, more specifically, a traditional Mexican approach to death.

Susan Masuoka discussed death with Pedro Linares in 1989 when he was eighty years old. Masuoka was working on the book *En Calavera*, a catalog associated with an exhibition of the Linares' work at the University of California-Los Angeles Fowler Museum of Art. Pedro Linares asked when the exhibition was to take place. Masuoka replied that it was five years away. With surprise that it was planned so far in the future, Linares remarked that he might be dead by then. If he were dead, he questioned, would he still be invited? Masuoka replied that she would send him an invitation, dead or alive. He seemed pleased and replied, "If I am dead I'll go *en calavera*. ... If I die before your opening, they'll make me [in the form of] a papier-mâché skeleton and send me to

Los Angeles like that." Everyone chuckled. He continued, "Whether in life or *en calavera*, I'll be there, I promise you. The important thing, though, is that you really do invite me." Masuoka reports that by that time everyone who heard the conversation was having a hearty laugh (Masuoka 1994, viii).

Conclusion

Humor is central to many of our folk beliefs and the practice of everyday communication systems (DuPré 1998, 47). It allows us to approach topics that might otherwise be uncomfortable. Humor is also a great equalizer. Freud claimed that humor can both distort reality and transcend it (Kuhlman 1984, 3). The Mexican attitude toward death, represented in Day of the Dead celebrations, uses humor to challenge the perceived reality experienced on this earth by the poor, by accepting and recognizing death as an equalizing truth that no one escapes. Death is humorously invited into the home and community with *ofrendas, calaveras*, feasting, and ritual activities at the cemeteries. Without involving humor, death would not be so acceptable. And for the working-class people of Mexico, because death is so pervasive in their everyday lives, avoiding the oppression of expected death would be difficult.

Calaveras are central to making humor work in Day of the Dead ceremonies. Garciagodoy proposed that humorous *calaveras* mask not only the difficulty of facing death, but also subordination and marginalization. Equalizing the status of the oppressed and the oppressors, *calaveras* question stereotypes of the downtrodden while poking fun at the wealthy. Those of the so-called leisure class are told that they are not the only group entitled to have fun. In fact, some *calaveras* flaunt the idea that there is plenty of fun to be had by everyone (1998, 204). They even ask the wealthy to join them in their merriment. But in this invitation is the understanding that if members of the ruling class partake, they will be exposed to mocking *calaveras*. They make visible class hierarchy. It is clearly the poor who do dangerous work, who live in the worst building structures, most susceptible to earthquakes and other disasters. It is the poor who engage in repetitive, unpleasant kinds of work that are dismissed and devalued, and it is the poor who die more readily because of an inability to pay for quality medical attention.

The *calavera*, in a humorous way, gives the wealthy time to think about their role in this subordination. They may purchase the works of Posada, the Linares family, and many other traditional artists. They may admire their poetry and ballads, their music, and their sense of humor. But ultimately, in enjoying the expressions of their humble compatriots, they must also consider the messages and belief systems represented.

The term "art" used to mean "to join or fit together," and the word "culture" comes from growth and cultivation (Lippard 1984, 358). In industrialized societies, these terms are too often associated with the elite. But today, some theorists, such as Thomas McEvilley, affirm that art's primary social function is to "define the communal self, which includes redefining it when the community is changing" (1992, 57). Likewise, William Ferris claimed that "art can make a community more human by bringing groups together" (1980, 19).

While many artists still concentrate on the individual expression, many more, along with critics, museum curators, and theorists, are becoming interested in ways that art connects instead of divides. Susan Friedman referred to the spaces where difference can come together as "borders." She wrote, "our survival as a species depends on our ability to recognize the borders between difference as fertile spaces of desire and fluid states of syncretism, interaction, and mutual interchange" (1998, 66). Perhaps some of those spaces are the borders between life and death, and wealth and poverty. Perhaps the laughing *calavera* can entice us to come together to face ideas and issues that we might more habitually want to avoid. If it is time for a restructuring of our world priorities and our relationships to one another; if it is time to move with less effort into each other's worlds and belief systems; and if we are brave enough to risk it, perhaps the *calavera* might help us along with a toothy grin.

Notes

1 1950 was the year of the original Spanish ed. *El Laberinto de la Soledad* (México D.F.: Cuadernos Americanos).

2 This information comes from a 1989 interview reported in Elizabeth Carmichael and Chloe Sayer's 1991 book, *The Skeleton at the Feast: The Day of the Dead in Mexico.* Sanchez de Escamilla believes her views are in keeping with general middle class belief in Puebla State. Along with her students, she participates annually in the competitive exhibition of creating a Day of the Dead *ofrenda*, or altar-like offering for the deceased.

3 Albert Camus believed that our angst comes from our strong wish to live, which is frustrated by our knowledge that we certainly must die (Garciagodoy 1998:186).

4 *Papeles picado* are cut paper banners, usually made from colorful tissue paper. Tradition says that because they are light, airy, and lacey, spirits can easily fly through them.

5 In the first few pages of her novel, *So Far from God*, Ana Castillo described an event in New Mexico where a wake for a baby was taking place. Everyone was crying, and the mother was asking God why she had to lose her daughter, when someone lets out a shriek. Everyone becomes silent and the priest goes over to the baby's coffin, which has been pushed open, "and the little girl inside sat up, just as sweetly as if she had woken from a nap, rubbing her eyes and yawning." Father Jerome is amazed and says prayers. As the child grows up, she claimed "that all humans bore an odor akin to that which she had smelled in the places she had passed through when she was dead" (1993:22–23).

6 Chicanos are Mexican-Americans, mostly from the west coast. The term is usually associated with individuals who take a political position with their identity.

7 For Mexican-Americans, as well as any other emigrant group, the car is seen as a symbol of the American dream. Dave Hickey called it "an icon of Life, Liberty, and the Pursuit of Happiness" (1997:70).

8 Dave Hickey discusses the reversal that takes place with bad and good taste, pointing out that Liberace cultivated them both. Hickey claimed that "bad taste is real taste, of course, and good taste is the residue of someone else's privilege ..." (1997:54).

9 Victor Turner defined ritual as "prescribed formal behavior for occasions not given over to techno-logical routine, having reference to beliefs in invisible beings or powers regarded as the first and final causes of all effects" (1982:79). David Morgan notes that ritual engages all the senses: smells, tastes, sounds, and sights. These sensations trigger the memories which helps participants face an unpredictable world (1998:54).

10 Barbara Kirshenblatt-Gimblett pointed out that the famous art critic Clement Greenberg even went so far as to argue for wealth as a precondition for being cultured. Kitsch was to be associated with the lower classes and was the opposite of aesthetic quality promoted by the avant-garde (1998:278). Greenberg would certainly have scoffed at the use of artificial flowers on graves and altars, the eating of sugar skulls, and perhaps, even the ephemeral material of the papier-mâché *calaveras*.

11 According to Brenner, writing in the 1960s, revolution meant "loyalty to native values," and confront-ing messy political situations. This meaning of revolution values honesty and a strong respect for work. The native is elevated as is the peasant and the laborer (1967:185–86). These are the kinds of values that Posada embedded in the character of the *calaveras* he illustrated. They are values that are also at the heart of the Day of the Dead celebrations. Politics, good living, and death are all intricately intertwined.

12 As Masuoka notes, the Judas figure is associated with the Holy Week between Palm Sunday and Easter. Traditionally during this time, papier-mâché Judas figures were lit and burned. The Judas figures, of course, are specifically Judas Iscariot, who betrayed Jesus. However, Judas figures can vary in form. Two common images are the devil and the skeleton. Like the *calavera*, the Judas fig-ure can be used to mock public figures. In this manner, Judas is not only Judas Iscariot, but the figure also represents wealthy landowners and unsavory businessmen. Masuoka points out that recent examples have "included Mexico City's former police Chief Arturo 'El Negro' Durazo, who ostentatiously misused public funds, and Fidel Velazquez, Mexico's long time labor leader, who was perceived as having served the interests of the decision-makers of the ruling party over those of his constituency" (1994:3). In 1991, Miguel Linares created a Judas figure of Saddam Hussein that was burned in response to the Iran-Iraq war (1994:4).

13 Although the Linares family is now internationally well known as the most famous papier-mâché artists in Mexico, and support themselves as full-time artists, they are by no means wealthy. Masuoka explains that, in the early 1990s, as an hourly wage, they made less than the minimum wage in the United States. Until 1991 they did not own a car, and when she wrote about them in 1994, they did not have a bank account (22).

14 Pedro Linares makes molds from plaster-of-Paris for some of his pieces. Figures are often constructed piece by piece. Some larger one-of-a kind figures are made with bamboo armatures. Sometimes

objects to be used as molds are purchased from markets. Plastic dolls, for example, help in constructing some of the figures. Brushes are made from cat hairs, which the Linares family claims are better than store-bought brushes (Masuoka 1994:12–15)

15 Leonardo Linares won the National Youth Prize for Folk Art in 1986. He said that it is his responsibility to not only make *cartonería*, but to teach classes throughout Mexico on how to make them. Masuoka reports that he clearly enjoys teaching (1994:24).

16 In 1984 the Museo Nacional de Arte e Industrias Populares in Mexico City held an exhibition of the work of Posada reproduced by Felipe Linares and his sons in papier-mâché form. In 1985 New York City's Museum of Contemporary Hispanic Art hosted a similar exhibition (Masuoka 1994:79).

References

Ades, Dawn. 1989. *Art in Latin America: The Modern Era, 1820–1980.* New Haven, CT: Yale University Press.

Beardsley, John. 1987. And/Or: Hispanic Art, American Culture. In *Hispanic Art in the United States*, ed. John Beardsley and Jane Livingston. New York: Abbeville Press.

Beezley, William.1997. Home Altars: Private Reflections of Public Life. In *Home Altars of Mexico,* ed. Ramón Gutiérrez. Albuquerque: University of New Mexico Press.

Brandes, Stanley. 1998a. The Day of the Dead, Halloween, and the Quest for Mexican National Identity. *Journal of American Folklore* 111: 359–380.

Brenner, Anita. 1967. *Idols Behind Altars.* New York: Biblo and Tannen.

Carmichael, Elizabeth, and Chloe Sayer. 1991. *The Skeleton at the Feast: The Day of the Dead in Mexico.* Austin: University of Texas Press.

Congdon, Kristin G., Catalina Delgado-Trunk and Marva Lopez. 1999. Teaching About the Ofrenda and Experiences on the Border. *Studies in Art Education* 40 (4): 312–329.

Doss, Erika. 1999. *Elvis Culture: Fans, Faith, & Image.* Lawrence: University Press of Kansas.

DuPré, Athena. 1998. *Humor and the Healing Arts: A Multimethod Analysis of Humor Use in Health Care.* Mahwah, NJ: Lawrence Erlbaum Associates.

Ferris, William R. 1980. Local Color: Memory and Sense of Place in Folk Art. In *Made by Hand: Mississippi Folk Art*, ed. Patti Carr Black. Jackson: Mississippi Department of Archives and History.

Friedman, Susan Stanford. 1998. *Mappings: Feminism and the Cultural Geographies of Encounter.* Princeton: Princeton University Press.

Garciagodoy, Juanita. 1998. *Digging the Days of the Dead: A Reading of Mexico's Día de Muertos.* Niwot: University of Colorado Press.

Gutiérrez, Ramón A. 1997. Conjuring the Holy: Mexican Domestic Altars. In *Home Altars in Mexico,* ed., Ramón Gutiérrez. Albuquerque: University of New Mexico Press.

Kuhlman, Thomas L. 1984. *Humor and Psychotherapy.* Homewood, IL: Dow Jones-Irwin Dorsey.

Lippard, Lucy. 1984. Trojan Horses: Activist Art and Power. In *Art After Modernism: ReThinking Representation*, ed. Brian Wallis and Marcia Tucker. New York: The New Museum of Contemporary Art.

Lippard, Lucy. 1990. *Mixed Blessings: New Art in a Multicultural America.* New York: Pantheon.

Lippard, Lucy. 1995. *The Pink Glass Swan: Selected Essays on Feminist Art*. New York: The New Press.

Masuoka, Susan N. 1994. *En Calavera: The Papier-mâché Art of the Linares Family*. Los Angeles: UCLA Fowler Museum.

McEvilley, Thomas. 1992. *Art and Otherness: Crisis in Cultural Identity*. Kingston, NY: McPherson and Company.

Mesa-Bains, Amalia. 1997. Afterword. In *Home Altars of Mexico*. ed., Ramón Gutiérrez. Albuquerque: University of New Mexico Press.

Paz, Octavio. 1961. *The Labyrinth of Solitude: Life and Thought in Mexico*. New York: Grove Press.

Pomar, María Teresa. ed. 1987. *The Life of the Dead in Mexican Folk Art*. Forth Worth: The Fort Worth Art Museum.

Poniatowska, Elena. 1991. The Great Cemetery of Dolores. In *Dia De Los Muertos*, ed., René H. Arceo Frutos. Chicago: Mexican Fine Arts Center Museum.

Sandoval, Denise and Patrick A. 2000. *Ital Arte y Estilo: The Lowriding Tradition*. Los Angeles: Petersen Automotive Museum.

Scalora, Salvatore. 1997. Flowers and Sugar Skulls for the Spirits of the Dead. In *Home Altars of Mexico*, ed. Ramón Gutiérrez. Albuquerque: University of New Mexico Press.

Traba, Marta. 1994. *Art of Latin America, 1900–1980*. Baltimore: Johns Hopkins University Press.

Turner, Kay. 1996. Hacer Cosas: Recycled Arts and the Making of Identity in Texas-Mexican Culture. In *Recycled Re-seen: Folk Art from the Global Scrap Heap*, ed. Charlene Cerny and Suzanne Seriff. New York: Harry N. Abrams.

Turner, Victor. 1982. *From Ritual to Theatre: The Human Seriousness of Play*. New York: Performing Arts Journal Publications.

Ybarra-Frausto, Tomás. 1991a. Mexican/Chicano Customs for The Day of the Dead. In *Dia de Los Muertos*. Chicago: Mexican Fine Arts Center Museum.

Ybarra-Frausto, Tomás. 1991b. Rasquachismo: A Chicano Sensibility. In *Chicano Art: Resistance and Affirmation, 1965–1985*, ed. Richard Griswold del Castillo, Teresa McKenna and Yvonne Yarbro-Bejarano. Los Angeles: UCLA Wight Art Gallery.

Machismo

Matthew C. Gutmann

> Haven't you also lost something for following your father?
> *Rodolfo Usigli,* El Gesticulador

Machos and Hombres

A re any of you married?" I asked the *mucbachos.*

"No, *todos solteritos* [all young and single]," said Felipe.

"That bozo's got two little squirts. He's the *macho mexicano*" said Rodrigo, pointing to Celso, the father of two children who lived with their mother in another city.

"What does that mean?" I inquired.

"Macho? That you've got kids all over," said Esteban.

"That your ideology is very closed," said Pancho. "The ideology of the *macho mexicano* is very closed. He doesn't think about what might happen later, but mainly focuses on the present, on satisfaction, on pleasure, on desire. But now that's disappearing a little."

"You're not machos?" I asked.

"No, *somos hombres* [we're men]." [1]

It is common to hear women and men in Colonia Santo Domingo say that although there used to be a lot of macho men, they are not as prevalent today. Some people who make this comment are too young to know anything firsthand about bygone machos, but regardless, they are sure there was more machismo before. Some older men like to divide the world of males into machos and *mandilones* (meaning female-dominated men), where the term *macho* connotes a man who is responsible for providing financially and otherwise for his family.[2] For older men, to be macho more often means to be *un hombre de honor* (an honorable man).[3]

It is far more common for younger married men in Colonia Santo Domingo to define themselves as belonging to a third category, the "nonmacho" group. "*Ni macho, ni mandilón* [Neither macho nor *mandilón*]" is how many men describe themselves. Others may define a friend or relative as "your typical *macho mexicano,*" but the same man will not infrequently reject the label, describing all the things he does to help his wife around the home, pointing out that he does not beat his wife (wife beating being one of the few generally agreed-upon attributes of machos). What is most significant is not simply how the terms *macho, machismo,* and *machista* are variously defined—there is little consensus on their meanings—but that today the terms are widely regarded by working class men in Colonia Santo Domingo, Mexico City, as pejorative and not worthy of emulation. For these younger men, then, the present period is distinguished by its liminal character with respect to male gender identities: as neither-macho-nor-*mandilón*, these men are precisely betwixt and between assigned cultural positions.

[...] Three general points bear mentioning from the outset. First, *macho* (in its modern sense) and *machismo* (in any sense) have remarkably short word histories. Indeed, tracing the historical permutations and modulations of these words is critical to understanding the ongoing discrepancies that exist popularly and in the social sciences regarding their meanings. Carlos Monsiváis (1981, 1992) in particular has linked the emergence of the ethos of machismo especially to the golden age of Mexican cinema in the 1940s and 1950s.

Second, machismo as discussed here is not reducible to a coherent set of sexist ideas. It is not simply male chauvinism. As Roger Lancaster (1992:19) stresses in his study of Nicaragua, "machismo is resilient because it constitutes not simply a form of 'consciousness,' not 'ideology' in the classical understanding of the concept, but a field of productive relations."[4] Determining the systemic character of machismo is predicated on following the historical tracks of the term. Because these lead in various directions in different times and circumstances in Mexico and Nicaragua, for instance, the structural and material content of machismo must be kept in mind.

Finally, I would like to touch on another central, recurring theme in many if not most meanings of machismo: the physical body. This theme manifests itself in beatings, sexual episodes, alcohol consumption, daredevil antics, and the not-so-simple problem of defining the categories of "men" and "women." Regardless of how confusing gender identities may seem, they usually share relations of mutual dependence with these somatic realms.[5]

Cowboys and Racism

In Mexican newspapers, academic literature, and dictionary entries, the terms *macho* and *machismo* have been used in contradictory ways. The definitions employed or implied in such official circles reveal not only a diversity of views regarding the substance of the terms, but also widely disparate conjectures as to the origins of the words and their meanings. Emphasizing sexuality,

Stevens (1973:90) calls machismo "the cult of virility," adding that "[t]he chief characteristics of this cult are exaggerated aggressiveness and intransigence in male-to-male interpersonal relationships and arrogance and sexual aggression in male-to-female relationships." Greenberg (1989:227) captures some of the ambivalence of machismo when he describes an episode in which Fortino, the protagonist of his study, "was being very macho, in a nonconfrontational, almost womanly manner." *Macho* thus may be identified with nonaggressive ("womanly") behavior.[6]

Many anthropologists and psychologists writing about machismo utilize characterizations like "manly," "unmanly," and "manliness" without defining them. They seem to assume, incorrectly in my estimation, that all their readers share a common definition and understanding of such qualities. Dictionaries are in conflict over the etymological roots of *macho,* sometimes tracing them to Latin and Portuguese words for "masculine" and "mule," and at other times tracing the cultural ancestry of *macho* to Andalusian soldiers of the Conquest, or to certain indigenous peoples of the Americas, or to Yankee gringo invaders in the early part of this century.[7]

In his essay "El machismo en México," one of the first scholarly discussions on the subject, Mendoza (1962) illustrates his analysis of Mexico's "national idiosyncrasy" with the words from several dozen folk songs, *corridos,* and *cantares* sung in the late 1800s and early 1900s. Especially noteworthy in this essay is Mendoza's distinction between what he calls the two classes of machismo: the first, authentic one is characterized by courage, generosity, and stoicism; the second, which is basically false, consists of appearances—cowardice hiding behind empty boasts. Mendoza is calling attention to an essential dualism in the history of the use of the word *machismo,* similar in some respects to what friends in Colonia Santo Domingo describe as the real machos of the old days and the buffoonish machos of today.

Yet in the songs and ballads cited by Mendoza the words *macho* and *machismo* do not appear. He uses the term *machismo* to represent Mexican male rebels and cowards in the Porfiriato (1877–1911) and the ensuing revolution of the 1910s, labeling a whole genre of folklore as exemplary of machismo, but he does not explain the curious absence of the phrase in the literature of the time.

In a brilliant essay written a few years later, Américo Paredes (1967) provides several clues as to the word history of *machismo* and in the process draws clear connections between the advent of machismo and that of nationalism, racism, and international relations. Building on an earlier (1966) paper, Paredes finds that prior to the 1930s and 1940s in Mexican folklore—a good indication of popular speech at the time—the terms *macho* and *machismo* did not appear. The word *macho* existed, but almost as an obscenity, similar to later connotations of *machismo* (which Santamaría [1959:677], for instance, defines as a "crude vulgarity for manliness and virility"). Other expressions, some also semantically related to men, were far more common at the time of the Mexican Revolution: *hombrismo, hombría, muy hombre,* and *hombre de verdad* (all relating to *hombre* [man]); *valentía* and *muy valiente* (relating to valor or courage); and so forth.[8] Despite the fact that during the Mexican Revolution the phrase *muy hombre* was used to describe courageous women as well as men, the special association of such a quality with men then and now indicates certain associations of words and phrases with maleness, regardless of whether the words *macho* and *machismo* were employed.

Making a connection between courage and men during times of war in Mexico—in which men have usually been the main, though assuredly not the only, combatants—is nevertheless not the same thing as noting the full-blown "machismo syndrome," as it is sometimes called. To oversimplify, if courage was valued during the Mexican Revolution, it was valued in both men and women, though the terms used to refer to courage carried a heavy male accent. Beginning

¿La mexicana abnegada? (The submissive Mexican woman?) Many bank guards in downtown Mexico City are women.

especially in the 1940s, the male accent itself came to prominence as a national(ist) symbol. For better or worse, Mexico came to mean machismo and machismo to mean Mexico.

Searching for a single national identity is a very modern project in Mexico as elsewhere. Often remembered for his blunt diagnosis of the country's "inferiority complex," Samuel Ramos (1934) is also frequently cited as the original critic of Mexican machismo. Once again, however, Ramos never used the term *macho* or *machismo*. Yet in Ramos the connections between *lo mexicano* and manliness (however defined) were striking. He centered his account of the nation's inferiority around the "well-known Mexican type, the *pelado*," whose conduct was one of "virile protest" (Ramos 1962:9). The *pelado* is a male proletarian, vulgar and poorly educated, Ramos reported, who himself associates "his concept of virility with that of nationality, creating thereby the illusion that personal valor is the Mexican's particular characteristic" (p. 63). The particular association by Ramos of negative male qualities with the urban working class has been a prominent theme in writings on Latin American masculinity and machismo ever since—what Mary Louise Pratt (1990:50) shows to be the "androcentrism of the modern national imaginings" in Latin America.[9] In contrast to Ramos, scholars like Paredes have linked machismo especially to Mexico's middle classes, and Limón (1989, 1994) effectively critiques the class prejudices of Ramos regarding macho *pelados*.[10]

One reason Ramos judged "the Mexican of the city" so harshly was his observation that "the *campesino* in Mexico is almost always of the indigenous race ... [and] his role is a passive one in the present life of his country" (p. 63) whereas the "active group" of Mexicans were the mestizos and whites who lived in the city—a view that is implicitly and partially shared by some of my friends in Colonia Santo Domingo today. In fact, in the eyes of many working class people in Mexico in the 1990s, the (white) Mexican elites are no longer to be trusted, because they have sold out the country for their own personal financial gain. So it is ironically left to the mestizo majority in the cities to maintain the banner of Mexican national identity, including in its (male) gendered aspects. Thus *mestizaje* comes to be equated in the minds of Ramos and some of his working class subjects with masculinity, and the two are in turn made complicit in the constitution of Mexicanness itself.

In Mexico, the consolidation of nation-state and party machinery throughout the Republic and the development of the country's modern national cultural identity took place on a grand scale during the presidencies of Lázaro Cárdenas and Manuel Avila Camacho (1934–40 and 1940–46, respectively). After the turbulent years of the revolution and the 1920s, and following six years of national unification under the populist presidency of Cárdenas, the national election campaign of 1940 opened an era of unparalleled industrial growth and demagogic rule in Mexico. Coincidentally, one of the campaign slogans of the ultimately successful presidential candidate, Avila Camacho, was: "Ca ... MACHO!" Paredes (1971:23) points out that although the president was not responsible for the use of the term *macho,* "we must remember that names lend reality to things."

As Paredes also perceptively points out, in a sense the Mexican macho is simply a joke that outsiders (foreigners) do not get. Indeed in Mexican movies, as Monsiváis (1981:107) quips, the *macho mexicano* is the Gran Macho Operático.[11] To the extent that the *macho mexicano* is a joke, both authors seem to imply, in like fashion those who grasp the humor will have their consciousness and agency restored to them, at least in part and in comparison to those who do not get the joke. Besides, although machismo in Mexico may take on quite exaggerated forms, it is hardly a phenomenon unique to that land.[12]

The word history of *machismo* is but a piece of the larger puzzle regarding the outlooks and practices codified in tautological fashion as instances of machismo. For Paredes, the peculiar history of U.S.-Mexican relations has produced a marked antipathy on the part of Mexicans toward their northern neighbors. The image of the frontier and the (Wild) West has played a special role in this tempestuous relationship, with the annexation of two-fifths of the Mexican nation to the United States in 1848 and repeated U.S. economic and military incursions into Mexico since then, putting the lie to proclamations of respect for national sovereignty. Trade between the two countries early on included the export of the Mexican *vaquero*-cowboy to the United States, Paredes reminds us. In the early nineteenth century, the frontiersmen of Texas and areas farther west were running point for the expanding Jacksonian empire, and their combination of individualism and sacrifice for the higher national good came to embody the ethos of machismo. Together with the pistol, the supreme macho symbol, such an ethos came to play a similar role in the consolidation of the Mexican nation. But today, after the fighting both in the United States and Mexico have long since ended, "*machismo* betrays a certain element of nostalgia; it is cultivated by those who feel they have been born too late" (Paredes 1971:37).

On the other side of the border, in the United States, the term *machismo* has a rather explicitly racist history; from the first appearance of the term in print in English that I can find (Griffith 1948:50–51), machismo has been associated with negative character traits not among men in general, but specifically among Mexican, Mexican American, and Latin American men.[13] Contemporary popular usage of the term *machismo* in the United States often serves to rank men according to their presumably inherent national and racial characters. Such analysis utilizes nonsexist pretensions to make denigrating generalizations about fictitious Mexican male culture traits.

Jorge Negrete and *LO Mexicano*

"You're macho, as we say. When I've needed you, you've helped me whole-
heartedly, and I'll do the same for you."
Pedro, resident of Jucbatengo, Oaxaca, quoted in Blood Ties, *by James Greenberg*

The consolidation of the Mexican nation, ideologically and materially, was fostered early on not only in the gun battles on the wild frontier, not only in the voting rituals of presidential politics, but also in the imagining and inventing of *lo mexicano* and *mexicanidad* in the national cinema. (Later both radio and television played starring roles in giving people throughout the Republic a sense of themselves as sharing a common history and destiny—in short, a national identity.) Although there were female leads in the movies of the period, on the silver screen it was the manly actors who most came to embody the restless and explosive potential of the emerging Mexican nation. And of all the movie stars of this era, one stood out as "a macho among machos." Ever the handsome and pistol-packing *charro* (singing cowboy), with his melodious and eminently male tenor, Jorge Negrete came to epitomize the swaggering Mexican nation, singing,

> I am a Mexican, and this wild land is mine.
> On the word of a macho, there's no land lovelier and wilder of its kind.
> I am a Mexican, and of this I am proud.
> I was born scorning life and death,
> And though I have bragged, I have never been cowed.[14]

In the rural cantinas, the manly temples of the golden age of Mexican cinema, the macho mood was forged. Mexico appeared on screen as a single entity, however internally incongruent, while within the nation the figures of Mexican Man and Mexican Woman loomed large—the former

> untamed, generous, cruel, womanizing, romantic, obscene, at one with fam-
> ily and friends, subjugated and restless ... [the latter] obedient, seductive,
> resigned, obliging, devoted to her own and slave to her husband, to her
> lover, to her children, and to her essential failure. (Monsivais 1992:18)

Other Mexican national archetypes followed Negrete, the actor Cantinflas playing a *pelado* more lighthearted than the one found in Ramos, and Tin Tan, another famous actor, cast as the U.S.-experienced *pachuco*.[15] The movies of the era carried titles like *¡Vámonos con Pancho Villa!* (Let's go with Pancho Villa!), *Allá en el Rancho Grande* (Out in the Rancho Grande), *Soy puro mexicano* (I'm all-Mexican), *Flor Silvestre* (Wildflower), *Salón México,* and *Nosotros los pobres* (We the poor).

The distinctions between being a macho and being a man were starting to come into clearer focus in the Mexican cinema of the 1940s:

> To be macho is now part of the scenery. To be macho is an attitude. There
> are gestures, movements. It is the belief that genital potency holds the key
> to the universe, all that. It goes from the notion of danger to the notion of
> bragging; that's the difference between macho and man *[hombre]*. As the
> song says, "If you've got to kill me tomorrow, why don't you get it over with
> now?"—that is being very manly *[ser muy hombre]*. "I have four wives"—that
> is being very macho *[ser muy macho]*." (Carlos Monsiváis, interview by author,
> 20 February 1993)

Then, at the end of the 1940s, Mexican machismo underwent a most refined dissection by Octavio Paz in *El laberinto de la soledad* (1950). Despite Paz's wish to speak only to a small group "made up of those who are conscious of themselves, for one reason or another, as Mexicans" (Paz 1961:11), this work more than any other has come to represent the authoritative view of essential Mexican attributes like machismo, loneliness, and mother worship. Therefore when Paz writes, "The Mexican is always remote, from the world and from other people. And also from himself" (p. 29), he should not be taken literally but literarily. It is a beautifully written book, and part of the reason for its elegance may be that Paz was creating qualities of *mexicanidad* as much as he was reflecting on them. As he put it in his "Return to the Labyrinth of Solitude," "The book is part of the attempt of literally marginal countries to regain consciousness: to become subjects again" (Paz 1985:330).

The "tough hombre" image is emblematic of many popular portrayals of the *macho mexicano* and of social science stereotypes of Mexican masculinity in general. This man ran a charcoal stall in the Mexico City Centro when I took his photo in 1991.

Paz (1961:35) writes with regard to men and women in Mexico, "In a world made in man's image, woman is only a reflection of masculine will and desire." In Mexico, "woman is always vulnerable. Her social situation—as the repository of honor, in the Spanish sense—and the misfortune of her 'open' anatomy expose her to all kinds of dangers" (p. 38). Biology as destiny? But there is nothing inherently passive, or private, about vaginas in Mexico or anywhere else. Continuing with Paz, just as "the essential attribute of the *macho*"—or what the macho seeks to display, anyway—is power, so too with "the Mexican people." Thus *mexicanidad*, Paz tell us, is concentrated in the macho forms of "caciques, feudal lords, hacienda owners, politicians, generals, captains of industry" (p. 82).[16]

Many Mexican men are curious about what it means to be a Mexican, and what it means to be a man. One is not born knowing these things; nor are they truly discovered. They are learned and relearned. For some, this involves a quest for one's patrimony. "Pedro Páramo is my father too," declares one of Mexico's bastard sons

(Rulfo 1955 [1959]:3). Even if he is an infamous brute, a father is a father. For the Mexican macho and for the nation, it is better to have a father than to be fatherless.

In Paz and in much of the literature of cultural nationalism in Mexico in recent decades,

> [t]he problem of national identity was thus presented primarily as a problem of *male* identity, and it was male authors who debated its defects and psychoanalyzed the nation. In national allegories, women became the territory over which the quest for (male) national identity passed, or, at best, as in Juan Rulfo's *Pedro Páramo* (1955), the space of loss and of all that lies outside the male games of rivalry and revenge. (Franco 1989:131)[17]

In Santo Domingo, another authoritative source of information about machismo and national identity in addition to Paz, one that people use in the stories they tell about themselves, is Oscar Lewis. Or at least people use what they have heard about his anthropological writings; Lewis is "remembered" far more than he is read.

In the social sciences Lewis continues to be the most cited reference with regard to conclusions about modern Mexican masculinity. The affinity of anthropologists and other social scientists to stereotypes of Mexican machismo exemplifies Giddens's (1990:16) point that "the practical impact of social science and sociological theories is enormous, and sociological concepts and findings are constitutively involved in what modernity *is*."

In fact, three particular sentences from Lewis's *The Children of Sánchez* are employed with astonishing frequency in anthropological texts to represent all Mexican males past, present, and future:

> In a fight, I would never give up or say, "Enough," even though the other was killing me. I would try to go to my death, smiling. That is what we mean by being "*macho*," by being manly. (Lewis 1961:38)

This specific passage is cited, for example, by Marshall (1979:89) in his discussion of machismo in Micronesia, by Madsen and Madsen (1969:712) in a paper on alcohol consumption in Mexico, and by Gilmore (1990:16) in his comparative survey of images of masculinity. A few sentences on page thirty-eight of *The Children of Sánchez* have thus come to shoulder a immense responsibility in anthropology: to provide a quotable sound bite defining Mexican masculinity/machismo.

Is this quotation really such a good and accurate description of Mexican male identity? If it were, then every male soul who finds himself south of the shallows of the Rio Grande and north of the highlands of Guatemala would have to, as if by ethnographic decree, at least try to go to his death smiling if he wished to retain his Mexican male credentials. I doubt very much if Lewis's intention was to summarize the life experiences and desires of all Mexican men in this short passage. Perhaps most revealing of all, the sentences in question are not even Lewis's own, but are actually part of a monologue by Manuel Sánchez, one of the Sánchez children. Manuel is nonetheless the man whose ideologically charged comments to Lewis on one particular day in the mid-1950s have frequently come to speak for all Mexican men since that time.[18]

Mandilones and Dominating Women

In Santo Domingo there are significant differences in the uses and meanings of the terms *macho* and *machismo*. These reflect, and often concentrate, contrasting urban and rural experiences, generational differences, class stratification, stages within individuals' lives, and, in the age of television satellites, the impact on people throughout Mexico of what others around the world say about them and their national peculiarities.

Returning to the term *mandilón*, which carries a meaning that is stronger than the English "henpecked" but not nearly as vulgar as "pussy-whipped," we see by its common daily use that it is an expression produced by a *machista* system, and that it is at the same time a response to machismo.[19] As Angela, Michelle, and I were walking through the *sobre ruedas* (open-air market) one day in October, shortly after we first met, Angela remarked that perhaps Michelle should buy a *mandil* (apron) "in Mateo's size" so that I could be a proper *mandilón*. Angela added that her son Noé, whom I had not yet met, was a *mandilón*. I asked her why, and she responded by saying that Noé washed dishes, cooked, and took care of his daughter. I wanted to know how Noé had come to do these things. "No *lo creía para ser macho mexicano* [I didn't raise him to be a *macho mexicano*]" came the answer. I wondered aloud if Noé would accept this appellation. Angela insisted that he would.

In early November, after I met him, I asked Noé about his being a *mandilón*. "No soy mandilón [I'm not a *mandilón*]" corrected Noé. "It doesn't bother me at all to help my wife. I share everything with her." But Noé rejected the title of *mandilón*, which he defined as, "he who is dominated by women."

Noé's younger sister Norma came by our apartment in January because her husband, Miguel, had not come home and I was the last person to have seen him. After a *futbol* playoff Miguel and I had gone over to the coach's house for tacos, beans, and beer. I had left hours earlier, but by 8 P.M. Mie still had not returned, and Norma was worried. Yet she could not go looking for him herself, she said, because that might make him look like a *mandilón* in the eyes of the other young men: a wife coming to fetch her (presumably) drunk husband.

Not labeling a man a *mandilón* is not merely a matter of helping him save face, however, because for many women as well as men it carries negative connotations. That is, being a *mandilón* is seen as a positive opposite of macho to some like Angela, but to others it is but an inverse form of the macho's empty boasting. In both cases described, the definitions of *mandilón* reflect an awareness of power differences between men and women, and a contradictory consciousness with respect to male identities.

"I don't want a man who's either macho or *mandilón*" one young woman told me.

"Why not *mandilón*?" I asked.

"Because who wants someone who can't stick up for himself, who's used to getting bossed around and likes it that way?" In other words, life is hard enough as it is, and a young woman can ill afford to depend on a *mandilón* as a husband. Instead, one needs a partner who can make things happen and not just wait for orders from others, his wife included.[20]

Among men in their twenties and thirties, it was rare to hear anyone claim the title of macho for himself. "Why, I wash dishes and cook," some would protest when called macho by a friend. Machos do neither of these things, nor do they spend a lot of time with their children, many felt. However, the most common comment used to fend off being categorized as macho was "I don't beat my wife." A grandfather of sixty-seven explained to me that he was no macho, and that his own father before him had not been one, either. "Why, he never drank a beer in front of the kids," my friend told me, "and he never beat his wife."

Angela calls her brother Hector one of the last of the dying breed of Mexican machos. But Héctor likes to joke that he is not a macho "*porque me ensillan* [because they (women) ride me]." For him, the Mexican playboy image from the cowboy movies of the 1940s typifies the golden age of machos with their "*charros, bravacones, ebrios, peleoneros, iresponsables, enamorados a las mujeres [charros,* braggarts, drunkards, fighters, irresponsibles, woman-lovers]." Angel García, who is active in the Christian Base Community in Colonia Ajusco, told me that for him machismo conjures up movie images of cowboys riding through the countryside, their *pistolas* firing away.

For some men today, "the macho" is also a playful role they can perform on demand. I stifled my displeasure one evening when, at her two-year-old granddaughter's birthday party, and in her capacity as patron saint of my research project, Angela took me by the hand and introduced me to several men who she said were "genuine representatives of Mexican machismo." After I had been so presented to one young man, Angela demanded of him, "Where's your wife?" A sly smile crossed the man's face. "I sent her to the bathroom," he answered. His wife was seven months pregnant, the man added, so he, like the good macho Angela accused him of being, had to send her to the bathroom a lot. Often, as in this case, such jokes were followed by remarks that revealed an acute sensitivity to the cultural beliefs about Mexican men that many people in Mexico think are held by North Americans. "That's really what you gringos believe about us, isn't it?" people would sometimes say to me when I raised the image of Mexican men preferring to go to their death smiling rather than lose face.

Another illustration of the influence of the United States on macho self-perceptions among Mexicans was my invitation to participate, on 5 July 1993, in the Mexico City–based nationally televised talk show *María Victoria Llamas.* Along with several Mexican men, I was invited to speak on the theme "A lo macho." It was hoped that my particular presence could be used to make two points: (1) that machismo was not just a problem in Mexico, and (2) that, based on my research, it was clear that not all men in Mexico were machos. I was informed that this would sound especially convincing coming from a North American anthropologist.[21]

People in Santo Domingo and throughout Mexico City are acutely aware of gringo images of Mexico and Mexicans, including those pertaining to Mexican masculinity. Many believe that North Americans feel their men are superior to Mexican men, as men, a perception gleaned from television, cinema, and the experience of migration to the United States. What many in Mexico may fail to recognize in ideological stances expressed in statements such as "My boyfriend may not be perfect, but at least he's no Mexican macho" is the mixture of anti-Mexican racism and sexist justifications for gender relations in the United States. In this way the perpetuation in the United States of stereotypes regarding Mexican machos and self-sacrificing women helps to obscure and preserve gender inequalities in the United States.[22]

Performing as Men

In the dramas that people in *colonias populares* offer about their own and others' marriages, the parts played by self-designated machos are not all playful by any means. But if not quite so common as the women who endure spousal abuse for decades, there are growing numbers of spirited and independent women who for one reason or another issue ultimatums to their husbands. If and when these are not met, such women file for and receive divorces from their *machos mexicanos*.

"We cheat on our wives because we're men," said one participant in a CAVI men's group that met to discuss domestic violence. Then he added, "and because we want to be macho." What does "we want to be macho" mean except that "to be macho" is an ideological stand that can be sanctified only by others—men and women—and by oneself? In my discussion with the *muchachos*, one of them said that they were not machos but rather they were *hombres* (men). Celso, however, insisted that, as men, by definition they were machos. He said that if they were going to call themselves something, *mandilón* and *marica* (queer) were obviously inappropriate. So what else did this leave except macho?

The description provided by Celso makes it appear that the youths rummage around in an identity grab bag, pulling out whatever they happen to seize upon as long as it is culturally distinct. One minute these *muchachos* identify themselves as machos who enjoy bragging about controlling women and morally and physically weaker men, clearly in tune with broader social mores. The next minute the same young men express bitterness at being the ones on the bottom. Often the two aspects of personal identities come into conflict—as, for example, when the *muchachos* enthusiastically sing along with the popular rock band Maldita Vecindad about their class hatreds:

> There in the street, shining like the sun
> It's his new car cruising, second to none
> Flying down the street, almost taking off
> Everyone watches it passing
> Windshield washer boy crosses not looking
> This is the car he's not missing
> Hear a shout and then a thud
> In this city there's too much blood.[23]

The *muchachos* do not identify with the driver in this song, and they see no contradiction in their simultaneous identification as domineering machos and as the dominated poor pitted in lifelong struggle against the rich, the ones who drive new cars.

The discussion one evening in the CAVI group also clarified an important point regarding some men's self-identification as machos. In the session on *celos* (jealousy), several men stated that they were no longer as jealous as they had once been. They spoke not only of the influence of recent sociocultural factors affecting women that had forced the men to reevaluate their own ethical standards—women working outside the home, the feminist movement, and educational levels achieved by women—but also of patterns more associated with stages in the life course. One man after another spoke of periods in his life when particular manifestations of male jealousy—and other features associated with machismo—were more pronounced and prevalent than at other times. In the cases of jealousy and violent outbursts against wives for assumed infidelity, for example, most men said that such behavior was more characteristic of the early years of their marriages.

Redefinitions

> [L]anguage is is at the same time a living thing and a museum of fossils of
> life and civilisations.
>
> *Antonio Gramsci*, Selections from the Prison Notebooks

Machismo, then, in the minds of many younger men and women, represents a kind of option. Whether the macho is seen as good or bad, a serious threat or merely a risible fool, men have the option of letting their heads be controlled by their bodies. And quite often today in Colonia Santo Domingo, the image of the macho is linked to the male body. Women never have the option of being truly macho in the sense that men do. Above all this is because a key component of a macho's machismo is his relationship to female bodies. In Santo Domingo there are many different notions of macho, but the one element that is most commonly a part of these definitions is that of wife beating. Together with men's sexual conquest of women, abusive male physicality is for many women and men the essence of machismo.

Whether Mexican society can be characterized as macho in some overriding sense is a matter of some importance, but once again it all depends on definitions and contexts. In financial and government circles, in the arts, the universities, and the media, men predominate and dominate. In terms of who rules Mexican society and its central institutions, the issue is so straightforward that male domination there is a classic example of hegemonic, taken-for-granted control. Yet to take a more marginal example, one that reveals the interests and desires of large masses of people in Mexico City, on selected metro lines during rush hours in Mexico City, several cars are specially designated for women and children. Women can ride on the men's cars, but no men are allowed on the women's. Signs announce the segregation, and guards armed with billy clubs enforce it.

Is this separation of women from men an acknowledgment of abusive male physicality? It is. Is this an example of machismo, or an attempt—at a semiofficial level, no less—to prevent such male molestations to the extent possible? The motives are no doubt entirely mixed at the level of city government and the metro system; "protecting women," as we have seen, is part and parcel of some systems of machismo. Yet overall in this case it is more a matter of recognizing a problem and seeking a (short-term) solution to it. At rush hour women overwhelmingly avail themselves of the no-men-allowed subway cars, a means of transit that does not even exist in other societies where women are routinely fondled and harassed by men on public transport. In this way gender identities are both recognized and to a certain extent created in Mexico City.[24]

Delineating cultural identities and defining cultural categories, one's own and those of others, is not simply the pastime of ethnographers. Despite the fact that creating typologies of Mexican masculinity can result in parodies without living referents, and overlooking for the moment the not unimportant issue of how men and women in Colonia Santo Domingo understand manliness and define what *ser hombre* means, there is purpose to the quest in the social sciences for better ways to categorize men in Mexico. Although it is likely that no one in the *colonia* would explicitly divide the population of men this way, I think most would recognize the following four male gender groups: the macho, the *mandilón,* the neither-macho-nor-*mandilón,* and the broad category of men who have sex with other men. But the fact that few men or women do or would care to divide the male population in this manner reveals more than simply a lack of familiarity with the methods of Weberian ideal typologizing. Masculinity, like other cultural identities, cannot be neatly confined in boxlike categories such as macho and *mandilón.* Identities make sense only in relation to other identities, and they are never firmly established for individuals or groups. Further, consensus will rarely be found as to whether a particular man deserves a label such as neither-macho-nor-*mandilón.* He will probably think of himself as a man in a variety of ways, none of which necessarily coincides with the views of his family and friends.

In terms of the last group of men, those who have sex with other men, this includes among others the *putos,* who have sex for money with other men and always play the active role, and the *homosexuales* (*maricas, maricones,* and so on), who are marked not only by their preference for male sex partners, but also more generally by the low cultural esteem in which they are held by many in society. I told Gabriel one day that in the United States a synonym for "coward" was *chicken* and asked him what an equivalent of *cobarde* might be for him. "*Puto* or *manca*" he responded, adding that in the north of Mexico they sometimes use *guajolote* (turkey) in the sense of cowardly fool. Nonetheless, men who have sex with other men are by some people's definition outside the bounds of masculinity altogether and would not even constitute a separate male gender type.

Yet although this taxonomy may indicate some important lines of demarcation, like all ideal typologizing it hopelessly obscures salient differences, which are so numerous that they can hardly be considered exceptions. And this is undoubtedly all the more true during liminal moments historically in which by definition cultural categories lack clearly circumscribed boundaries. No man today in Santo Domingo fits neatly into any of the four categories, even at specific moments, much less throughout the course of his life. Further, definitions such as these resist other relevant but complicating factors such as class, ethnicity, and historical epoch. *"El mexicano es muy hablador; habla mucho y no cumple* [The Mexican man is a big talker; he talks a lot but doesn't come through]," one young man told me. So who represents the more archetypal *macho mexicano:* the man who wants many (male) offspring and later abandons them, or the man who wants few, works hard to earn money for them, and calls these his manly duties? This is why attempts, even the more sophisticated ones, at quantifying Mexican masculinity on more-macho-or-less-macho scales inevitably become mired in problems of randomness, procedural errors, and, most of all, an inability to capture the existence and influence of contradictory consciousness, hegemony, and ideology among the men under investigation.

To unravel these stereotyped social roles, we must return to the point raised by Lancaster (1992): machismo, in whatever guise, is not simply a matter of ideology.[25] Machismo in Colonia Santo Domingo has been challenged ideologically, especially by grassroots feminism (see Massolo 1992a and Stephen 1996) and more indirectly by the gay and lesbian rights movements. But it has also faced real if usually ambiguous challenge through the strains of migration, falling birthrates, exposure to alternative cultures on television, and so on. These economic and sociocultural changes have not inevitably led to corresponding shifts in male domination, whether in the home, the factory, or society at large. But many men's authority has been undermined in material, if limited, ways, and this changing position for men as husbands and fathers, breadwinners and masters has in turn had real consequences for machismo in Santo Domingo.

Fidel Aguirre, a technician working in a laboratory outside the *colonia,* took pains to explain to me early one evening, "With women working outside the home it's not just a question of them having their own money now, as important as this has been. What's also involved is that women have met all sorts of different people, which has changed them forever. And this has meant that the men have changed, for if they don't, more and more they're getting left behind by women. Let me tell you, this is what's happening."[26]

To be a macho for most people in Colonia Santo Domingo involves qualities of personal belligerence, especially though not only as directed toward women, and in this sense it is very tied to appearances and style. In substance, this veneer of arrogance and hostility derives on the part of some men from feelings of superiority—and repeated and regular actions to back up these sentiments. At the same time, in the manner of Mendoza (1962) and Paredes (1967), the buffoon in Santo Domingo may seek to hide deep fears of physical inadequacy and losing male prerogative behind the guise of the macho. Women in particular talk of men who match the second description, referring to them in terms of disdain, ridicule, and even pity, and sometimes speaking of the inability of these men to sexually satisfy their wives.

Indeed, to the extent that men and women in Santo Domingo in the 1990s viewed it as a negative quality and practice, we may say that machismo had been transformed in part from a hegemonic into an ideological position that was being more openly challenged, as well as defended, in people's everyday discussions and activities in the *colonia.*

Cultural Nationalism

Authoritative discussions of machismo, or what later came to be known as machismo in some form (Ramos 1934; Paz 1950), have all made connections between the macho who "represents the masculine pole of life" (Paz 1961:81) and the broader social and political world of twentieth-century Mexico. Just as Lafaye (1976) has shown with regard to the Virgen de Guadalupe, so too with Mexican masculinity: it has not always represented the same kind of national symbol, but rather has been used for different purposes at various times to emphasize particular cultural nationalist qualities by a vast array of social forces.[27]

In Colonia Santo Domingo, as elsewhere in the Republic, the fate of machismo as an arche-type of masculinity has always been closely tied to Mexican cultural nationalism. Recall Cesar's comment to me about drinking: "More than anything we consumed tequila. We liked it, maybe because we felt more like Mexicans, more like *lugareños* [homeboys]."

For better or for worse, Ramos and Paz gave tequila-swilling machismo pride of place in the panoply of national character traits. Through their efforts and those of journalists and social scientists on both sides of the Rio Bravo/Rio Grande, the macho became "the Mexican." This is ironic, for it represents the product of a cultural nationalist invention: you note something (machismo) as existing, and in the process help foster its very existence. Mexican machismo as a national artifact was in this sense partially declared into being. Surely Paz is not the only literary figure in the world today whose authoritative descriptions about national characteristics are so continually cited that their statements become tautological arguments for the existence of these presumed traits in the first place.

And from the beginning, the portrayal of machismo (or its *pelado* forerunner) has been uniquely linked to the poor, unsophisticated, uncosmopolitan, and un–North American. From the 1920s on in Mexico, the bourgeoisie and the middle classes were, in Monsiváis's words, "obstinate in seeing nationalism as the most fruitful for their progress and internal coherence" (1976:194). The *macho-pelado,* always eminently male, represented either Mexico's homespun rural past, as did Jorge Negrete, or the essential backwardness of the nation, rural and urban, which needed to be exposed and eradicated. Regardless of the nostalgic allusion, "being *mexicano*" has been a male Mexican project. On the other side of the class ledger, nearly all union leaders and many leftist intellectuals in Mexico for much of this century have championed the cause of national progress by promoting the heroic figure of the proletarian male militant. In all versions, Mexican masculinity has been at the heart of defining a Mexican nation in terms of both its past and its future.[28]

Yet to whatever extent cultural traits like masculinity could ever have been justifiably called exclusively national in character, those days are past. Cultural processes are driven today by global ethnoscapes as never before (Appadurai 1991). In Colonia Santo Domingo in the mid-1990s, young women were watching the Miami-based, Spanish-language talk show *Cristina.* The subject of one of the first *Cristina* programs to be broadcast in Mexico concerned hospitals mixing up babies in neonatal rooms. One guest on the show was a Latino man who in the course of his story mentioned that he had been with his wife all through labor and delivery (a circumstance far more common in the United States than in Mexico, which perhaps says more about restrictions imposed by the hospitals in Mexico than it does about the desires of mothers and fathers in that country). The show's host, Cristina, interrupted the man's narrative and remarked, "That's what we'd like to see more of: real macho Latinos!" Her intention seems to have been to suggest that only real macho fathers could endure the traumas (blood and pain?) of childbirth. Where this leaves mothers in her view was not discussed, but nonetheless viewers in Mexico were treated to a Cuban-born, Miami-reared television personality defining for them the requisite components for good macho fathers.

Like religiousness, individualism, modernity, and other convenient concepts, machismo is used and understood in many ways. And history in the form of nationalism, feminism, and socioeconomic conjunctures impinges directly on gender identities in Mexico, including identities of masculinity and machismo and how they are variously regarded.[29] Either we can accept that there are multiple and shifting meanings of macho and machismo, or we can essentialize what were already reified generalizations about Mexican men in the first place. Like any identity, male identities in Mexico City do not reveal anything intrinsic about men there. The contradictory consciousness of many men in Colonia Santo Domingo about their own gender identities, their sense and experience of being *hombres* and machos, is part of the reigning chaos of their lives at least as much as is the imagined national coherence imposed from without.

Notes

1 The word *hombre* may have special resonance for aficionados of Hollywood Westerns. Expressions like "He's a tough hombre" are regularly used to conjure up images of Mexican bandits for whom life means little and sexual conquest is but part of daily life. Historically there is more than a coincidental relationship between Mexican male identities and cowboys.

2 The word *mandilón* comes from *mandil* (apron) and translates literally as "apron-er."

3 Behar (1993:40) cites an incident several decades ago involving a woman who denounced her husband in front of municipal authorities in a village in San Luis Potosí using these words: "The fact is that he's no man. He's no man because he's not responsible for his family. He never treats his family well. He treats them worse than animals!"

4 However, machismo is not necessarily the same beast in every cultural context, as we will see.

5 I have greatly benefited from discussing the topic of machismo with Carlos Monsiváis and Roger Lancaster. My gratitude is due as well to Gilberto Anguiano and Luz Lernández Gordillo of the Diccionario Español Mexicano project at the Colegio de México for their help in researching the word histories of *macho, machismo, mandilón,* and other terms relevant to male identities in Mexico.

6   For a psychological-anthropological analysis of machismo, see also Gilmore and Gilmore 1979. The role of the social sciences in the United States has not been incidental in popularizing the terms *macho* and *machismo*—for instance, in national character studies and their progeny. See, for example, Peñalosa 1968. For early published references in English to *macho*, see Beals 1928a:233, 1928b:288; and Mailer 1959:19, 483–84. For *machismo*, see Griffith 1948:50–51.

7   On the etymology of *macho*, see Gómez de Silva (1988:427) and Moliner (1991:II:299–300). On diverse and contradictory aspects of the cultural history of *macho* and *machismo*, see Mendoza 1962; Santamaría 1942:210, 1959:677; and Hodges 1986:114.

8   Even though the classic novel of the Mexican Revolution, Mariano Azuela's *Los de abajo* (first published in 1915), at one point uses the expression *machito* (1915 [19585]:70; translated as simply "a man" in Azuela 1962:79), this does not constitute a widespread use of the word *macho* or even a familiarity with the term in the sense of machismo or any of its derivatives.

9   See Bartra 1992 for more on Ramos, Paz, and *lo mexicano*. For a recent study of these "imaginings" outside Mexico, see Bolton's (1979) investigation of machismo among Peruvian truckers.

10 A review of recent literature regarding machismo and Chicanos is outside the scope of the present study, but in addition to Limón 1989 and 1994, interested readers may profitably consult Baca Zinn 1982; Mirandé 1986; and Almaguer 1991.

11 Monsiváis is conjuring up the image of the great theatrical (operatic) macho. See also Gaarder 1954.

12 Examining masculine imagery in Brazilian popular music, Oliven (1988:90) writes that "with respect to the formation of Brazilian social identity, machismo appears as a fundamental factor."

13 Representative examples in the U.S. media of popular stereotyping of Mexican and Latin American men as uniformly macho may be found in Reston 1967 and McDowell 1984.

14

>   Yo *soy mexicano, mi tierra es bravia.*
>   *Palabra de macho, que no hay otra tierra más linda*
>   *y más brava que la tierra mía.*
>   *Yo soy mexicano, y orgullo lo tengo.*
>   *Nací despreciando la vida y la muerte,*
>   *Y si he hecho bravatas, también las sostengo.*

From the song "Yo soy mexicano."

15 It will also be recalled that the *pachuco* is the character who, not coincidentally, opens Octavio Paz's examination of Mexican essence around this time, *El laberinto de la soledad* (1950). During this period, the role of the United States, and of Mexican migrants to the United States, most of whom were men, in defining Mexicanness was often emphasized by artists and other cultural critics.

16 Mellifluous, reasoned, and eminently accessible, *Laberinto* is the canonical text not only of foreigners seeking to find out about Mexico, but of many Mexicans trying to understand themselves. A friend who directs traffic in a supermarket parking lot just outside Santo Domingo commented to me one day that, like me, his brother in a village in the state of Puebla enjoyed reading books. The last time he was in the village for a visit, my friend told me, his brother was reading a book he had borrowed from the library: *El laberinto de la soledad*. For his brother it was like reading a public opinion poll in the newspaper; *this* is what Mexican men are like, it declares, and if you're not like this then you're not a real Mexican man.

17 My thanks to Jean Franco (personal communication), who first suggested that I expand the final section of an earlier paper (Gutmann 1993a), the result of which is the present chapter.

18 Another U.S.-born writer, Ernest Hemingway, is additionally responsible for popularizing ideas about Latin heroics, also known as machismo, in the United States. See Capellán's (1985) discussion of defiance in the face of death on the part of Hemingway's characters.

19 Another way to refer to a *man-as-mandilon* is to say, "*El es muy dejado* [He's very put upon]."

20 There is a superficial resemblance between these statements and those made to Abu-Lughod (1986:89) by a Bedouin woman about "real men": "My daughter wants a man whose eyes are open—not someone nice. Girls want someone who will drive them crazy. My daughter doesn't want to be with someone she can push around, so she can come and go as she pleases. No, she wants someone who will order her around.'" To seek an independent man would seem a similar objective in both cultural contexts. Yet there is also an important distinction in that my friend in Santo Domingo did not equate, as apparently the Bedouin woman did, such male independence with the domination of women but rather with the ability to take care of oneself and one's family—that is, to dominate "outside" circumstances.

21 The ethnographic authority of anthropologists to expound on issues of supposed "national character traits" has a long history in Mexico and elsewhere, stemming back to World War II and the need at that time to place clear national labels on enemy and allied characters (see Fabian 1983:46 ff. and Yans-McLaughlin 1986). It is unclear how long it will take contemporary anthropologists to undo such simplistic "boundary maintaining" schema.

22 The imposition by the media and by social scientists of totalizing cultural histories on countries like Mexico has been effectively challenged with regard to various sites and issues by Herzfeld 1987; Anderson 1991; and Stern 1995.

23
> *Ahí está en la calle, brilla como el sol*
> *En su auto nuevo, qué orgulloso va*
> *Vuela por la calle, gran velocidad*
> *Todas las personas lo miran pasar*
> *Limpia parabrisas, cruza sin mirar*

El niño no puede el auto esquivar
Sólo se oye un grito, golpe y nada más
Demasiada sangre en esta ciudad.

From the song "Un poco de sangre," on the album *El circo*. The love of the stereotyped macho for automobiles and trucks is notorious; one linguistic commentator writes about the everyday usage of the term machismo, "[T]he high rate of road accidents in L/A [Latin America], particularly perhaps in Mexico, is due to notions of *machismo;* Mexicans are, admittedly, somewhat direct and impatient in their ways but the tussle to make the crossroads first ... was activated just as much by the feeling that it would be 'sissy' to get beaten to it" (Gerrard 1952 [1972]:99).

24 Diane Davis (personal communication) also notes that the decision to segregate men and women has as much a class logic as a gender logic. Initially at least, riders on the metro were often working class men and middle class women.

25 However, it does include this aspect, as Fernandez Kelly (1976) makes clear in a paper on some of the ideological foundations of the notion of machismo.

26 For a similar analysis involving an opposite response by a different stratum of men—the New Men's Movement in the United States—see Kimmel and Kaufman 1994.

27 On Mexican national identity, nationalism, *mexicanidad,* and *lo mexicano,* see Gamio 1916; Vasconcelos 1925; Saenz 1927; Ramos 1934; Paz 1950; Ramirez 1977; Bonfil Batalla 1987; and Bartra 1992. For English surveys and analyses of this material, see Schmidt 1978 and especially Lomnitz-Adler 1992. On the Virgen de Guadalupe in particular, see also Bushnell 1958; Wolf 1958; and Alarcon 1990.

28 See Stern 1995, who argues that archetypes of masculinity and femininity were also central to Mexican national self-definitions in the late colonial period.

29 For a detailed study of nationalism in modern Europe and its relationship to male identity, homosexuality, homoeroticism, and men's domination of women, see Mosse 1985.

References

Appadurai, Arjun. 1991. "Global Ethnoscapes: Notes and Queries for a Transnational Anthropology." In *Recapturing Anthropology.* Richard G. Fox, ed. pp. 191–210. Santa Fe, NM: School of American Research.

Franco, Jean. 1989. *Plotting Women: Gender and Representation in Mexico.* New York: Columbia University Press.

Giddens, Anthony. 1979 (1990). *Central Problems in Social Theory: Action, Structure and Contradiction in Social Analysis.* Berkeley: University of California Press.

———. 1990. *The Consequences of Modernity.* Stanford, CA: Stanford University Press.

Gilmore, David D. 1990. *Manhood in the Making: Cultural Concepts of Masculinity.* New Haven, CT: Yale University Press.

Gramsci, Antonio. 1929–35 (1971). *Selections from the Prison Notebooks.* New York: International.

Greenberg, James. 1989. *Blood Ties: Life and Violence in Rural Mexico.* Tucson: University of Arizona Press.

Griffith, Beatrice. 1948 (1973). *American Me.* Westport, CT: Greenwood.

Lafaye, Jacques. 1976. *Quetzalcóatl and Guadalupe: The Formation of Mexican National Consciousness, 1531–1813.* Benjamin Keen, trans. Chicago: University of Chicago Press.

Lancaster, Roger, 1992. *Life Is Hard: Machismo, Danger, and the Intimacy of Power in Nicaragua.* Berkeley: University of California Press.

Lewis, Oscar. 1951 (1963). *Life in a Mexican Village: Tepoztlán Restudied.* Urbana: University of Illinois Press.

——. 1952. "Urbanization without Breakdown." *Scientific Monthly* 75:31–41.

——. 1961. *The Children of Sanchez: Autobiography of a Mexican Family.* New York: Vintage.

Limón, José. 1989. "*Carne, Carnales,* and the Carnivalesque: Bakhtinian *Batos,* Disorder, and Narrative Discourses." *American Ethnologist* 16(3):471–86.

——. 1984. *Dancing with the Devil: Society and Cultural Poetics in Mexican-American South Texas.* Madison: University of Wisconsin Press.

Madsen, William, and Claudia Madsen 1969 "The Cultural Structure of Mexican Drinking Behavior." *Quarterly Journal of Studies on Alcohol* 30(3):701–18.

Marshall, Mac. 1979. *Weekend Warriors: Alcohol in a Micronesian Culture.* Palo Alto, CA: Mayfield.

Massolo, Alejandra. 1992a. *Por amor y coraje: Mujeres en movimientos urbanos de la ciudad de México.* Mexico City: El Colegio de México.

Mendoza, Vicente T. 1962. "El machismo en México." *Cuadernos del Instituto Nacional de Investigaciones Folklóricas* (Buenos Aires) 3:75–86.

Monsiváis, Carlos. 1976 (1983). "La nación de unos cuantos y las esperanzas románticas (Notas sobre la historia del término 'Cultura Nacional' en México)." In *En torno a la cultura nacional.* Héctor Aguilar Camín, ed. pp. 159–221. Mexico City: Instituto Nacional Indigenista/SepOchentas.

——. 1981. *Escenas de pudor y liviandad.* Mexico City: Grijalbo.

——. 1992. Las mitologías del cine mexicano." *Intermedios* 2:12–23.

Paredes, Américo. 1966. "The Anglo-American in Mexican Folklore." In *New Voices in American Studies.* pp. 113–27. Lafayette, IN: Purdue University Press.

—— 1967. "Estados Unidos, México y el machismo." *Journal of Inter-American Studies* 9(1):65–84.

—— 1971. "The United States, Mexico, and Machismo." Marcy Steen, trans. *Journal of the Folklore Institute* 8(1):17–37.

Paz, Octavio. 1950 (1959). *El laberinto de la soledad.* Mexico City: Fondo de Cultura Económica.

——. 1961. *The Labyrinth of Solitude: Life and Thought in Mexico.* Lysander Kemp, trans. New York: Grove.

——. 1985. "Return to the Labyrinth of Solitude." In *The Labyrinth of Solitude and Other Writings.* Yara Milos, trans. pp. 327–53. New York: Grove.

Pratt, Mary Louise. 1990. "Women, Literature, and National Brotherhood." In *Women, Culture and Politics in Latin America.* pp. 48–73. Berkeley: University of California Press.

Ramos, Samuel. 1934 (1992). *El perfil del hombre y la cultura en México.* Mexico City: Espasa-Calpe Mexicana.

——. 1962 (1975). *Profile of Man and Culture in Mexico.* Peter G. Earle, trans. Austin: University of Texas Press.

Rulfo, Juan. 1955 (1986). *Pedro Páramo.* Mexico City: Fondo de Cultura Económica.

———— 1959. *Pedro Páramo.* Lysander Kemp, trans. New York: Grove.

Santamaría, Francisco J., 1959. *Diccionario de mejicanismos.* Mexico City: Porrúa.

Stern, Steve. 1997. *Women and Social Movements in Latin America: Power from Below.* Austin: University of Texas Press.

Stevens, Evelyn. 1973. *"Marianismo:* The Other Face of *Machismo* in Latin America." In *Male and Female in Latin America.* Ann Pescatello, ed. pp. 89–101. Pittsburgh: University of Pittsburgh Press.

Usigli, Rodolfo. 1947 (1985). *El Gesticulador.* Mexico City: Editores Mexicanos Unidos.

God Is Not Dead

The Decline of Catholicism in Latin America

Lisa Lopez

S ince the Conquistadores came to conquer the New World, Latin America has been characterized by devout adherence to the Roman Catholic faith. However, for the past two decades, there has been a significant decline of Catholicism in the region, enough to spark serious discussion amongst scholars and people of faith. Many Latin Americans have increasingly converted to Protestantism, or Evangelicalism, which is the preferred term in Latin America, or have declared themselves atheist, especially in countries like Chile and Brazil. The Catholic Church's hold on state and moral authority is decreasing rapidly, due in large part to technology, mass media, and competition. People are now more exposed to varying opinions and free to choose their beliefs. In addition, Latin America has become more liberal throughout the years, and its people's changing religious practices.

Catholicism in Latin America

Daniel H. Levine, a professor of political science at the University of Michigan, argues that Latin American Catholicism in the 20th century was like a "lazy monopolist," as its power and position were virtually guaranteed by law, custom, and a network of elite connections. Due to its hierarchical nature and identification with traditional elites, the Catholic Church has been faulted for Latin America's slow progress into modernization. Supposedly, the Church sole interest was preserving its privileged position in the legal and social structures that historically was the source of its influence and power.

Lisa Lopez, "God is Not Dead: The Decline of Catholicism in Latin America," *Washington Report on the Hemisphere*, vol. 35, no. 12, pp. 8–11. Copyright © 2015 by The Council on Hemispheric Affairs. Reprinted with permission. Provided by ProQuest LLC. All rights reserved.

Despite its elitist history, the Church also played an influential role in criticizing military regimes and sponsored various Catholic missions during the Colonial period. The 1960s witnessed the emergence of the "progressive church," marking a transformation of the Catholic Church from an elitist institution to the "church of the poor." The transition, which occurred after the Second Vatican Council in 1962, was rapid and dramatic, occurring within two decades. Along with attention shifting toward the popular classes, there was also a transition from short-term charity to searching for long-term solutions to poverty and other issues facing the masses. Churches in Chile and Brazil began to support social justice reforms, and bishops were increasingly interested in land reform, literary campaigns, and rural cooperatives. Liberation Theology, which examines the meaning of faith in relation to the commitment to abolish injustice and build a new society, was the driving force behind progressive Catholicism in the 1960s and 1970s. On top of this, the Church began to move from condemning only specific rulers or regimes as unjust to labeling entire economic, cultural, and political systems as sinful, particularly legal systems that allowed abortion, contraception use, and homosexual rights. This helped to mark the Church as the highest moral authority throughout Latin America.

Recently, Catholic leaders have been concerned over the growth of Protestantism, the emergence of *Católico a mi manera* (Catholic in my own way), and those who have declared no religion at all. From this concern has arisen the *Comunidades Eclesiales de Base* (Base Ecclesial Communities; CEBS) and the Catholic Charismatic Renewal (CCR) as a response to the increasing perception of the Church as archaic and traditional. With ties to Liberation Theology and originating within the United States in the late 1960s, these movements are directed by lay people and based on independent Bible study. It is an attempt to reconcile Pentecostal practices, like baptism in the name of the Holy Spirit, with core Catholic devotions to the Virgin Mary and other saints. There have always been alternatives to Catholicism in Latin America, but these have usually been suppressed, hidden, or incorporated into Catholic practices. Now, the Church is struggling to convince the Latin American population that it can meet their needs.

Protestantism in Latin America

Enter Evangelical Protestantism. This Christian denomination has three main beliefs: the complete authority and reliability of the Bible, the need to be saved through a personal relationship with Jesus, and the duty of spreading the message of Christ to others. Beginning in the 1940s, waves of Protestant missionaries first focused their attention on rural and indigenous populations and then expanded their hold in the cities. Indigenous groups were easily converted because they tended to reject Catholicism, the religion used by the conquistadores to justify the repression and slaughter of indigenous peoples.

Data has suggested that the decline of Catholicism in Latin America is largely accompanied by a rise in Protestantism. According to a Pew survey, 69 percent of Latin American adults identify as Catholics, which is down from an estimated 90 percent for much of the 20th century. Since

84 percent of those surveyed said they were raised Catholic, the evidence suggests there was a 15 point drop in one generation alone. Forty percent of the world's Catholics are found in Latin America, but the survey found that 19 percent of Latin Americans now describe themselves as Protestants. Most converts state they wanted a more "personal connection with God." Evangelists have had trouble in Andean countries like Venezuela, Colombia, Ecuador, Peru and Bolivia, as well as in Mexico. In countries like Brazil, Chile, and Guatemala, however, they have claimed a great deal of territory.

Part of the attractiveness of Evangelicalism comes from its promise of liberation from sin, poverty, and oppression. It is believed that a political transformation could come through a religious and moral one; religious leaders believe that if infidelity and immorality were eliminated, poverty could be cut in half in one generation. This belief stems from the fact that Evangelists promote women's participation, greatly discourage acts like gambling, and do not consume alcohol. The greatest support for the socio-economic advancement based on spiritual renewal comes from the emerging middle class persons, who converted while they were poor and now live a comfortable lifestyle.

The divine healing professed by Evangelicals and the possibility of a new life, which is greatly attractive to people who have urgent physical and emotional needs because of poverty, alcoholism, violence, disease, and a marginalized status, make the religion particularly appealing. Evangelical denominations are more personable because leaders tend to be from the community and thus speak the native language easily unlike Catholic priests that can be sent out to practice the faith from anywhere in the world. They also speak in a way that is easier for people to follow, with visuals and engaging conversations. The development of local leaders and resources has enabled Evangelicals to cut ties with foreign missionaries and in some cases establish homegrown churches. Thus, the Evangelical churches have become safe for the underprivileged groups of the region.

Monopolistic to Pluralistic

After having dominated the area as the primary religion in Latin America for centuries, Catholicism has had to make room for alternative voices. Despite their emergence, other Christian denominations and atheism continue to be the minority and usually lack a defining voice. However, after 500 years, hegemonic Catholicism has been replaced by religious pluralism, especially in large urban cities where different denominations compete for space, attention, pubic goods, and members.

Today, it is easier than ever to access information, and the Catholic Church can no longer control its dissemination. The growth of cities and literacy rates along with increased access to mass media has contributed to this trend. Due to this opening up of communication, anyone can compete for space, attention, and followers, and thus the religious scene has become pluralistic. A variety of churches, chapels, mass media programming, and campaigns have been able to spread their message to the streets, squares, beaches, sport stadiums, jails, and even nightclubs. Church leaders are no longer the final authority. Catalina Romero, an Evangelical leader from Peru, states that "understanding persons as friends of God is quite different than looking upon them as serfs, in the same way that inviting them to follow God's project is different than ordering them to follow the law," an assessment that alludes to what she sees as being the Catholic Church's faults. The Church can no longer monopolize the moral sphere in the name of religion now that its leaders share the airwaves, TV screens, and public platforms with representatives from other churches.

Intense competition and new markets create a need for new rules of co-existing. In order for Catholicism and Evangelicalism to survive, they have had to learn to compete effectively in a pluralistic environment with competitive products of mass appeal and marketing skills.

Church and State

An omnipresent triad of politicians, clergy, and military officials used to affirm the presence of the Church when religion and state were heavily intertwined in Latin America. However, the rise of a pluralistic environment has changed that. Most churches support some sort of political democracy and open civil society in which they can be heavily involved within civic networks tied to institutions like schools, media outlets, and health centers. As Evangelical churches become more popular, they have followed in the footsteps of the Catholic Church by making deals with government officials and providing support in exchange for material goods and legitimation. Evangelicals and other Protestant denominations simply ask for the same legal treatment the Catholic Church enjoys, ranging from exemptions to benefits. Atheist and humanist movements call for government neutrality toward religion and non-religion. The separation of church and state, although preferable, is unlikely to occur any time soon in Latin America; therefore, all religions should at least be given equal influence within the government and society.

Left-wing politicians have increasingly dominated Latin American politics, which has further altered the relationship between church and state. Catholic orthodox doctrines forbidding the use of contraceptives, the ordination of women, and gay marriage are no longer popular and create more problems than they solve. In the wake of Latin America's shift to the left, the Church must accept these evolving social standards in order to remain relevant. The loss of Catholic influence has allowed for more progressive bills like same-sex marriage and abortion to pass in Latin America. Argentina was the first to legalize gay marriage, followed closely by Uruguay, Brazil, and some states in Mexico. Also, for the last two decades in Chile, Catholic spokesmen have advocated against new legislation on divorce, decriminalization of sodomy, equal status for children born in and outside of marriage, and the emergency contraception pill, but have been unsuccessful. This signals that there is a possibility for change within the Catholic Church. Part of Evangelism's success has been its ability to be more open to liberal ideas.

Social and Political Implications

As waves of communication introduce new ideas to avid listeners looking for a community to belong to, Latin Americans have been able to find a religion that fits their needs and beliefs instead of needing to change beliefs. The decline of conservative Catholicism has been accompanied by a flourishing of liberal ideology and practices and a transition to hearing the plight of the masses instead of the few elite of each country. Within this changing climate, the Roman Catholic Church has continued to perform their most important task of providing social services to those most in need.

Although there has been a push for greater separation of church and state, it is undeniable that a religious denomination, whether Catholic or Evangelical, still has much influence in the political process. However, now the people of Latin America have more options when it comes to practicing religion and finding social services that can improve their lives.

Section V: Recommended Readings

Botta, S. (2013). *Manufacturing otherness: Missions and Indigenous cultures in Latin America.* Newcastle upon Tyne, UK: Cambridge Scholars.

Faudree, P. (2013). *Singing for the dead: The politics of Indigenous revival in Mexico.* Durham, NC: Duke University Press.

Gutmann, M. C. (2006). *The meanings of macho: Being a man in Mexico City,* 6th edition. Berkeley, CA: University of California Press.

Kellogg, S. (2005). *Weaving the past: A history of Latin America's Indigenous women from the Prehispanic period to the present.* New York, NY: Oxford University Press.

Penyak, L. M., & and Petry, W. J. (Eds.). (2015). *Religion and society in Latin America: Interpretive essays from conquest to present.* New York, NY: ORBIS.

Section V: Post-Reading Questions

1   What are the major components of the Day of the Dead celebration?

2   Outline the historical variations associated to the meaning of the terms *macho* and *machismo.*

3   Historically, what factors led to the decline of Catholicism as the dominant religion in Latin America?

SECTION VI

ECONOMY AND SOCIAL DEVELOPMENT

Editor's Introduction

Drugs and poverty are two relevant issues in the study of modern Latin America and the Caribbean. Their socioeconomic and global impact is explored in the last section of this anthology. As such, both issues are historically intertwined as agents for the rise of drugs as a global commodity leading to the emergence of transnational corporations like cartels that resort to violence as a means of controlling territory, corruption of government and local authorities, suppression of democratic institutions, and subjugation of the poor by fear and death.

Gootenberg (2006) rigorously assesses the history and socioeconomic conditions that allowed cocaine to become a globally traded product. The introduction of cocaine as an anesthetic and "miracle" drug and subsequent availability as a tonic component of sodas such as Coca-Cola were contributing factors to an increase in its desirability and demand. In his article, Gootenberg describes the exchange chains established originally during Colonial times and the role that Germany and the United States played in subsequently expanding the trade of cocaine to a global market.

Caracas is the geographic setting for Fernandes's (2010) ethnographic discussion of poverty, Hugo Chavez, and the rise of post-neoliberalism in Venezuela. The failure of neoliberal austerity policies aimed to stimulate a stagnant economy and reduce social spending strengthened a small proletariat opposition movement, thereafter leading to social unrest, government disintegration, and the rise of *Chavismo* as an anti-neoliberal alternative.

Section VI: Key Terms

Alkaloid

Bolivarianismo

Caracazo

coca

cocaine

Coca-Cola

coca syrup

drugs

export commodities

Gran Viraje

homelessness

Hugo Chavez

Maria Lionza cult

pure salts

social welfare state

substitution industrialization

transnational commodity networks

unemployment

urban barrios

urbanizaciones

Cocaine in Chains: The Rise and Demise of a Global Commodity, 1860–1950

Paul Gootenberg

> The rising cultivation, consumption, and export of this so precious article of our agricultural production [coca]—once widely known and used for health purposes
> —will replace tea and coffee themselves. La Crónica Médica (Lima), 1889

This [...] treats coca and cocaine as essentially world export commodities rather than as menacing drugs. Commodity perspectives make good sense for the period at hand, 1860–1950, from the years Andean coca leaf first hit world markets to the birth of today's vast circuits of illicit cocaine. During this formative century both goods were still considered legitimate or even progressive articles of world commerce, as the epigraph suggests. Taking coca and cocaine as typical goods rather than uniquely spiritual or pariah substances may also temper some of the passionate politics that entangle these Andean products today.[1] Even the words used to describe current drug trades assume a fantastic quality. Discourse on drugs, rather than using terms appropriate to a capitalist market, reverts to images of a "feudal" crusade between evil "drug lords" and knightly "drug czars," drug "cartels" or "plagues" and haplessly "enslaved" consumers.

Andean coca leaf and cocaine make an especially strong case study on commodity chains in Latin American history. Neither existed as a significant commodity until the late nineteenth century, so their complex social transformations into marketable and exportable goods can be historically tracked. Coca and cocaine, rather than entering undifferentiated world markets, became organized into distinctive transnational

Paul Gootenburg, "Cocaine in Chains: The Rise and Demise of a Global Commodity, 1860–1950," *From Silver to Cocaine: Latin American Commodity Chains and the Building of the World Economy, 1500–2000,* ed. Steven Topik, Carlos Marichal, and Zephyr Frank, pp. 321–351. Copyright © 2006 by Duke University Press. Reprinted with permission.

commodity networks, and these networks have analytical significance, or so I argue here. Placing coca into spatially embedded relationship chains may also help to demystify drugs, usually perceived in loaded binaries of "supply" and "demand."

Conceptually, I see tension between sociological commodity chain approaches and much of neoclassical or institutional economics, though it is a good thing to try to bridge them. After all, the concept of global commodity chains, in which world markets are socially structured and power-segmented, originated in Immanuel Wallerstein's world systems theory and more-over has the constructivist spirit of the anthropological "social life of things." For historians, the commodity chain can work as both a descriptive and an analytical tool.[2] It helps grasp power differentials between actors in the "core" and "periphery" of chains, though not in the deterministic spirit of yesterday's dependency theory. By focusing on flows rather than objects or sites, a commodity chain approach challenges distinctions between *national* economies and polities still dear to neoclassical and institutional economists. In short, this holistic view helps us to overcome traditional divides between internal and external factors and between economic and noneconomic factors in Latin American history, binaries shared by neoclassical and dependency perspectives.

[…] I try to demonstrate the utility of thinking about coca and cocaine in discrete global commodity chains over extended time. The quantitative data derive from motley sources that do not lend themselves to reliable aggregates or comparisons.[3] Nor do I dwell on illicit tastes and trades in cocaine, which in any case (save for a brief eruption around 1905–20) were modest before the 1970s. […] The first, 1860–1910, saw the creation of world commodity networks around coca and cocaine. Two commercial chains linked nascent Andean coca to overseas markets, the Germany-Europe-Andes circuit and the United States–Andes circuit. The second period, 1910–1950, saw mounting political and market constraints on coca and cocaine, in part related to international narcotics control. Three new commodity chains arose which worked to displace existing Andean coca and cocaine: a hemispheric network managed by the United States, a Dutch-European colonial network, and an imperial pan-Asian Japanese network. These chains, which crumbled during World War II, were prelude to the illicit circuits of cocaine which tied the eastern Andes back into the outside world by the 1970s.

Making Global Commodities: Coca and Cocaine, 1860–1910

With deep roots in Andean culture, coca did not become an exportable commodity until the late nineteenth century. Coca leaf is produced by a shrub that is among the oldest domesticated plants of the Andean region, grown in mid-range subtropical Amazonian regions and closely associated with Andean cultural life and identities. The dried leaf is carried upland for mastication (so-called chewing) by highland peoples, *coqueros* who have prized coca for thousands of years for its stimulant properties (as part of ritualized high-altitude work routines), for purposes of health and nutrition (benefits it probably provides), and for spiritual and community sustenance. During the Inca era (1420–1532 A.D.), coca was declared a prestige item, off-limits to the toiling peasant masses, with no explicit exchange value, though much use likely escaped state regulation. After the Conquest of the 1530s, the Spanish partially commercialized coca, after heated religious debates about its devilish nature, establishing plantations in the Andean *montaña* for supplying mine workers in silver mining complexes such as Potosí across the high Andes. Coca use expanded. By the close of the colonial era, coca chewing constituted both a substantial business (helping monetize exchanges between lowlands and highlands) as well as a widespread marker of (degraded) Indian caste. Coastal populations and white elites did not generally indulge in coca, which they regarded as a suspiciously "Indian" habit.

Scholars often ponder why coca, unlike tobacco or coffee, proved unassimilable into the new pantheon of Europe's colonial stimulants in the early modern era, and remained a limited regional commodity in the colonized territory of today's Peru and Bolivia.[4] The negative aesthetics of chewing or its early ethnic connotations are cited as well as the fragility of coca leaves in shipment to Europe. However, perhaps it is better to see coca as indirectly a strategic commodity, as a local input into the seventeenth-century Peruvian forced-labor silver regime vital to expanding world commerce. Perhaps coca's recognition and embrace by the West ought to be seen as merely delayed for three centuries, to the mid-nineteenth century; later, as industrialized cocaine, coca accelerated into one of history's most profitable world commodities in the illicit drug trades of the 1970s.

The nineteenth-century world revolutions of commerce and science sparked renewed appreciation for coca and for its alkaloid, cocaine, first isolated in 1860. Interest emanated from Europe but sparked active responses in the Andes. Much had to change for coca to become a bona fide world commodity: its scientific, medical, and ethnic prestige had to rise in Europe and North America as well as in republican Peru and Bolivia; it needed "modern" uses and outlets, public spokesmen and colonizing planters, not to mention working networks of laborers, investors, processors, shippers, and consumers. To make a complex story short, these factors came together quickly after 1850 as European botany and medicine settled coca's (previously disputed) stimulant power, as industrializing societies embraced novel mass health stimulants (famously in this case with Vin Mariani and Coca-Cola) and touted modern medical marvels (cocaine as local anesthesia after 1885), and as the Andean nations of Peru and Bolivia desperately sought new export goods in the wake of the devastating War of the Pacific in 1879–83.

The German Connection

Broadly speaking, the first impulse to Andean coca and cocaine production came from "Greater" Germany and to a lesser extent France and Britain in the mid-nineteenth century; by 1900 Germany took the lead in scientific interest in cocaine and in its production. These influences were felt deeply in Peru (the largest exporter) and by the Peruvians who organized the initial coca trades.

Interest in coca as a modern stimulant was awakened by the development of German alkaloid science. Reports of such German-speaking nineteenth-century travelers as Alexander von

Humboldt, Johan Jakob von Tschudi, and Eduard Poeppig sparked a veritable race to discover coca's active principle. Leading German chemists such as Friedrich Wöhler requested bulk samples of fresh coca—a great rarity in Europe—from the Austrian *Novara* scientific mission in the late 1850s, which the chemistry student Albert Niemann used in his isolation of *Kokain* in 1860. Viennese medical men, most famously the young Sigmund Freud, played a major early role in research and promotion of cocaine's medical uses. Particularly galvanizing was Karl Koller's discovery in 1884 of cocaine's local anesthetic properties, which revolutionized Western surgery.[5] All of them used scarce medicinal cocaine hydrochloride, which E. Merck manufactured in Darmstadt from modest but now regularized imports of dried Bolivian and Peruvian leaf. European interest in coca had steadily awakened since the 1850s; after 1885, a decade-long coca boom began.

Along with "scientific" alkaloid cocaine, medical, commercial, and popular fascination with herbal coca leaf grew as well. New stimulants became coveted, especially by "brain workers," living amid the exertions and neurotic disorders of modern societies. Global "coca mania" was particularly pronounced in France and Britain (and later reached its height in the United States) and had distinctive cultural roots and associations, some with imported Andean accents. In 1863 a Corsican entrepreneur, Angelo Mariani, launched his remarkably successful Vin Mariani, a mixture of coca and Bordeaux wine, which captivated the world with its arty and sophisticated marketing campaigns. Cyclists and opera singers typified the epoch's coca drinkers. Between 1863 and 1885, Mariani became the single largest user of Andean coca, and French medical interest filtered to Peru. British medical men, some obscure and some famous, also focused on coca as a health stimulant (rather than on German cocaine) and would long defend coca tonics and medicine on their own therapeutic terms. With the mid-1880s boom, the royal Kew Gardens (and later the Imperial Institute), which had worked similar wonders with Amazonian cinchona and rubber, began a crash program of coca research and botanical experiments in their colonies in India, Ceylon, and beyond (as did the Dutch, French, and even Germans in Cameroon).[6]

German interests, however, through the port of Hamburg, dominated the field (see Table 6.1.1). Merck enjoyed the experience, Andean connections, and product prestige, though the quantities it made were modest— less than one kilo a year—before 1884. After cocaine was adopted for use during surgery, production rose quickly to over 500 kilos annually in 1890, 1,500 in 1898, and more than 2,400 kilos by 1902. Merck produced about a quarter of the world's cocaine, and for a decade it was the firm's most profitable single product line. Merck transformed cocaine from an experimental medical novelty into a marketable commodity, as international prices dropped from about $1 per grain in 1884 to about 2 cents a grain by 1887. Other German firms also jumped into cocaine, among them Gehe & Co., Knoll, Riedel, and C. H. Boehringer & Sohn, some with American branch houses.

The turning point for Merck came in 1884–86, when prices and output jumped five and twenty times respectively with the use of cocaine as an anesthetic and for other medical purposes. The spike sparked a much-debated and alarming "crisis" in international coca supply. Merck's strategy was to encourage Peruvian suppliers of "crude cocaine," a semiprocessed (80–90 percent pure)

Table 6.1.1 Kilograms of cocaine produced and of coca and cocaine imported by Merck, 1879–1918

YEAR	MERCK PRODUCTION	COCA IMPORTED		CRUDE COCAINE
		FROM PERU	FROM JAVA	IMPORTED FROM JAVA
1879–80	0.05	25		
1880–81	0.05	25		
1881–82	0.09	58		
1882–83	0.30	138		
1883–84	1.41	655		
1884–85	30	8,655		
1885–86	70	18,396		
1886–87	257	3,629		
1887–88	300			
1888–89	303			
1889–90	511			
1890–91	557			
1891–92	436			
1892–93	505			
1893–94	626			
1894–95	645			
1895–96	791			
1896–97	831			
1897–98	1,509			
1898–99	1,553			
1899–1900	1,564			
1900–1901	1,418			
1900–1902	1,886			
1902–1903	2,454			
1903–1904	2,157			
1904–1905	2,246			
1905–1906	2,146		58,967	919
1907	1,881		94,018	1,647
1908	3,642		220,429	3,721
1909	4,183		238,066	3,721
1910	5,241		186,127	3,183
1911	4,681		261,254	4,080
1912	6,049		422,776	6,552
1913	8,683		724,189	10,683
1914	6,212		487,245	7,295
1915	265		203,972	2,966
1916	44		68,380	829
1917	1,246			
1918	1,738		6,744	72

Source: H. R. Friman, "Germany and the Transformation of Cocaine," in Paul Gootenberg, ed., Cocaine: Global Histories (New York: Routledge, 1999), Tables 4.1 and 4.2.

jungle cocaine sulfate cake, and to this end it and other German firms sent agents to Lima. Crude cocaine shipped far more easily and cheaply than bulk leaf and lasted longer. Merck processed it into medicinal-grade cocaine in Germany for its global distribution networks. This product also fitted a marked German cultural and medical preference for "pure" scientific cocaine. By 1900, almost all German imports—more than 6,000 kilos yearly at the peak in 1903–5, worth nearly £100,000—arrived in the form of crude cocaine, so that shipments of coca leaf became obsolete. The Germans' success in promoting crude cocaine was also a prime reason that rival colonial coca projects (British, Dutch, and the American Rusby mission for Parke-Davis) were largely abandoned by the 1890s.[7] Crude cocaine was in fact too successful: with world production surpassing 15 metric tons by the early twentieth century, medicinal markets were saturated. (England, France, Italy, Switzerland, and Russia also engaged in cocaine processing in a modest way for national markets.) Merck quickly diversified into other drug lines. As profits and prospects fell, German firms soon formed a cocaine "syndicate" (1905) with monopsonistic buying, cartel pricing agreements, and strong organizational ties to the German state. By 1910, the European cocaine network was no longer primarily market-driven.

A decisive factor in the emergence of coca and cocaine as a discrete commodity chain is the way European (largely German) interests infiltrated and shaped the Peruvian end of things. In the 1860s and 1870s, such Peruvian medical and cultural spokesmen as Manuel A. Fuentes and the physicians Tomás Moreno y Maíz, José Casimiro Ulloa, and José de los Ríos overcame traditional elite prejudices and began to seriously reevaluate native coca as a good and now marketable resource. French medicine held sway, and indeed, the major Peruvian worker in the field after the War of the Pacific, the remarkable Alfredo Bignon, was a naturalized French pharmacist working in Lima. But commercial developments, which made Peru the monopoly supplier of world coca and cocaine by 1900, followed German cues and connections (plus some American coca trends). In a little-known burst of pharmaceutical experiments in Lima in 1884–87—a local version of Freud's famed *Coca Papers* of the same years—Bignon perfected an original and simplified method for distilling crude cocaine, which was soon promoted by Lima medical circles and by two official Peruvian coca commissions. By 1886, German pharmacists and businessmen like Meyer and Hafemann in Lima established themselves as the main cocaine processors, sending their product on via German merchant houses (Pruis, Dammert, and others) to Hamburg.[8] Mannheim's C. F. Boehringer also sent its sole chemist to Lima as early as 1885.

But it was the dedicated Arnaldo Kitz, an immigrant German merchant in the capital and commercial agent for Merck, who went farthest to the source of supply: the eastern Andes, ancestral homeland of coca. By 1890, Kitz had marched off to isolated Amazonian Pozuzo, home of a legendary "lost" Austrian peasant colony of the 1850s, to establish the region's first working cocaine factory. Bignon's process became known as the Kitz formula in producing zones. By 1892, Peru's earnings from crude cocaine surpassed its revenues from coca leaf. In the mid-1890s, Kitz shifted operations to nearby Huánuco, with its rich *montaña* (Chinchao-Derrepente zone) haciendas. For the next sixty years, this district would remain the capital of Andean cocaine-grade coca, delivering most of its output to Germany until World War II. Committed Peruvian hacendados, drawing thousands of migrating peasant workers and sharecroppers, colonized or "industrialized" these coca lands from 1885 to 1910, with the help of a few Croatian immigrants. By 1900, Huánuco province was home to about a dozen cocaine manufactories (of about twenty scattered throughout the country), with a regional elite based on coca and cocaine estates. The industry became concentrated and dominated by the flamboyant regional and national political boss, Augusto Durand. These complex local structures of production—particularly of the central Huánuco region—were oriented and connected over thousands of miles to a handful of German pharmaceutical concerns.

Around 1901 (according to German consuls), Peru's legal cocaine zenith, total production peaked at 10,700 kilos of crude cocaine, which required the use of some 1,600 metric tons of raw coca leaf. Peru still also exported 610 tons of coca leaf (more than half of that northern Trujillo coca to the United States) out of an estimated national production of 2,100 tons. As usual, those numbers don't quite add up, but the export boom likely left some three-quarters of Peruvian coca in traditional indigenous circuits, much of that grown in the far Cuzqueño south.[9] Together, and fleetingly, coca and cocaine constituted Peru's fifth-highest export earner and continued to excite the developmental imagination of liberal national elites. Peru's success here, guided by German cues, was likely at the expense of neighboring Bolivia, the only other commercial coca producer. By 1900, Bolivia had failed to industrialize any of its productive Yungas coca zones (which previously exported to France and the United States) and Bolivian sales to modern commercial users in the northern hemisphere faded away. But to grasp these Andean circuits roundly we need to explore another coca commodity chain: the one between the United States and Peru.

The North American Connection

North America's interest in coca and cocaine grew after 1860 (explosively after 1884), but in contrast to Germany, which focused on scientific cocaine, the United States had a pronounced medical, cultural, and political-economic bias toward coca leaf. By 1900, Americans were the world's largest and most avid consumers and boosters of both substances, by then seemingly domesticated all-American goods. By 1910, however, American thinking and policies dramatically shifted against both coca and cocaine, and the United States began its long global campaign to banish both products. Over the long term, Americans' attitudes toward coca must be seen in the context of expanding informal influence in the Andean region.

North America's fascination with coca leaf, sparked by exported European curiosity, took on distinctively American tones. By the 1870s American medical men, pharmacists, entrepreneurs, and hucksters were actively discovering coca. It was soon among the most widespread additives in popular patent remedies and tonics, prescribed for a vast range of conditions and ills, real and imagined. Most were related to "neurasthenia," the American condition of nerve exhaustion linked to the fast pace of modern urban life. Thus although coca had begun as a brain worker's salve, by the 1890s its use was spreading across (or down) the social (and racial) spectrum, sometimes by way of concoctions spiked instead with pure cocaine.[10] Pioneering American drug firms, such as Detroit's Parke-Davis Company, specialized in coca medicines. Dozens of leading U.S. physicians experimented with, wrote on, and debated the benefits of coca (and later cocaine), though its appeal derived mainly from the herbalist or eclectic healer tradition, still a vibrant alternative to European-style allopathic medicine. The American romance with coca resonates in Dr. W. Golden Mortimer's classic 1901 tome *History of Coca: "The Divine Plant" of the Incas* (still a wonderful source on coca) and of course lives on in our coca-laced national soft drink, Coca-Cola, launched in 1886 as a dry southern imitation of Mariani's popular health beverage and one of modernity's pioneering consumer commodities. By the early 1900s, the United States imported 600–1,000 metric tons of coca annually, mainly for this popular market.

The United States actively promoted the trade in Andean coca. In 1877, besides modest Bolivian sales, Peru exported only 8,000 kilograms of coca. When coca grew scarce from 1884 to 1887, debates on its supply raged in American pharmacy journals and domestic growing schemes were suggested. Parke-Davis sent its pioneer ethnobotanist, Henry Hurd Rusby—a towering figure in American pharmacy—on a legendary mission to scout out supplies, processing methods, and native coca therapies in Bolivia. The U.S. Navy and consuls in La Paz and Lima worked to identify and secure coca supply routes. In the 1890s, U.S. commercial attachés in Lima honed contacts with local cocaine makers (even the German Kitz) and helped Peruvians to upgrade their shipping and leaf-drying techniques. Peruvian coca producers responded well to these signs and to market signals, more than doubling their coca exports during the 1890s. Bolivia, saddled with tortuous transport costs, gradually dropped out of overseas sales, and by 1910 was focusing on regional commerce to migrant coqueros in Bolivia, northern Argentina, Chile, and even southern Peru.

American pharmaceutical companies and physicians reacted enthusiastically to the discovery of cocaine's anesthetic powers in 1884 and tested its gamut of modern medical uses (though soon enough they realized cocaine's dangers and illicit lures). By the mid-1890s, major firms—among them Parke-Davis, Schlieffelin, Mallinkrodt, and the New Jersey branch of Merck—competed vigorously with German suppliers.[11] By 1900, they refined a total of five to six metric tons of cocaine, about a third of the world supply; total U.S. consumption (including imports from Europe) peaked at around nine tons in 1903, or some two-thirds of all global usage of some fifteen tons. Even tariff politics played their part: high effective tariffs on cocaine, with herbal coca entering free, decidedly favored home production of cocaine from imported leaf. Peruvian cocaine processors themselves perceived this bias. American consumers' taste for coca, expanding with the spectacular success of Coca-Cola and countless imitators after 1900, and cheaper and faster shipments from the Andes deterred the United States from following the Germans in switching to large-scale imports of Peruvian crude cocaine.

Indeed, after 1900 U.S. buyers focused increasingly on a distinctive northern coca-leaf circuit in western La Libertad, instead of Huánuco's Amazonian cocaine lands or the Cuzco's Indian-leaf zone. Grown under drier conditions, Trujillo-branded leaf was deemed more flavorful, less alkaloid, and best for tonics, such as the secret "Merchandise No. 5" used in Coca-Cola. In fact, it was a German national, Louis Schaefer (a Boehringer chemist sent to Lima in 1885), jumping across chains, who established this business in the United States, which was soon transformed into Maywood Chemical Works, Coca-Cola's chief syrup intermediary with Peru. La Libertad's Sacamanca and Otuzco districts evolved into the long-term supply shed of its leaf, prepared specially for Coca-Cola, organized and managed by the regional merchant clans of Goicochea and Pinillos.[12] In short, the German and North American chains developed around different cultural, medical, business, and political principles and were even articulated to distinguishable zones and networks within the Andes.

Finally, one need note the initial impact of Americans' fervor against cocaine. Americans' growing fear and loathing of cocaine (and less rationally of coca) was the flip side to their early enthusiasm. Cocaine was symptomatic of the love-hate "American disease" of drugs as cure-all and scourge, to paraphrase the medical historian David F. Musto. By 1900, dominant medical, reformer, and governmental opinion began to turn against licit coca and cocaine, along with alcohol and true narcotics, and especially against spreading illicit use by the "dope fiends" of the racialized underclass.[13] By 1915, the United States had become a lonely crusader against cocaine, portraying Germany as an evil drug empire. U.S. controls of coca and cocaine, legally erected between 1906 and 1922, had many paradoxical effects, many still with us today, such as the prohibition of harmless coca leaf. As cocaine demand became regulated and reduced, using an intricate system of coca controls, the outcome was a high degree of cooperation between the state and pharmaceutical companies in defining the trade. Indeed, by the 1920s only two New Jersey firms—now fully nationalized Merck and the Maywood Chemical Works, Coca-Cola's partner—dealt with coca and cocaine, and the business assumed a monopoly character. In effect, for control purposes U.S. legislation systematized the long-standing American penchant for leaf imports.[14] The result was a cartel-like state-governed coca chain—in that sense, not so different from the formally cartelized European chain of cocaine. By 1910, global coca—in two distinctive chains tied to differing product zones in the Andes—came under conflicting pressures.

Divvying up Global Coca, 1910–1950

The period from 1910 to 1950 represents cocaine's declining middle age, between the drug's licit peak and its full global prohibition. From production of fifteen tons or more in 1905, total use was probably halved by 1930; by 1950 the U.N. set legal world medicinal needs at under four metric tons. Three factors drove this steady fall: a decline in medical usage (anesthesia) by substitutes and in medical opinion; anticocaine laws and campaigns by states and international organizations (whose efforts were focused mainly on narcotics); and withdrawal from the market and diversification of vulnerable producers and coca planters. As yet, illicit cocaine barely compensated for market blockage, after its fleeting emergence from surplus pharmaceutical stocks from the 1910s to the early 1920s. The United States, the largest consumer market, initiated national restrictions with the 1906 FDA Act, which was followed by a federal ban in the 1914 Harrison Act and a full-fledged import control system by 1922.[15] Less successfully, the

United States also pushed global cocaine controls at the Hague conventions of 1912–14 and at successive Geneva antinarcotics conventions sponsored by the League of Nations starting in 1924–25.

Rather than go away, cocaine divided into a new trio of politically structured and geographically defined global commodity chains. The first was a Dutch colonial mercantilist Java-Europe chain, which by 1915 swiftly displaced Peruvian producers. The second was Japan's state-sponsored pan-Asian circuit, launched in the 1920s in reaction to League and industrial imperatives. The third chain was the residual United States–Andes nexus: increasingly linked to corporate privilege (mainly Coca-Cola) and drug control (under Harry Anslinger's Federal Bureau of Narcotics) and on the Peruvian end dividing into coca and cocaine circuits and contending national projects. This market encrustation is hardly unexpected for such a declining and politicized commodity. Global markets of coca and cocaine, built in the prior period, ceased to exist.

The Dutch Colonial Coca Boom, 1905–1930

The rapid rise of the Dutch to prominence in the world coca and cocaine trades took interested parties by surprise, especially the Peruvians, who until 1900 felt they enjoyed a natural birthright to the world coca market. In 1904 the Dutch island of Java (now a part of Indonesia) exported only 26 tons of coca leaf; this figure soared to 800 tons in 1912 and to 1,700 tons in 1920, glutting the world market. The Dutch built an especially productive and integrated industrial cocaine regime, but it was dismantled by decree almost as quickly as it arose.

Dutch scientific and commercial interest in coca dates to the 1850s, and plantings began in the mid-1880s, when such botanical experiments spread among the European colonial powers. One advantage was accidental: the abnormally high-alkaloid coca bush Javanese planters received from the colonial botanical gardens at Buitenzorg descended from one special strand of *Erythroxylon novogranatense*, obtained from Kew. It contained twice the cocaine content of quality Huánuco leaf (up to 1.5 percent), but in a form so difficult to refine that it was practically useless for herbal coca products. Given Peru's swift entry into crude cocaine in the 1885–1900 era, not much interest was evinced in Javanese coca, though small lots reached European buyers.

After 1900, several factors refocused Dutch interest in coca, spurred on by national botanical specialists like A. W. K. de Jong and Emma Reens. One was the establishment in 1900 of Amsterdam's large Nederlandsch Cocainefabrieck, subsidized by the state bank, which took advantage of patented German technology to extract cocaine from coca leaves imported from Java. The second factor was steady investment in the productivity of plantations and the quality of their yields. Cheaper Asian field labor, four annual harvests, economies of scale and technical rationalization, and intercropping with colonial rubber and tea projects, all made the efficient Javanese plantations outpace the haphazard peasant-style coca culture of the Andes. By 1911 they captured a quarter of the world market, filtered through Amsterdam into a high-margin fully integrated cocaine industry (see Table 6.1.2).[16] The disruptions of World War I spurred Europeans to rely more heavily on this coca corridor. Dutch industrial-grade coca also made it to Japan, Belgium, France, and even the United States. In the 1920s, impressed by its reliable quality, New

Jersey Merck acquired its own plantation in Java, which performed well into the 1930s. Three world cores of industrial cocaine now existed: Darmstadt, northern New Jersey, and Amsterdam, with an enlarged Nederlandsch Cocainefabrieck (NCF), the biggest single producer. Together they dramatically reduced prospects for Peruvian coca (wiped off European markets from 1908 to 1915) and crude cocaine, now confined to depressed German processors. The values of Peruvian coca and cocaine exports dropped by some 95 percent by the 1920s. Peruvians watched these developments haplessly, having neither the time, the capital, nor the expertise to respond.[17]

Paradoxically, almost as quickly as it arose the Dutch cocaine network receded. By 1920, Javanese coca basically satisfied the full world demand (twelve tons) for cocaine; prices plummeted and revenues zigzagged throughout the 1920s. To diversify, the NCF even began to make novocaine, cocaine's closest and fully synthetic substitute. Price controls emerged to manage the surplus. Assisted by the League of Nations (interested mainly in drug-control formulas), a new formal European cocaine syndicate, the European Convention of Cocaine Producers, was formed in 1924, with eight members. It included the Nederlandsch Cocainefabrieck and the three largest German makers, with only small domestic French, British, German, and Russian firms still apart. At first this development signified more planned purchases from Java but also steadily declining cocaine quotas. A Dutch national Association of Coca Producers also formed, which soon worked to downsize itself and diversify into alternative crops. In the late 1920s, Dutch production systematically fell. From 1929 to 1931, in contradictory political moves, the Netherlands opted to comply with the export controls of the League's Geneva Manufacturing Limitation Accord, despite unhappiness with the United States' drug crusade, in part to protect its colonial opium monopolists. With a tiny home market, the annual output of the NCF withered to 250–300 kilos.[18] Japan's invasion of Java in World War II snapped the chain, and the subsequent U.S.

Table 6.1.2   Coca Exports from Java, 1904–1935 (kilograms)

YEAR	COCA	YEAR	COCA	YEAR	COCA
1904	25,836	1915	1,089,076	1926	1,043,000
1905	67,000	1916	407,984	1927	709,000
1906	122,000	1917	271,911	1928	385,000
1907	200,000	1918	661,968	1929	585,000
1908	417,000	1919	994,203	1930	354,000
1909	373,000	1920	1,676,621	1931	304,000
1910	430,000	1921	1,137,373	1932	209,000
1911	750,000	1922	1,283,503	1933	161,000
1912	1,075,000	1923	907,335	1934	105,000
1913	1,332,000	1924	1,118,000	1935	125,000
1914	1,353,270	1925	1,008,000		

Note: 1,000 kilograms = 1 metric ton.
Source: D. F. Musto, "International Traffics in Coca through the Early Twentieth Century," *Drug and Alcohol Dependence* 49 (1998): Table 5.

occupation led to the mandated destruction of remaining coca plants in Java. It had been a brief but spectacular political marriage of state, industry, and colonial planter. (And a reminder today that coca could easily escape the Andes for other tropical realms if pressures mount.)

Japanese Imperial Cocaine

Even less is known about Japan's cocaine network of the 1920s and 1930s than about the Netherlands'. It may have been spurred by the Dutch example, as well as by intriguing chain crossings. By the 1930s, Japan was one of the largest producers and purveyors of cocaine to Southeast Asia, although the size (and legality) of this state-sanctioned trade remain clouded in controversy.

The first Japanese involvements with coca and cocaine were responses to Western initiatives. Jokichi Takamine, a brilliant Japanese chemist (still known for synthesizing adrenaline), had worked for Parke-Davis in the 1890s, at the height of the firm's cocaine age, and brought his expertise back to Japan's expanding Sankyo Pharmaceuticals; he became its vice president in the late 1910s. Colonial sugar interests in Formosa (Taiwan) began to invest in coca around the same time; processors purchased Javanese and Peruvian coca and crude cocaine until they achieved self-sufficiency in the 1930s. In 1917, Hoshi Pharmaceuticals actually acquired a major coca tract smack in the middle of Peru's Huallaga valley, the Tulumayo property; it was a source not only of quality coca but probably also of know-how about the larger business. Other firms developed plantations in Java.[19] Another influence was a group of German pharmaceutical firms that used Japanese companies for shadow transshipments (banned to China) from 1912, when export controls on opiates and cocaine were imposed, through the 1920s. Given the surplus of cocaine in Europe, these transfers became substantial: some years saw more than 4,000 pounds of cocaine pass through Japan in this semilicit trade.

Japan's role in narcotics in general has been read in two contrary ways. International warnings were sounded from the start. In one sense, drug trafficking fitted Japan's Asian-oriented industrialization process and expansive trade sphere. Japan sought self-sufficiency after the trade disruptions of World War I, and close relationships of the state and large firms were a basic feature of Japanese business culture. Pharmaceuticals represented an important element of scientific modernization. To the Japanese, drug exports were a normal business. Japan—which never experienced a domestic drug scare—did not share in the Western ideal of demarcating illicit and legal substances (and later, of course, left the League of Nations). A second view—rooted in concerns of the United States and the League during the 1920s and in testimony at the Tokyo war crimes trials—sees Japan's involvement as extraordinary or nefarious. It was based on deliberate deception (to Western drug-control bodies) and on militarist or imperialist profiteering in illicit sales across Asia.[20] Without falling into conspiratorial Japan bashing, we can at least think of the Japanese chain as emerging from the shadows of growing League jurisdictions over drugs. An increasingly autonomous Asian coca and cocaine network appeared from 1920 to 1945.

By 1920, Japan itself produced more than 4,000 pounds of cocaine, which then doubled to 8,000 by 1922. Official figures for the 1930s shrank to just under 2,000 pounds, though League officials and some historians believe that figure was doctored for external consumption. (This is a hard charge to prove, though Steven Karch has tried to prove it.) Exports across Asia officially dropped to negligible levels, though complaints were registered about Japanese firms and reporting practices, as well as reports of smuggling, such as the vials branded "Fujitsuru" and "Taiwan Governor" in India. Some specialists have noted diplomatic cooperation between Japan and international drug officials, at least until the invasions of Manchuria and China, where opiate sales became a contentious issue. The firms that made cocaine and morphine were among Japan's largest: Hoshi, Sankyo, Koto, and Shiongo Pharmaceuticals, which enjoyed growing links to major trading trusts (such as Mitsui and Mitsubishi) and to interlocking governmental, colonial, and military officials. We know that in 1934, Taiwan's Kagi district kept 694 acres under intensive coca cultivation as earlier plots on Iwo Jima and Okinawa were abandoned. Formosa harvested some 300,000 pounds of leaf annually in the late 1930s, mainly for the Taiwan Drug Manufacturing Co. Ltd. Imports of Peruvian leaf were officially discontinued in 1938 (in fact, Peru nationalized Tulumayo, which had a colorful subsequent history of its own).[21]

By World War II, the whole pharmaceutical industry, self-sufficient in imperial Japan, came under the government's jurisdiction. In that sense, if cocaine was indeed marketed for nonmedical purposes across occupied Asia—and the evidence mainly concerns opiates—the state bore responsibility. In any case, the Taiwanese coca industry was demolished by war and the Japanese pharmaceutical sector was reorganized, without cocaine, under the American occupation in 1945 (its previous practices an explicit charge of U.S. war tribunals). A two-decade autonomous coca sphere abruptly ended.

The United States–Andes Chain, 1910–1950

The United States–Peru chain, despite these competitors and its relative quantitative decline, proved to be the most resilient and significant in the long term. Modern trade in coca and cocaine germinated in Peru in the 1890s, with North America the defining consumer market; the United States' anticocaine policies of the early twentieth century incubated in this peculiar relationship. And in the 1960s and 1970s, when illicit cocaine took off, the new chain began in eastern Peru and worked its way famously to Miami and Hollywood. This is the historically central cocaine chain, even if it was marked by the shrinking of legal exchange during most of the century.

Aggregate statistics—the decline seen from Peru—show that coca trades, mainly to the United States, fell from an average 584,000 kilos (over a million pounds) in 1909–13 to 242,000 in 1919–23 to 128,000 in 1929–33, before climbing to the 300,000–400,000-pound range during World War II (for emergency war uses). Crude cocaine exports, mainly from greater Huánuco, fell from over 10 metric tons in their peak (1903–4, mainly to Germany) to one ton (i.e., 1,000 kilos) in 1927 and to an unstable 200–900 kilos throughout the 1930s (see Table 6.1.3). By the 1920s, no crude cocaine entered the United States (its import was strictly prohibited by law), but Peruvians had new buyers in Japan and France (and in about ten other countries that kept small national alkaloid lines). But by the mid-1930s, a politically risky

Germany, with six firms still making cocaine, was effectively Peru's sole remaining cocaine customer. Combined export revenues slumped below 200,000 soles throughout the 1930s. Because of falling prices, the total drop in the values of coca and cocaine exports was more than nine-tenths of their early twentieth-century peak. It was a shattering collapse, especially given the initial national hopes for cocaine. Economically, coca and cocaine became marginal for Peru, except in a few regions.

Peru's coca and cocaine circuits became reconfigured, as can be seen by a survey of coca regions. (Bolivia's production was now confined entirely to traditional or borderlands users.) The notable fact is that as the Peruvian cocaine industry came under market and legal constraints, it neither modernized itself into an integrated or technologically upgraded industry, as some people called for it to do, nor switched to illicit trade (which appeared nowhere until the 1950s).

Table 6.1.3 Peruvian exports of coca and crude cocaine, 1877–1933 (kilograms)

YEAR	COCA	COCAINE	YEAR	COCA	COCAINE
1877	8,000		1914	477,648	979
1888	29,000	1,730	1915	393,404	1,353
1890	6,677	930	1916	265,834	1,576
1891	128,543	3,215	1917	306,535	1,896
1892	377,762	4,550	1918	167,449	2,967
1897	494,000	4,200	1919	385,583	596
1898	406,718	4,346	1920	453,067	1,637
1899	312,112	4,500	1921	87,849	157
1900	565,730	7,745	1922	124,357	778
1901	610,100	10,688	1923	190,000	192
1902	933,284	8,268	1924	169,850	967
1903	1,026,000	10,000	1925	216,714	621
1904	911,000	9,500	1926	204,209	1,048
1905	1,489,598	6,788	1927	142,797	980
1906	1,210,652	5,914	1928	150,092	625
1907	654,103	6,057	1929	101,273	236
1909	496,328	5,266	1930	191,609	–
1910	495,729	5,524	1931	169,524	246
1911	768,017	5,434	1932	96,647	420
1912	769,751	2,944	1933	85,721	918
1913	392,918	3,267			

Source: D. F. Musto, "International Traffic in Coca through the Early Twentieth Century," *Drug and Alcohol Dependence* 49 (1998): Table 6, p. 153.

A major shift was the move of coca leaf back to the home market of traditional users. During the boom of the late 1890s, as much as a quarter of Peru's coca was reported in export channels (though that figure is questionable); by the 1930s and 1940s the tradable share was far smaller, around 3 percent by most estimates. In part, this market involution reflected the steady multiplication of Peru's rural folk and their intensified migratory labor during the twentieth century. Coca for traditional uses went from under 4.8 million kilos in the mid-1920s to 5.4 million by 1930 to over 6 million by 1940, and to 8–11 million kilos by the 1950s. Regionally, this surge translated into an advancing coca frontier, heralded by national agronomists, mainly to the newer southern tropical regions (especially Cuzco's La Convención valley), close to the indigenous "Mancha India." In the early 1940s, in a crude guess, one expert estimated Peru's entire leaf crop at 6.8 million pounds, with 6 million used by the nation's 2 million male chewers (women, who certainly did use coca, didn't count). Peru's triad of internal coca circuits were defined as northern (La Libertad, largely for export for cola flavorings), at 1.6 million pounds, or 19 percent of the total crop; central (greater Huánuco, for crude cocaine and central regional leaf trades), at 2.24 million pounds, or 34.5 percent; and southern (mostly Cuzco) at 3 million, or 46.5 percent. Even the coca specialists evidently jumbled the numbers; for example, confusing here pounds and kilos.[22] Seen as regional networks, northern leaf growers (in the Otuzco and Sacamanca districts) remained tied to the powerful Pinillos export clan, who exported two-thirds of local coca crops to Maywood Chemical, Coca-Cola's agent in the trade. Spotty experiments in crude cocaine making also registered in the north. In the center, Huánuco's economic hub remained crude cocaine, however depressed and technologically backward, as its traditional elite lost hold. Now local Chinese merchants plied provincial coca trades to the upland mining town of Junín, and new peasant-driven coca frontiers were opening up in Monzón and downstream Tingo María. About six to ten crude cocaine workshops, still using Kitz's techniques from the 1890s, carried on the industry, basically part-time, mainly on demand; that is, for special orders from abroad. They were led by a new regional magnet, Andrés Avelino Soberón, a merchant with close ties to German consigners but always struggling to diversify (even into the closed United States cocaine market). The third zone around southern Cuzco was less strategic with low-alkaloid home-market leaf and was the sole area that saw campaigns to upgrade coca agricultural practices among colonizing hacendados.

Peruvian politics of coca and cocaine after 1910 were also related to developments at the other end of the chain. In a great turnabout between 1905 and 1925, foreign campaigns against cocaine filtered to Peru via science, politics, and markets. In medical science, the new idea of cocaine as a poisonous or addictive narcotic paradoxically mutated in Peru into growing sentiments against coca as backward or harmful to national development. Combined with racism against the country's Indian majority, this view fueled a novel hygienics movement against coca by the 1930s, since toxic coca "degenerated" Peru's "Indian race." Cocaine, ironically, was still considered a modern or model Western good, with no local abuse. Peruvian officials actively ignored pressures from the United States and the League of Nations to restrict cocaine and coca after 1920.[23] In part defending Huánuco interests, officials sincerely felt that global antidrug campaigns discriminated against a Peruvian product. By the mid-1920s, Peruvian health officials embraced a few modern narcotics controls, but only in the mid-1940s did such regulation be-come transformed into police functions, in a prelude to the actual criminalizing of legal cocaine making in 1947–49. Meanwhile, during the 1930s a vociferous countermovement arose, led by Dr. Carlos Enrique Paz Soldán, to nationalize and modernize the entire coca and cocaine industry in a large state monopoly, in outright resistance to encroaching global constraints on cocaine. One of Peru's most respected and outspoken medical figures, Paz Soldán was appalled by cocaine's falling fortunes as well as spreading coca use by the Indian peasants. The idea, which had deep local appeal, was for Peru to face the world as the sole sanctioned exporter of medicinal cocaine hydrochloride. Although the United States opposed this statist scheme, during World War II Merck's cocaine specialist, Emile Pilli, also lobbied for modernization of the industry, including home production of "pure salts" of cocaine. Thus external market and political pressures led to schizophrenic and increasingly statist discourses on coca and cocaine. Commodity segmentation worked in strange ways.

The United States still managed the far end of this hemispheric chain (save for the shrink-ing Hamburg entrepôt until the eve of World War II) with increasingly defined drug controls around coca and cocaine. The chief characteristics of the United States' cocaine network were specialization in coca chains (and "de-cocainized" coca syrup); state-assisted monopolies in cocaine processing; a total (and largely effective) prohibition in the domestic market; and the intensification of global campaigns against still-licit coca and cocaine elsewhere. However, global prohibitions bore fruit only after World War II with the destruction of the three extant chains, Dutch, Japanese, and German, and Peru's entry into the Allied political sphere. The United States had been the undisputed world capital of coca and cocaine use and a pioneer in the popular abuse of cocaine, and after 1910 it worked passionately to reverse that equation. There is little doubt that illicit (as well as medicinal) use of cocaine largely dried up in the United States after 1920, though the reasons remain unclear. Popular coca products were successfully eliminated, with the notable exception of booming and now cocaine-free Coca-Cola (the com-pany voluntarily de-cocainized its coca leaf after 1903). One factor was a political economy of control that emerged out of the prior North American penchant for coca leaf and (by 1920) the concentration of coca handling in two firms, New Jersey Merck and nearby Maywood Chemical, Coca-Cola's ally.[24] Rather than regulate thousands of pharmacists, dentists, and physicians at the retail level, the United States pinched cocaine at the top. By 1920, these two firms had become close intermediaries of the emerging federal antidrug bureaucracy (the Federal Bureau of Narcotics, or FBN), trading in intelligence and favors and ensuring that only bulky supervised coca leaf entered the port of New York. Every detail of the distillation process—of Merchandise No. 5, Coca-Cola's secret extract, made by Maywood from Trujillo leaf, and of Merck's high-grade medicinal cocaine—was tightly regulated by the FBN. For a long time this system functioned well, hastening the disappearance of illicit cocaine in the 1920s as well as helping to ensure the monopoly successes of Coca-Cola against competitors (and its monopsony with Peruvian coca dealers). Coke and Maywood focused exclusively on northern Peru, forging a closed

Table 6.1.4   U.S. coca imports: medicinal (cocaine) and nonmedicinal (cola), 1925–1959 (kilograms)

YEAR	COCA LEAVES		
	TOTAL IMPORTS	MEDICINAL	NONMEDICINAL
1925	72,254.578	72,254.578	
1926	133,347.054	133,347.054	
1927	114,594.886	114,594.886	
1928	110,667.347	110,667.347	
1929	61,617.962	61,617.962	
1930	89,699.155	89,699.153	
1931	221,235.522	122,748.931	98,486.591
1932	101,624.340	101,624.340	
1933	81,699.046	81,699.046	
1934	85,551.171	81,070.364	4,480.807
1935	110,330.782	94,468.901	15,861.881
1936	171,389.634	101,855.814	69,533.820
1937	189,598.231	101,384.362	88,213.869
1938	208,581.675	101,041.220	107,540.455
1939	263,814.726	123,138.430	140,676.296
1940	352,200.544	146,189.403	206,011.141
1941	420,388.955	127,484.210	292,904.745
1942	360,655.921	80,849.520	270,806.401
1943	447,395.986	207,408.941	239,987.045
1944	202,057.238	67,555.235	134,501.985
1945	316,224.374	45,359.188	270,865.186
1946	228,782.927	90,718.971	138,063.956
1947	315,237.057	180,183.930	135,053.127
1948	289,375.064	289,375.064	
1949	142,078.358	142,078.358	
1950	112,742.530	112,742.530	
1951	130,849.918	130,849.918	
1952	112,354.213	112,354.213	
1953	150,183.138	150,183.138	
1954	125,392.754	125,392.754	
1955	141,290.354	141,290.354	
1956	184,095.849	184,095.849	
1957	90,482.508	90,482.508	
1958	112,501.219	112,501.219	
1959	135,222.544	135,222.544	

Note: Cola leaf not clearly separated before 1930; separate reporting (but not imports) ceases after 1947.
Source: U.S. Department of Treasury, Federal Bureau of Narcotics, *Traffic in Opium and Other Dangerous Drugs in the Year 1960* (Washington: GPO, 1960), Table 10.

corporate-family commodity chain with the Pinillos clan; they even won their imports their own congressional judicial status, as "special-leaf imports." As legal and illegal cocaine dwindled and addiction to Coca-Cola rose, these special nonmedicinal imports grew to an ever larger portion of Peruvian coca shipments. By World War II, the United States consumed twice as much coca in beverages (more than 200,000 kilos annually) than was used in making residual medicinal cocaine (see Table 6.1.4). By the mid-1920s, a diversified Merck, the monopoly U.S. cocaine maker, turned to imported leaf from its own plantations in Tjitembong, Java, in effect building its own in-house state-governed coca-cocaine commodity chain. Merck looked to Peru only during the war; by the mid-1950s, seeing little use, it gave up making cocaine altogether and simply bought and distributed Maywood's legal Coca-Cola cocaine residue. In effect, all American cocaine became a byproduct of the Coca-Cola empire.

American cocaine politics abroad was partly a sideshow of a more general antinarcotics diplomacy, by which the United States, with few colonial interests, became the main force behind the erection and extension of an idealistic world system of cocaine prohibitions, via ongoing Geneva conventions of the League of Nations. The first targets were the Germans, then the Japanese, and finally after 1945 the errant Peru and Bolivia. To some extent this campaign slowly worked by defining and shrinking legitimate cocaine spheres after 1920; it also backfired, by spurring the expansive Japanese shadow chain. Overall, the interwar period represents the greatest paradox in drug control: while a multiplicity of legal global cocaine chains existed, the United States experienced an idyllic era in respect to cocaine as an active domestic social problem. Moreover, the United States still exerted little or no limiting control at the periphery—in coca-growing areas—the stated goal of American diplomats since 1915. In the 1920s and 1930s, partly to pressure Peru and partly to support Coca-Cola, U.S. officials began taking a deep interest in Peruvian coca and cocaine. The main achievement was cultivating an FBN–State Department drug-intelligence web in Peru, facilitated by the contacts of Maywood and Coca-Cola Company executives. Slowly, more and more North American notions of modern drug control filtered to Peru, despite the Peruvians' (and Bolivians') resistance to imported anticoca ideals.[25] FBN records reveal scant direct American meddling in Andean drug policies before World War II, though a good deal thereafter. However, in a larger sense the United States structured the options available for Peru in this realm by its ban on cocaine imports, by curtailing world markets, and by obstructing national schemes of drug control.

World War II was the turning point. During the war itself—significant for commodity chains of all kinds—the United States severed Peru's participation in the Japanese and German markets, and Japanese-occupied Java fell off the Western map. The United States' focus fell on Peru just as Good Neighbor ties multiplied during the course of the conflict, and afterward intensified with the advent of the Cold War. Cocaine became defined strategically within the wartime meanings of "licit" and "contraband" trades. Collaborating agents from the United States and Peru began watching all facets of the network.[26] By 1945, even many Peruvian officials saw the need for restrictions on coca and cocaine and recognized the commercial dead end of Huánuco's limping industry under the United States' postwar hegemony. An anticoca consensus gathered at the new

American-inspired United Nations drug agencies, exemplified by the U.N.'s touring Commission of Enquiry into the Problem of Coca Leaf in 1947. Peru, under the anticommunist military regime of Manuel Odría, rushed dramatically in 1947–49 to outlaw the making of cocaine and began, at least on paper, to regulate the Indian coca bush under the auspices of a newly declared national coca monopoly. Thus in 1950 ended—at least in its licit market phase—a commodity chain born almost a century before.

Such were the commodity chains developed by licit coca and cocaine during their rise and demise as modern global drugs between 1860 and 1950. These were not simply interconnected markets of supply and demand, but institutionalized channels for the flow of science and medicine, political ideas, information and influences and varied attempts at monopoly and drug control. They were segmented by changing cultural tastes and by shifting colonial and neocolonial spheres. They reflected varied levels and forms of international power as well, between motley unequal actors and relationships involved in the growing, processing, marketing, regulation, and use and misuse of these substances. They were even discursive links, as cocaine shifted from a heroic modernizing commodity to a marginal one of rival spheres, until its postwar construction as menacing illicit substance, powered by a feudal rhetoric of criminality and violence.[27] In many ways over the long run, these commodity chains and the tensions along and between them helped create the initial legitimacy of coca and cocaine in the nineteenth-century market, and helped structure their progressive illicitness over the twentieth century.

Illicit Cocaine Chains, 1950–2000

Since 1950, in some sense, commodity chains of coca and cocaine have become both more and less market-driven phenomena, and this illicit boom may indeed reflect, as some cynics suggest, the revenge of the coca periphery. This era is the transnational stuff of covert police records and drug-culture legends, portrayed in Hollywood's *Traffic* and *Blow*. After 1950, Andean cocaine, outlawed everywhere, escaped all state regulation and carved out its own underground niches and chains, invoking a cast of new criminalized actors. Clearly, except to politically blinded officials of the Drug Enforcement Administration (DEA), it was government and international prohibitions that pushed cocaine so radically into illicit free markets. One intriguing plot line of the story is that once cocaine was proscribed, Cold War circuits of illicit cocaine basically reverted to their original geographic spaces in the eastern Amazon and to historic links with the United States. The jungle export *pasta básica* of cocaine of the 1970s was essentially Bignon's and Kitz's old 1890s crude cocaine sulfates, now forwarded to outside criminal refiners in Colombia rather than to Merck chemists in Darmstadt. A few seasoned specialists of the Huánuco industry reinvented themselves as pioneers of illicit cocaine, which hardly existed before, though land-hungry peasants rather than regional elites became the true driving force behind this new kind of coca expansion. With the declassification of DEA archives, one can trace such developments back to 1950, to precisely the point where the trail of legal cocaine peters out.[28] Underground cocaine blazed a sinuous path across Peru and Bolivia in the 1950s and 1960s, marked by intensifying struggles between U.S. drug agents and aspiring Andean entrepreneurs, experimenting with smuggling routes through Chile, Cuba, Brazil, Panama, Mexico, and taste-testing incipient coke markets in Havana and New York City. A culture and a chain of illicit cocaine were constructed between 1950 and 1973, their paths set by politics and risk profits rather than by efficiency or factors of production. They were pushed to the fore by American pressures well before the deluge of the 1970s, as glimpsed in mounting quantities of Andean "coke" seized at U.S. borders from the late 1950s on.

After 1970, cocaine flooded into the United States to fill in the market niches carved out by speed, heroin, and marihuana, popular products of the 1960s drug culture, under siege in Richard Nixon's declared crackdown on drugs. Coke surfaced among the elite of Hollywood and the rock scene, who liberally publicized their new gourmet "soft" drug. Colombians of Medellín, well-located entrepreneurs under a weak state, soon consolidated as the core middlemen in this trade, re-fining and passing on with spectacular markups Peruvian and Bolivian peasant product to a diaspora of far-flung Colombian sellers in Miami and New York. As the United States invigorated its suppression of cocaine after 1980, huge segmented retail markets were discovered (middle America, ghetto crack, Dominican gangs) and coca frontiers for illicit export spread massively into the deep jungle recesses of the Huallaga Valley and Bolivia's Chaparé. Further steps against cocaine—wholesale eradication campaigns since the drug wars during the administrations of Ronald Reagan and George H. W. Bush—have led to spirals of illicit production and violence and steep drops in prices, precisely the opposite of the United States' stated objectives. Chains shifted, too: the rerouting of smuggling in the 1980s, at one time from Medellín to Miami, then from Cali to northern Mexico, obeyed the basic laws of drug suppression and commodity chains.

By the early 1990s, illicit cocaine commanded an estimated productive capacity in the range of 1,000 metric tons in a chain involving hundreds of thousands of employees (farmers, processors, guards, money launderers, corrupted officials, smugglers, street dealers, and rehab councilors) along the route, with millions of avid consumers throughout the world and revenues ranging from $50 billion to $100 billion annually. This volume was a hundred times greater than Peru's peak legal cocaine output in 1900, and with the premium in price guaranteed by its prohibition, cocaine has taken its place among the most valuable single commodity chains in world history.[29] Since the late 1970s, the coca crop sown for illicit export has dwarfed domestic-use low-potency leaf for the first time in coca's long history. It is the most dramatic commodity network ever pio-neered by Latin American peasants and businessmen. In some ways coca culture is comparable to coffee culture, but it raises serious issues as to why such a lucrative export success story, inequities and all, is found only in Latin America's illicit commerce. Half of the world's 14 million regular cocaine users are North Americans, white and black, rich and poor, who snort some 250–300 tons yearly. In their use of the product they surpass surviving indigenous coqueros of the Andes, who now probably number fewer than five million, despite a recent revalorization of ritual use. Coca is used in a few minor commercial Peruvian and Bolivian concoctions (teas, toothpaste, and the like). Save for Coca-Cola's, there are no legal international exports.

The current stage, starting in the mid-1990s, has largely pushed illicit coca out of eastern Peru and Bolivia into southern Colombia, and trans-shippers are fleeing Mexico for more dispersed Caribbean sites. This chain is just unfolding, given the pressure exerted by the United States on Colombia to stop the flow of cocaine and now heroin. Reports suggest that overall capacity peaked around 2001 and that coca is again being planted in Peru and Bolivia. New links are being forged through Brazil (a huge emerging consumer capital) and southern Africa and on to the third-ranked markets in Europe and fragments of the former Soviet empire. Illicit cocaine, goaded on by foolhardy drug policies, could end up replicating the geography of early-twentieth-century commodity coca, globalized to such exotic venues as Indonesia, Taiwan, and West Africa—indeed, anywhere helicopters and herbicides don't yet reach.

Notes

Laura Sainz, my spouse, helped this essay happen by caring for Dany; Domenica Tafuro worked on the tables. Thanks to participants at the two symposiums on Latin America and global commodity chains (Stanford, 2001; Buenos Aires, 2002), particularly David McCreery and Steve Topik, for incisive comments, and to Steve for taking cocaine as the serious commodity it is.

1 See Gootenberg, ed., *Cocaine*, 12–14, for economic vs. poststructural views of drugs; the volume is organized by global commodity chains. For global drugs, see Stares, *Global Habit*; Pomeranz and Topik, *The World That Trade Created*, chap. 3. A new working group of the Social Science Research Council, Beyond Borders, studies illicit economies as commodity flows.

2 Gereffi and Korzeniewicz, eds., *Commodity Chains and Global Capitalism*; Bellone, "The Cocaine Commodity Chain and Development Paths in Peru and Bolivia." Appadurai, ed., *The Social Life of Things*, discusses "commodity ecumene"; Mintz, *Sweetness and Power*, discusses the cultural life of commodities.

3 A work on aggregates is Musto, "International Traffic in Coca through the Early Twentieth Century"—a team effort to collate global statistics on historical coca trades. A commodity chain approach can correct flaws in such aggregates by stressing differences in providence and flows rather than artificially standardized quantities. Example: using a poorly defined "cocaine equivalent" (based on reduction of all coca commerce to a standard cocaine alkaloid content), Musto ignores robust regional trade in coca leaf for traditional use (chewing in Bolivia) or coca preparations (such as beverage syrups from northern Peru for the United States and Europe). He overestimates world cocaine consumption in the early twentieth century and underestimates the social significance of alternative coca trades.

4 Goodman, *Tobacco in History*, 49–51; Schivelbusch, *Tastes of Paradise*; Kennedy, *Coca Exotica*, chaps. 5–7. For a "commodity" look at drugs, see Courtwright, *Forces of Habit*.

5 Freud, *Cocaine Papers*. See Kennedy, *Coca Exotica*, 57–58, for an account of the *Novara* mission.

6 Martindale, *Coca, Cocaine and Its Salts*, 388–92. French coca culture needs research, though there are popular essays on Mariani and his famed advertising.

7 Friman, "Germany and the Transformation of Cocaine"; Rusby, *Jungle Memories*, chaps. 1, 8; "Production and Use of Coca Leaves" and "Exports of Crude Cocaine from Peru," *Bulletin of the Imperial Institute* (London) 8 (1910): 388–92; "Mr. Clements R. Markham on 'Coca-Cultivation,'" *Chemist and Druggist* (March 17, 1894): 387–89.

8 Gootenberg, "From Imagining Coca to Making Cocaine"; Spillane, *Cocaine*, 51.

9 On Kitz, see Gootenberg, "Rise and Shine of a National Commodity," and Tamayo, *Informe sobre las colonias de Oaxapampa y Pozuzo*, 111–12. Statistics are from "Cocaine-Manufacture in Peru," *Chemist and Druggist* (April 9, 1904). Also see Garland, *El Perú en 1906*, 180–82, 213. Thanks to Juri Soininen, a Finnish graduate student, for correcting these numbers.

10 Searle, *A New Form of Nervous Disease Together with an Essay on Erythroxylon Coca*; Mortimer, *History of Coca*; Gootenberg, "Between Coca and Cocaine."

11 Spillane, *Cocaine,* chap. 3, and "Making a Modern Drug."

12 For the syrup circuit, see Gootenberg, "Secret Ingredients"; Pilli, *Coca Industry*.

13 Musto, *The American Disease*; Spillane, *Cocaine*, chaps. 5–8.

14 Gootenberg, "Secret Ingredients."

15 Gootenberg, "Reluctance or Resistance?"

16 De Kort, "Doctors, Diplomats, and Businessmen"; Karch, *A Brief History of Cocaine*, chaps. 2, 6; Reens, "La coca de Java."

17 Derteano, "Informe que presenta el consul sobre la coca de la isla de Java"; Paz Soldán, *La coca peruana*.

18 De Kort, "Doctors, Diplomats, and Businessmen"; coca eradication was a U.S. condition for the (brief) Dutch reoccupation of Indonesia after 1945.

19 Friman, *Narcodiplomacy*, chap. 3; Meyer, "Japan and the World Narcotics Traffic"; Karch, "Japan and the Cocaine Industry of Southeast Asia."

20 Friman, *Narcodiplomacy,* is a balanced account of the Japanese and German drug trade.

21 Karch, *Brief History of Cocaine,* chap. 10, guesses Japan's production at seven metric tons (above world licit supply) on the basis of his own acreage-alkaloid ratios. Tulumayo had a remarkable history: originally owned by Kitz, then Durand, nationalized (despite protests by Japanese managers) in 1937, it became the U.S. Tropical Agricultural Station at Tingo María and then the epicenter of illicit cocaine in the 1960s.

22 Pilli, *Coca Industry*, 4–5, 8. Pilli also has an estimate—by bulk?—of 70 percent chewing, 15 percent exports, 15 percent cocaine manufacturing. Paz Soldán, *La Coca Peruana*, xvi, has Cuzco 50 percent, Huánuco 21 percent, La Libertad 7 percent, Ayacucho 17 percent, others 5 percent. Also Gerbi, *El Perú en marcha*, 183–87 (Table 18).

23 Gootenberg, "Reluctance or Resistance?" 56–63; Paz Soldán, "El problema médico-social de la coca en el Perú"; Gagliano, *Coca Prohibition in Peru*, chaps. 6–7.

24 Gootenberg, "Secret Ingredients"; Pilli, *Coca Industry*; U.S. Department of the Treasury, *Traffic in Opium and Other Dangerous Drugs*, Table 10.

25 Gootenberg, "Reluctance or Resistance?"; McAllister, *Drug Diplomacy in the Twentieth Century*.

26 Gootenberg, "Reluctance or Resistance?" 63–70.

27 Commodity chains (which can go beyond economics) are akin to two spatial conceptions of power: Bourdieu's "fields" of contested/capitalized power and Mann's four territorial bundles of power. See Wacquant and Bourdieu, *An Invitation to Reflexive Sociology*; Mann, *The Sources of Social Power*. The global commodity chain approach assumes the continuum and complicity of state market, and society and of licit and illicit spheres.

28 Gootenberg, "Birth of the Narcs"; U.S. Department of the Treasury, *Traffic in Opium and Other Dangerous Drugs*.

29 For today's networks, see Clawson and Lee, *The Andean Coca Industry*, Table 1.1, Fig. 1.4; Painter, *Bolivia and Coca*, Table 3.10; U.S. Bureau of International Narcotics and Law Enforcement Affairs, *International Narcotics Control Strategy Report*, "Policy and Program Overview," 35–45; Forero, "Hide and Seek among the Coca Leaves."

References

Appadurai, Arjun, ed. *The Social Life of Things: Commodities in Cultural Perspective*. Cambridge: Cambridge University Press, 1986.

Bellone, Amy. "The Cocaine Commodity Chain and Development Paths in Peru and Bolivia." In Roberto Patricio Korzeniewicz and William C. Smith, eds., *Latin America in the World-Economy*. Westport, Conn.: Greenwood, 1996.

Clawson, Patrick L., and Rensselaer Lee III. *The Andean Coca Industry*. New York: St. Martin's Press, 1996.

Courtwright, David T. *Forces of Habit: Drugs and the Making of the Modern World*. Cambridge: Harvard University Press, 2001.

De Kort, Marcel. "Doctors, Diplomats, and Businessmen: Conflicting Interests in the Netherlands and Dutch East Indies." In Paul Gootenberg, ed., *Cocaine: Global Histories*, 126–43. London: Routledge, 1999.

Derteano, M. A. "Informe que presenta el consul sobre la coca de la isla de Java." *Boletín del Ministerio de Relaciones Exteriores del Perú* 15 (1918): 347–48.

Forero, Juan. "Hide and Seek among the Coca Leaves." *New York Times*, June 9, 2004.

Freud, Sigmund. *Cocaine Papers*. Ed. Robert Byck. New York: Stonehill, 1974.

Friman, H. Richard. "Germany and the Transformation of Cocaine." In Paul Gootenberg, ed., *Cocaine: Global Histories*, 83–104. London: Routledge, 1999.

———. *Narcodiplomacy: Exporting the U.S. War on Drugs*. Ithaca: Cornell University Press, 1996.

Gagliano, Joseph. *Coca Prohibition in Peru: The Historical Debates*. Tucson: University of Arizona Press, 1994.

Garland, Alejandro. *El Perú en 1906*. Lima: Imprenta del Estado, 1907.

Gerbi, Antonello. *El Perú en marcha: Ensayo degeografíaeconómica*. Lima: Banco de Crédito, 1943.

Gereffi, Gary, and Miguel Korzeniewicz, eds., *Commodity Chains and Global Capitalism*. Westport. Conn.: Greenwood, 1994.

Goodman, Jordan. *Tobacco in History: The Cultures of Dependence*. London: Routledge, 1993.

Gootenberg, Paul. "Between Coca and Cocaine: A Century or More of U.S.-Peruvian Drug Paradoxes, 1860–1980." *Hispanic American Historical Review* 83, no. 1 (2003): 119–50.

———. "Birth of the Narcs: The First Illicit Cocaine Flows in the Americas, 1947–1973." Unpublished manuscript, 2004.

———. "From Imagining Coca to Making Cocaine: Inventing a National Commodity in Peru, 1850–1890." Unpublished manuscript, 2000.

———. "Reluctance or Resistance? Constructing Cocaine (Prohibitions) in Peru, 1910–50." In Paul Gootenberg, ed., *Cocaine: Global Histories*, 46–82. London: Routledge, 1999.

———. "Rise and Shine of a National Commodity: Peruvian Cocaine, 1885–1910." Unpublished manuscript, 2000.

———. "Secret Ingredients: The Politics of Coca in U.S.-Peruvian Relations, 1915–65." *Journal of Latin American Studies* 36, no. 2 (2004): 233–65.

———, ed. *Cocaine: Global Histories*. New York: Routledge, 1999.

Karch, Steven B. *A Brief History of Cocaine*. Boca Raton: CRC Press, 1998.

———. "Japan and the Cocaine Industry of Southeast Asia, 1864–1944." In Paul Gootenberg, ed., *Cocaine: Global Histories*, 146–64. New York: Routledge, 1999.

Kennedy, Joseph. *Coca Exotica: The Illustrated History of Cocaine*. New York: Cornwall, 1985.

Mann, Michael. *The Sources of Social Power*. Cambridge: Cambridge University Press, 1986.

Martindale, William. *Coca, Cocaine and Its Salts*. London, 1886.

McAllister, William B. *Drug Diplomacy in the Twentieth Century: An International History*. London: Routledge, 2000.

Meyer, Katherine. "Japan and the World Narcotics Traffic." In Jordan Goodman et al., *Consuming Habits: Drugs in History and Anthropology*. London: Routledge, 1995.

Mintz, Sidney W. *Sweetness and Power: The Place of Sugar in Modern History*. New York: Viking, 1985.

Mortimer, W. Golden. *History of Coca: "The Divine Plant" of the Incas*. New York: J. H. Vail, 1901.

Musto, David F. *The American Disease: The Origins of U.S. Narcotics Control*. New York: Oxford University Press, 1973.

———. "International Traffic in Coca through the Early Twentieth Century." *Drug and Alcohol Dependence* 49, no. 2 (1998): 145–56.

Painter, James. *Bolivia and Coca: A Study in Dependency*. Boulder: Lynne Reinner, 1994.

Paz Soldán, Carlos E. *La coca peruana: Memorandum sobre su situación actual*. Lima: SNA, 1936.

———. "El problema médico-social de la coca en el Perú." *Mercurio Peruano* 19 (1929): 584–603.

Pilli, Emile. *The Coca Industry of Peru*. Rahway, N.J.: Merck, 1943.

Pomeranz, Kenneth, and Steven C. Topik. *The World That Trade Created*. Armonk, N.Y.: M. E. Sharpe, 1999.

Reens, Emma. *La coca de Java*. Thesis. Paris: Université de Paris, 1917. Abbrev. trans. (chapter 4) in Steven Karch, *A History of Cocaine: The Mystery of Coca Java and the Kew Plant*. London: Royal Society of Medicine Press, 2003.

Rusby, H. H. *Jungle Memories*. New York: McGraw-Hill, 1933.

Schivelbusch, Wolfgang. *Tastes of Paradise: A Social History of Spices, Stimulants, and Intoxicants*. New York: Pantheon, 1992.

Searle, William S. *A New Form of Nervous Disease Together with an Essay on Erythroxylon Coca*. New York, 1881.

Spillane, Joseph F. *Cocaine: From Medical Marvel to Modern Menace in the United States, 1884–1920*. Baltimore: Johns Hopkins University Press, 1999.

———. "Making a Modern Drug: The Manufacture, Sale and Control of Cocaine in the United States, 1880–1920." In Paul Gootenberg, ed., *Cocaine: Global Histories*, 21–45. London: Routledge, 1999.

Stares, Paul B. *Global Habit*. Washington: Brookings Institution, 1996.

Tamayo, Augusto. *Informe sobre las colonias de Oaxapampa y Pozuzo y los Ríos Palcuzu y Pichir*. Lima: Ministerio de Fomento, 1904.

U.S. Bureau of International Narcotics and Law Enforcement Affairs. *International Narcotics Control Strategy Report*. Washington: Government Printing Office, 2000.

U.S. Department of the Treasury, Federal Bureau of Narcotics. *Traffic in Opium and Other Dangerous Drugs*. Annual reports. Washington: Government Printing Office, 1926–72.

Wacquant, Loic, and Pierre Bourdieu. *An Invitation to Reflexive Sociology*. Chicago: University of Chicago Press, 1992.

Wallerstein, Immanuel. *The Modern World-System: Capitalist Agriculture and the European World-Economy in the Sixteenth Century*. New York: Academic Press, 1974.

Poverty, Violence, and the Neoliberal Turn

Sujatha Fernandes

E pa-le, Johnny!" shouts Yorman, a lanky, brown-skinned young man who flicks away his cigarette and comes up behind Yajaira and me to take over control of Johnny's wheelchair and push him up the ramp that leads to the front gate of our apartment building.

"Epa-le, Yorman!" says Johnny, relieved that he will not have to struggle up the ramp, at midnight, when he is exhausted.

Orlando, Yorman's smoking buddy, holds the gate open for Johnny as we enter into the apartment complex, and there is another round of greetings as we see Iván, Bao, and Yancry, smoking in the cool darkness of the open patio beneath the apartments.

"Epa-le Johnny, hola Señora Yajaira." The young men then nod in greeting to me, and I nod my head back. Yorman, Orlando, Iván, Bao, and Yancry are the local drug dealers in the Residencia José Felix Ríbas, Sector III of the popular Caracas parish of El Valle. When I first began doing my field research in the barrios of Caracas, residing in the home of Johnny and Yajaira, I was aware that I could move freely in Sector III because the local drug dealers had seen me with Johnny. Johnny, who has been a paraplegic for thirty years following a car accident in his youth, commands respect in the eyes of the dealers because of the energetic way he lives his life. He is a community activist who works with street children and he has a special rapport with the drug dealers and street children of Ríbas, where he has lived for many years. The dealers understood that I was in the barrio as Johnny's friend, and when I arrived home in the morning or night, they left me alone because they knew who I was. The same went for Yajaira, Johnny's *compañera*, who had moved from Barrio Marín in San Agustin to live with Johnny in El Valle a few years earlier.

The Residencia José Felix Ribas is a complex of housing projects constructed for victims of the flood tragedy in the neighboring town of La Guaira, which left over 10,000 dead and 150,000 homeless soon after Chávez came to office in 1999. Former residents of La Guaira came to live in the city and remake their lives and homes in these rapidly constructed housing blocks. After several years of living in the blocks, the residents still had no cooking gas; there were frequent problems with water leakage and plumbing; a lack of sanitation services produced cockroaches and rats; and in four years the complex system of gang control and drug dealing that characterizes every major barrio in contemporary Caracas had evolved.

Unlike the gated communities in the east of Caracas, with doormen and security guards outside the front of the complexes and then several bolted security gates leading to the apartments, the popular residencies have few security gates. In Ribas, there are two main gates, one in the north of the complex and one in the east. Each building also has its own gate that leads onto an open patio. The eastern gate of the complex serves no real purpose, as it is surrounded by low and broken-down walls, which the younger residents easily jump over to get in and out. The northern gate is monitored by the drug dealers, who have their "business" in a small shack at the side of the gate. Moreover, the outside and inside gates are never locked, because only one resident per household has the gate keys. When I began to stay with Johnny and Yajaira, they gave me a key to their front door, but I had no gate keys, and I did not need these. There is an unspoken agreement among residents that when you open the gate you leave it resting on the frame rather than pulled locked, so that people can come in and out without keys.

A middle-class acquaintance visiting me once from the east of Caracas was shocked at this "poor security," but what he did not understand was that security for the residents of Ribas does not lie in the locks on the gates but rather in the gangs that control the territory and monitor who goes in and out. In the barrios, the concept of public space is entirely different from the middle- and upper-class gated communities and condominiums, known as *urbanizaciones*. While most middle-class residents have few common areas for public interaction and recreation, the streets, patios, and doorways of the barrios are generally crowded with children playing baseball, girls and boys flirting, women gossiping, and men playing dominoes or smoking. What underlies the relative sense of security in public spaces are the arrangements between sets of competing gangs in the sector, who have marked out their territory and delineated their responsibility for their area. At times the gangs even display a sense of commitment to residents of the community. The gang leaders and drug dealers of Ribas are generally on hand to assist Johnny up the ramp and through the gates, to help him push his car when it breaks down, or to help Yajaira carry home her groceries.

But this balance is extremely precarious and residents tend to stay home after about ten at night, when violence may erupt between competing gangs. The large holes blown by a bazooka in the façade of the local shopping mall across the road are testament to the kinds of artillery found in the barrio. Most of the time the residents joke about these intergang exchanges; when the gunshots begin, the residents pretend not to notice and if asked they generally use the euphemism of *fuegos artificiales*, or firecrackers, to refer to the shooting. Violence has become routinized in the lives of the residents. Sadly, these kinds of shootouts can happen even during the day; they can erupt out of nowhere, and innocent residents can get caught up in the middle of a situation and be hurt or killed. This is more often the case when the police become involved. The corrupt and inefficient nature of the police force means that they are sometimes bought off by gangs, or they do not have the resources to attend to complaints in the barrios, but they frequently make incursions into the barrios, disrupting the relative equilibrium established by the gangs.

One afternoon on my way home, I was stopped by a police officer at the outside east gate of Ríbas and told that I could not enter. Several neighbors were standing around, trying to find out what was going on, but the police had cordoned off the area for nearly two hours. When I could finally get inside to my building, I saw that there was fresh blood on the ground in our open patio. Victor, the four-year-old boy from the apartment next to ours, came over and told us that the police were chasing a gang member who had come running into our building complex, knocking on all the doors to be let in. Victor's *abuela* opened the door. The police shot the young man right there, on the doorstep of Victor's house, in front of Victor and his abuela.

Everyday violence is one of the most pervasive indications of how neoliberalism reshaped the contours of society. Neoliberal policies, consisting of the privatization and deregulation of state enterprises, trade liberalization, and the flexibilization of labor markets, were introduced into Venezuela during the period of the 1990s. The retreat of the state from social welfare and service provision, and its greater orientation toward an international market, left popular sectors to fend for themselves in a situation of growing desperation and impoverishment. Large-scale unemployment and poverty led to the proliferation of street gangs, violent crime, and the illegal drug trade as a means of survival. But as Jean and John Comaroff argue, rising criminality in postcolonies is not simply a response to the poverty and scarcity produced by structural adjustment. Rather, it is part of a much more troubled dialectic of law and dis/order, whereby criminal violence appropriates the rule of law and operations of the market, creating parallel modes of production, social order, and governance under conditions of deregulation and privatization.[1] Nor is it the case that under neoliberalism the state simply disappears. While the state retreats from its role as a benefactor and protector, it reenters as a repressive force, carrying out sporadic raids against barrio residents.

[...] I look at the changing nature of the state in Venezuela during the 1990s and early years of the new century and the shifting dynamics of state-society relations. I explore the impact of neoliberal reforms on the relationship between the state and the urban barrios, and I consider the social effects of neoliberal reforms. [...] to outline the transition to a post-neoliberal state under Chávez, with certain key areas of social policy governed by principles of welfare liberalism, and others subject to the market.

The Making of the Neoliberal State: 1989–98

Marginality and the violence of contemporary urban life are related to processes of growing urban segregation, a deterioration in the conditions of public services, and the transition from a protectionist to a neoliberal state. The insertion of Venezuela into a global order required new forms of efficiency and competition that put pressures on the state-based developmental model pursued by previous governments. The shift of resources away from infrastructure, health care, education, and other social services led to a sustained increase in social inequality. These changes were also racialized, with those at the bottom of the social scale—mostly the black, indigenous, and mixed-race population who form the majority—hit hardest by the changes.

After the collapse of the military dictatorship in 1958 and the transition to democracy, the new Acción Democrática (AD) government pursued strategies of Import Substitution Industrialization (ISI) and prioritized social welfare. Héctor Silva Michelena refers to the period of the 1960s and 1970s as one of economic expansion and redistribution, where the economy generated oil wealth that could be used to increase social spending, provide subsidies for basic goods, and pay high wages to the working classes.[2] But after 1980, this pattern was interrupted by a decline in oil prices and an increase in international borrowing costs.[3] On February 18, 1983, otherwise known as "Black Friday," the currency collapsed, leading to a period of depreciation, hyperinflation, and economic stagnation.[4] The crisis produced by Black Friday was related to massive spending, illegal use of state funds, and unrestrained foreign borrowing, which had increased from $9 billion to nearly $24 billion under the administration of Luis Herrera Campíns during the early to mid-1980s.[5] As a response to rising interest rates, the government of Herrera Campíns devaluated the currency and initiated a set of controls over the economy to prevent the massive flight of private capital.[6] Yet during the administrations of Herrera Campíns (1979–84) and Jaime Lusinchi (1984–89), the economy continued to experience high inflation, disequilibrium in the principle macroeconomic indicators, a deterioration in public-sector salaries, the flight of private capital, and internal and external indebtedness.[7]

Despite his populist, anti-IMF rhetoric during the 1988 election campaign, when Carlos Andrés Pérez attained the presidency in 1989 he declared his plans to adopt neoliberal austerity measures. On February 16, 1989, just a few weeks after his inauguration, Pérez announced the Gran Viraje (Great Turn), a program that sought to dramatically reshape and restructure the economy, political institutions, and cultural foundations of Venezuelan society. The program consisted of austerity measures such as dismantling government subsidies to local industries, deregulating prices, privatizing public enterprises, and reducing social spending. Through these measures, the government sought to increase the competitiveness of Venezuela in the global economy through the growth and diversification of exports and to reduce the role of the state in the domestic economy.[8] But Pérez underestimated the widespread opposition to these proposed reforms, and within ten days the initial measures had sparked the largest anti-austerity protest in Latin America, which came to be known as the *Caracazo*.

Soon after Pérez's announcement of the neoliberal measures, in anticipation of the removal of subsidies and competition, local manufacturers cut back on production. Sellers hoarded goods in order to drive prices up, causing shortages and a growing anger among the urban poor. Subsequently, on February 26, the government announced that gas prices would double in accordance with global market prices. When people went out to catch public transport to work on the morning of Monday, February 27, they found that bus fares had doubled. Protests against the fare increases in the town of Guarenas outside Caracas and at the Caracas bus terminal soon spread across the city.[9] Fernando Coronil and Julie Skurski argue that the decision to raise gas prices in an oil-exporting nation was seen as a violation of the imagined shared ownership of the country's petroleum resources, a rupture of the moral bond between state and pueblo.[10] Men, women, and children came down from the cerros in large numbers to participate in a *saqueo popular* (popular looting) of grocery stores and processing plants. By six in the evening, the main arteries of the city were blockaded, and there was no transport, forcing protesters to return home by foot. With no authorities on the scene, the looting continued into the night. In the early hours of February 28 the army was dispatched onto the streets and there was a massive and violent crackdown. Thousands of people were killed or wounded in the streets by the armed forces, and others stayed terrified in their homes.[11] State violence reimposed conditions of stability and set the groundwork for a new order.

Despite some adjustments and delays, the original neoliberal package was implemented through most of Pérez's presidency.[12] The first stage of the reforms in 1989 included cuts in public spending and trade and financial-sector liberalization. There were successes in reducing imports, but the economy contracted by 8.6 percent and poverty rose over 20 percent. By 1991, oil prices had risen, which led to higher economic growth, but poverty continued to rise dramatically.[13] The Privatization Law in 1992 set the groundwork for privatization of key industries. Over the years 1989–93, the market came to play a much more prominent role in the economy as the state was scaled back.

Under Pérez, there was a transition from a protectionist to a neoliberal state. A combination of external pressures and internal political realignments produced changed roles for the state and new modes of governance under neoliberal regimes. But in contrast to the scholarship that refers to the eclipse or decline of the state,[14] there is growing evidence to suggest that the "nation-state" is simply being rearticulated as the "neo-liberal nation-state."[15] The state takes on new functions as representative of global economic forces in the national realm and a terrain of competing interests as domestic groups raise their demands.[16] The VIII Plan of the Nation, devised under Pérez, has a section titled "The New Role of the State." It states, "The new strategy requires a strong and efficient state that promotes competition and stimulates the expansion and consolidation of a modern market economy."[17] In Venezuela, the orientation toward private initiative and a global economy was channeled through the state, as powerful economic groups such as the media corporation Cisneros group used their local political connections to deepen their involvement in international markets.[18] In contrast to the protectionist state, which is described in the VIII Plan as a "direct participant in private economic activity," "discretionary and centralized distributor of oil rents," and "inefficient administrator of social wealth," the neoliberal state should be a "promoter and efficient regulator of private activity," "generator of adequate macroeconomic conditions," and "efficient administrator of the public budget."[19] According to this logic, the neoliberal state should reduce its field of action, focusing on assigning public resources only to areas strategic for encouraging private investment.

In order to carry out the neoliberal package, Pérez had to distance himself from his election promises and the ad party machine, relying increasingly on his ministers, a team of technocrats known as the IESA boys. Technical institutes such as the Institute of Higher Management Studies (IESA) and the Center for the Dissemination of Economic Knowledge (CEDICE) and business groups such as the Grupo Roraima were sites for the diagnosis of the economic crisis and the articulation and dissemination of neoliberal economics. Over a decade of changing political leadership, the pared-down state apparatus, driven by a technocratic agenda and oriented toward global markets, came to have an irreducible presence independent of the ideological stripes of those in power.

Social policy under Pérez's neoliberal framework was also reoriented from its emphasis on providing equity, universal access to social welfare, and redistribution toward the privatization of social services and compensatory programs designed to mediate the effects of structural adjustment reforms. As Norbis Mujica Chirinos has argued, social policy came to be guided by the criteria and values of the market—economic efficiency, individualism, and competition.[20] Pérez's social policy was encapsulated in the program Plan de Enfrentamiento de Pobreza (Plan for Confronting Poverty, PEP), which included a mother-infant nourishment program, school nutrition programs, youth training and employment, day care centers, programs of assistance in popular economy, a project of urban improvement in the barrios, and a program of local social investment, among others.[21] Under a second phase of social policy, Pérez implemented the Mega Proyecto Social (Mega Social Project), in 1992. The Mega Proyecto Social complemented the PEP providing investment in areas such as water, infrastructure, education, health, housing, social security, and environment. But while the funding for the program was initially projected at Bs 123,000 million, it was reduced to a credit of Bs 57,300 million, to be financed from assets sold off through privatization.[22] The responsibility for social services was increasingly delegated to NGOs and civil society groups, without the corresponding resources. The VIII Plan states, "It is imperative to improve the management of basic public services and incorporate civil society into the instrumental tasks of social policy and culture."[23] The program of day care centers was outsourced to 850 NGOs financed by the state and reached only 9 percent of Venezuelan children.[24] In a time of limited public resources, the burden for subsistence and welfare was shifted onto social sectors.

The government began to show signs of disintegration by late 1992, due to increasing discord between the AD and Pérez's technocratic cabinet, particularly over issues such as the minimum salary, as well as a coup attempt by Hugo Chávez on February 4 and a second coup attempt on November 27. Rafael Caldera was elected in 1993 on an openly anti-neoliberal and social Christian program, as part of a coalition of parties known as Convergencia Nacional. For his first year and a half in office, Caldera employed a hybrid mix of neoliberal and anti-neoliberal policies. As Julia Buxton outlines, Caldera's initial economic policy, known as the Sosa Plan, combined spending cuts with increases in taxation, and it had some success in closing the fiscal gap. But Caldera also had to deal with a banking sector crisis, which led to massive capital flight. Caldera fell back on neoliberal strategies of exchange controls, currency devaluation, and spending cuts in order to deal with the crisis. By the end of 1994, inflation had increased to 70.8 percent, unemployment had risen to 8.5 percent, poverty continued to rise, and public infrastructure was plagued by blackouts and shortages.[25]

Under Caldera, the PEP was replaced by a new social program, the Plan de Solidaridad Social (Plan of Social Solidarity), launched in 1994. The plan attempted to combat poverty through constructing a healthy economy that would reduce unemployment and increase salaries. This was followed by the Plan de Recuperación y Estabilización Económica (Plan for Recuperation and Economic Stabilization, PERE), where social programs were listed under a section for strategic social action. Caldera revived the neo-liberal package in April 1996 in consultation with the IMF, as a program of macroeconomic stabilization known as Agenda Venezuela, although no formal agreement was signed with the IMF. As part of this program, the Caldera administration privatized the steel company, attempted to auction off the aluminum industry, and deepened the partial privatization of the oil company.[26] The Agenda Venezuela also contained a social component of fourteen programs, some carried over from earlier plans, such as mother-infant nourishment, school nutrition, youth training and employment, and day care centers. It was fairly similar to plans such as the PEP, with the exception that it utilized more direct subsidies in order to confront extreme poverty.[27]

But these social programs had little effect in mediating the impact of structural adjustment. Compensatory programs were short term and targeted small sectors of the population. By 1997, greater foreign investment and a rise in oil prices allowed for greater economic growth, but social indicators did not improve. By this time the official rate of unemployment was 12 percent, inflation had reached 103 percent, and real incomes had fallen by 70.9 percent since 1984.[28] The effectiveness of programs such as day care centers depended less on the state and more on the capacity of NGOs, which had increased to between 2,500 and 2,600 community-based organizations, private development groups, and private agencies.[29]

The shift away from protectionist to neoliberal orders produced new processes of class formation across Latin America. Alejandro Portes and Kelly Hoffman point to the appearance of a transnational elite class that included managers, executives, and elite workers.[30] Similarly, in Venezuela there was a shift in the power base of domestic elites, as some groups that flourished under the protectionist state declined and others adapted to the new conditions of liberalization by diversifying and moving to export-production. For example, in the automobile parts sector, the Sivensa Group shifted over half of its production to export, thus retaining its leading position within the industry. Others like Grupo Polar expanded by investing in domestic industries.[31] The retreat of the state from redistributive functions such as progressive taxation, controls, and regulation led to a concentration of power and resources in this transnational elite.

At the same time, a large and impoverished informal proletariat emerged which consists of the urban poor and former public-sector employees and factory workers.[32] Official statistics report that the informal sector in Venezuela grew from 34.5 percent of the labor force in 1980 to 53 percent in 1999, although these figures likely underreport the true number.[33] During the same period, unemployment went from 6.6 to 15.4 percent of the urban labor force.[34] As a result, many Venezuelans were unemployed or underemployed with no job security. Large numbers of urban poor, as well as the downwardly mobile middle classes, increasingly turned to street vending as a way of supporting themselves and their families following layoffs or after difficulty securing formal sector employment.[35] Some vendors left formal sector employment because they preferred the freedom of self-employment. Some even managed to accumulate enough capital to own and operate several stalls, where they employ workers to sell their merchandise. But for the most part, vendors are self-employed individuals who are vulnerable to loan sharks for purchase of their stalls and equipment, and they barely scrape a living day to day. And while these informal sector occupations have arisen in the absence of the state, vendors are still subject to policing and harassment by virtue of their permanent illegality, as well as problems of crime and insecurity.

Poverty had always been a major social problem in Venezuela, even under the social welfare state, but during the 1980s and 1990s it increased substantially. In 1978, 10 percent of the population lived in poverty and 2 percent lived in extreme poverty.[36] Between 1984 and 1995, those living below the poverty line went from 36 to 66 percent, and those in extreme poverty tripled from 11 to 36 percent.[37] By 1998, 81 percent lived below the poverty line and those living in extreme poverty had risen to 48 percent. In December 1997, there were 3 million homes in poverty and more than 1.6 million homes in situations of extreme poverty. Even during moments of economic growth, poverty continued to rise, defying the notion that the benefits of economic growth would trickle down to poorer classes.

The increase in poverty was related to a number of factors including the large scale loss of employment, higher prices and reduced purchasing power due to inflation, and reduced government spending on social programs. Purchasing power of the minimum wage was reduced by more than two-thirds between 1978 and 1994. There were major cuts in social spending, including cuts of over 40 percent in education, 70 percent in housing, and 37 percent in health. A downwardly mobile middle class gradually took over the public health care and education system, which was less accessible to the poor because of the registration fees for schools and costs of treatment supplies at hospitals.[38] Unemployment, inflation, and cuts in social spending impacted most strongly the poorest 40 percent of the population, whose income share fell from 19.1 percent in 1981 to 14.7 percent in 1997, while the wealthiest increased their share of income from 21.8 to 32.8 percent.[39] The effects of this unequal redistribution of income can be seen in processes of growing urban segregation and social polarization.

War on the Urban Poor: From a Benefactor to a Repressive State

Structural changes in Venezuelan society during the 1990s dramatically transformed the nature of urban life and the relationship of the barrios to the state. During the period of ISI, the barrios provided industrial labor for factories, public-sector personnel, and domestic labor for the middle and upper classes. In turn, the state intervened in the barrios through a system of clientilist redistribution of goods and services.[40] As Elizabeth Leeds identified in Brazil, the relationship between the shantytowns and the outside polity "was a symbiotic one, with each side extracting some good or service from the other."[41] But given the shift away from formal employment to informal employment, declining jobs in the public sector, and the reduction in redistributive social spending, the shantytowns came to constitute what Javier Auyero calls "a space of survival for those excluded from the rest of society."[42] The severing of the symbiotic relationship between the barrios and the outside world resulted in a growth of elaborate strategies of survival and parallel economies, and a state that became more repressive even as it failed to provide basic security for barrio residents.

The declining employment opportunities for barrio residents gave rise to a range of informal and sometimes illegal survival economies, one of the most lucrative among young barrio men being drug dealing. For an account of these survival economies, some suggestive evidence can be obtained from looking at popular culture forms such as rap music. It must be noted that rap lyrics are not a transparent account of working-class experience, as the lyrics are mediated by record labels and the commodification of the "ghetto" as it is marketed to middle-class audiences. But it is still the case that rap music is produced by and resonates strongly with barrio youth, who identify the lyrics with their own experiences. In their song "Malandrea negro" (Black Delinquency), the Venezuelan rap group Guerrilla Seca say that it is the poverty, hunger, and desperation of the barrios that leads to drug dealing for some as a means of survival. Trying to find meaningful work for unskilled black youth is practically impossible: "I go on desperately, looking for work is a joke." Even for those who want to find work in the formal economy there are few opportunities: "I look for legal cash, but destiny is changing me." If one needs money and there are no legal opportunities, then the turn to crime and the informal, underground economy is the only path, according to the rapper, especially when one has children to support. Similarly in the chronicle of street life "Historia nuestra" (Our History), the rapper Budu from Vagos y Maleantes relates that he began dealing drugs, "empecé en el jibareo," at the age of seventeen. While the parents of the rapper dreamed of his being an engineer, he dreamed of being a criminal.

The drug trade provided one form of economic subsistence for all those involved in the production, manufacture, and sale of drugs. According to Eithne Quinn, who has studied representations of the drug trade in American gangsta rap, the informal economy of the drug trade reflects a capitalist ethos of "the meteoric rise of the fledgling entrepreneur; the rejection of traditional notions of communal responsibility in an age of individualism; the 'ruthless' startup business organization; and the marketing and distribution of a 'dangerous' product."[43] In the song "Puro lacreo" (True Delinquent), the rapper Colombia from Guerrilla Seca describes a drug business. The dealers are managers who own and oversee the entire business and are intimately familiar with the production process. As compared with the degradation of wage labor or service work, the dealers themselves direct their business. The dealers are concerned with many aspects of a startup business. There is much demand, "everyone wants cocaine and rocks," but they need to establish a good name for themselves in the barrio and protect themselves against crackdowns by the police. As long as they have control over their zone and are street smart about how they do business, no one will mess with them. The song ends with guns being fired into the air, emphasizing that in the end it is violence and the cartel's monopoly over the means of violence in the barrio that maintain their control over trade.

Another example of a lucrative informal-sector activity that doubled as what Auyero calls a "surrogate social security system" was the Maria Lionza cult, a popular spirit possession cult that focuses on healing.[44] In addition to employment and income generated by the healing ceremonies, the sale of cult-related products distributed through street merchants was a mode of informal economy.[45] Given the lack of public services for barrio residents during the 1990s, the Maria Lionza cult came to constitute an alternative form of health care. Indeed, the "clinics" of the cult mimicked allopathic clinics, where patients are given a number and asked to sit in a waiting room. They then go into consulting rooms where they meet with the *materias*, the mediums who oversee the rituals. Patients are given "prescriptions," or pieces of paper with suggested cures, usually involving ways to remove a spell that has been cast on the person and is creating his or her ill health. Materias conduct spiritual "operations" which do not involve actual surgery but imitate the procedures and instruments of regular surgery. In the absence of health care services, the clinics of the cult came to serve as a surrogate form of consultation for barrio residents. One of the most popular clinics known as the Centro Madre Erika in Petare received close to 20,000 patients per week during the 1990s.[46] In addition to spiritual services, the center invited medical doctors to speak on topics such as teenage pregnancy and infant health, substituting for the services that an absent state no longer provided.

At the same time as the neoliberal state retreated from its integrationist roles as service provider and public sector employer, it reentered as a repressive force, maintaining the shantytowns in a state of permanent crisis and illegality. The liberal state had been involved in repressive interventions into the barrios since the early period of democratic rule when a guerrilla movement arose to contest the conditions of "pacted" or elite democracy. But in the late 1980s, combat between guerrillas and the police was replaced by tensions between gang leaders and urban security forces. As drugs began to circulate in the popular neighborhoods in large quantities during the 1980s, some former guerrillas left behind militant politics and began to enter the drug trade. According to Juan Contreras from the parish 23 de Enero, several leftist activists who had experience in doing expropriations of territory, using arms, and planning military operations began to use these techniques to their own benefit, setting up small drug cartels in the barrios and staking claim over their territories. At this time, the state formed various paramilitary units designed for urban combat. In 1994, they created urban squads known as the *Angeles Guardianes* (Guardian Angels), based on civil security forces in use at the end of the 1970s in the United States.[47] Another unit for urban control set up during the 1990s was the *Cascos Blancos* (White Helmets).[48] In public discourse the phrase "Plomo contra el Hampa" or "War against Delinquency" became common and has justified the use of severe punishments for acts of juvenile crime.[49]

Public security services became more repressive at the same time as they became more corrupt and underresourced. In the last few decades there has been an increase in crime and a decline in protective security for the poorer sections of the population who live in barrios. Ana María Sanjuán comments that in 1999 the homicide rate in Venezuela had risen 20 percent from the previous year.[50] This number was greater in Caracas, where the number of homicides sometimes reached the hundred mark on weekends. Official statistics for the year 2000 reported a total of 7,779 homicides in Venezuela.[51] An overwhelming number of these homicides take place in the barrios, and a personalized system of punishment and retribution has evolved to make up for the absence of state security forces enforcing the law on behalf of poorer citizens.

The absence of state protection for citizens was all too apparent to me through an incident that happened during my fieldwork. During a research trip in January 2005, all the money was stolen from my bank accounts, following my use of my credit card at an automatic teller machine in a neighborhood known as Las Mayas. My card was duplicated after I used it and all my bank accounts were wiped out over a period of two weeks. A friend took me to the police station in the middle-class neighborhood of Chacao, hoping that we could get attention for our problem. When we arrived at the station, I noticed that it was fully staffed, with several police officers in new-looking uniforms who were pleasant and courteous to the people waiting for help with their complaints.[52] When I reached the counter and explained what had happened, they said that I would need to go to the police station in El Valle, since the crime was under the jurisdiction of that station. The difference between the police station in Chacao and El Valle was striking. The station in El Valle had large numbers of people waiting to be attended to and only one police officer on duty, who disappeared inside his office for long periods of time. When I went to the counter and explained what had happened I was told that I would need to wait.

As I took my seat among the plastic orange chairs in the waiting area, I began to converse with the people around me. The woman on my left told me that her brother had been killed and she was trying to file a report so that his killer could be apprehended. On my right, a tired-looking woman said that her ex-husband was physically harassing her and she was trying to get a protection order against him. They had both come in several times, waiting for four or five hours at a time without having their complaints attended to.

When it was finally my turn to be attended to, several hours later, I was able to see at close hand the scarcity of resources for the barrio police stations. The attending officer asked me to go outside and find a place to make copies of my bankcard and other important documents, and while I was at it, he asked if I could photocopy a few forms for the station as well, since there was no functioning copier at the station. He typed up my report on an ancient typewriter that broke down at least twice. He entered my data into a word processor, and then printing out the data took another hour on an old dot matrix printer that skewed the text. Finally, the officer led me to another room and pressed my fingers onto an inkpad, but there was no ink, and he could not take my fingerprints. By this stage both the officer and I were shaking our heads in disbelief. It was clear to me that the police are overburdened and underresourced when it comes to citizen protection in the barrios.

The result of this underresourcing has been widespread corruption among the police, who abuse their position in order to extract personal benefits. Freddy Mendoza, a community activist, related to me that it was frequent for police to arrest residents of the barrio, particularly youth, and then release them for a certain amount of money. Freddy also told the story of a town clerk who had reached his position through deals with the political party COPEI in the 1990s. The clerk, known as "pica pollo" because he sold chicken, used to gamble until two or three o'clock in the morning, and when he lost all his money he would go to the police module and extort money from detainees so he could continue gambling. If they paid him, then he would release them. Paying bribes to police has become an accepted practice. Budu related to me an incident with the police:

> Once I was smoking a marijuana cigarette. I was in the doorway of my house and the police arrived—nearly six of them—and they caught me because me and my friend didn't realize in time. I had the marijuana. They saw me, and they said, "We're going to take you." I said, "ok, but don't handcuff me because I'm a public figure and I don't want people to see me like a kid." They asked, "How much do you have there?" "I have twenty thousand bolívares." "ok, give it to us." And they took my twenty thousand bolívares and gave me back my cigarette ... There were eight of them and between the eight they shared the twenty thousand bolívares.

Twenty thousand bolívares is the equivalent of about $US9.50, and shared between eight police officers amounts to a little over 2,500 bolívares ($US1.20) per person. But corruption ranges from this kind of petty extortion and bribing to larger, regular payments by drug dealers, which can substitute nicely for the paltry salaries paid by the state.

As the state underwent changes during the period of the 1990s, it retreated from its role as a benefactor providing public services such as health, education, and security, and reentered the lives of barrio residents as a repressive state. Barrio residents were left to fend for themselves and often created elaborate strategies of survival that included illegal activities such as drug dealing and crime. When Chávez came to power in 1998, he promised to bring back the benefactor state and reverse processes of exclusion and segregation. The next sections [...] examine the changing nature of social policies under Chávez and the shift to a post-neoliberal state.

The Reconfiguration of the State Under Chávez, 1998–2007

Hugo Chávez was elected in the December 1998 general elections mainly because of his proposals to transition Venezuela away from the neoliberal model. In contrast to the neoliberal state shaped under Pérez and Caldera, Chávez conceived of a developmental, benefactor state that would act as a "promoter of private economic activity, regulator of economic agents, stimulator of the accumulation of physical and human capital."[53] The state would directly administrate policy and guarantee social justice and security, while involving social sectors in the construction of a participatory democracy.[54] Soon after taking office, Chávez initiated the process of rewriting the constitution as a method of reforming the state. Many of those elected to the constituent assembly had been human rights advocates under previous governments, and they incorporated a broad concept of human rights as both civil rights and social rights of public health, education, and welfare. The new constitution was completed over the next few months and approved by referendum in December 1999.

However, despite his anti-neoliberal rhetoric and legislation, during his first period of office from 1998 to 2001, Chávez followed many of his predecessors' policies. Initially, there was a strong emphasis on short-term macroeconomic policies of fiscal discipline and monetary control, practically identical to that pursued under the Agenda Venezuela. In July 1999, the Chávez government announced the ratification of nine of the fourteen social programs of Agenda Venezuela. In his Plan Bolívar announced in 2000, Chávez proposed short-term civic-military interventions to address the most urgent social problems.[55] There was also a move to centralize social programs within large state ministries.[56] Chávez's early period was marked by a contradictory orientation that combined macroeconomic adjustment policies with compensatory social programs, in contrast to the model of development he had proposed.

During this period, the Chávez administration collaborated with the World Bank, which continued its social programs in Venezuela. Shifts were taking place within leading development institutions themselves, away from the more aggressive structural adjustment policies toward "inclusive" poverty reduction and good governance goals. As David Craig and Doug Porter argue, by the end of the 1990s, the millenarian vision of global market integration was under siege. Development failure and zero net growth brought into question neoliberalism's trust in free markets and self regulation. The United Nation Development Program (UNDP) proposed a set of Millennium Development Goals (MDGS) in 2000, which included the eradication of extreme poverty, universal primary education, and the reduction of child mortality, among other goals. The idea was that economic growth resulting from neoliberal market integration would not on its own reduce poverty, and there would need to be a focused moral commitment from poor countries and their citizens to address social problems.[57] In December 2002, the World Bank proposed the Interim Country Assistance Strategy (ICAS) designed to help Venezuela meet the MDGS by 2015. This included a $60.7 million Caracas Slum Upgrading Project with the state institution FUNDACOMUN. The WB also committed funds to public health services, urban transport, and finance.

However, starting in 2001, the Chávez government was ready to make a break with its predecessors' social policies, including its ties to the WB and international agencies. In November 2001, the Chávez administration passed a package of forty-nine laws which included the Organic Hydrocarbons Law to establish majority government ownership of all oil-related mixed companies, and the Lands Law, which made idle land subject to expropriation.[58] After 2002, the growing independence of the Chávez administration was due to its increased control over the state-owned oil company PDVSA and was also a consequence of the spectacular rise in oil prices, from US$24.13 per barrel in December 2002 to $84.63 in December 2007, which made more funds available to state coffers. As Thad Dunning argues, "Venezuela is again a rentier state in the midst of an oil boom."[59] In July 2002, the government proposed the Plan Estratégico Social 2001–2007 (Strategic Social Plan, PES), which had three sub-objectives: "the universalization of social rights, the reduction of the inequality of wealth, income and quality of life, and the appropriation of the public realm as a collective good."[60] At the center of this new social policy were the missions, a comprehensive series of publicly funded and administered poverty alleviation programs.

Two of the main goals of the missions were introducing universal education and health care. This was initially done by bypassing the established institutions and setting up programs in the barrios through a parallel set of institutions. The key educational missions included the adult literacy and elementary education programs Mission Robinson I and II; work-study program Mission Ribas; and a university program, Mission Sucre. Unemployed and informal sectors were incorporated into these programs in large numbers as both instructors and students, helping to partly alleviate poverty by providing them with small stipends for their involvement. In mid-2003, Chávez introduced the Barrio Adentro (Inside the Barrio) program of local health clinics, staffed by Cuban doctors, in 320 of Venezuela's 335 municipalities.[61] By mid-2005, he had added another two programs, Barrio Adentro II and III for additional medical services. In March 2005, there were over 5,000 Comités de Salud (Health Committees), which were created to supervise and help out with the Barrio Adentro program.[62]

In addition to educational and health programs, Chávez encouraged barrio residents to create a range of committees and cooperative organizations. In an executive decree in 2002, Chávez established the basis for Comités de Tierra Urbana (Urban Land Committees, CTU), in order to rationalize land tenancy through surveys, distribution of land deeds, and development of property belonging to the community.[63] Since most dwellings in the barrios were constructed through a process of massive squatting as people moved to Caracas from the countryside, few homeowners possess deeds or titles to their land. In March 2005, there were more than 4,000 Urban Land Committees in the urban capitals of Venezuela, which had distributed about 170,000 property titles.[64] The Chávez government also set up Casas Alimentarias (soup kitchens), where needy children and single mothers from the barrios receive one free meal a day. In 2004, 4,052 Casas Alimentarias were established in Venezuela.[65] Mission Mercal was a series of subsidized supermarkets also designed to improve nutrition.

By around 2005 it is possible to identify a shift in the nature of the Venezuelan state to a post-neoliberal state. Julia Buxton argues that the development agenda of the Chávez government places an emphasis on sustainable economic growth based in technological innovation, macroeconomic policy management, and basic social services provision. Fiscal and monetary policies are compatible with social policies. There is a disproportionate focus on the poor and a redistribution of assets and land. All these factors differentiate the agenda of the Chávez government from the targeted poverty reduction approach associated with MDGS, which still retain a jaundiced view of the state, focus on private-sector and trade-led growth, measure development by economic and not social indicators, and lack any emphasis on land redistribution.[66] In the post-2002 order, neo-liberalism was no longer the dominant policy.

Conclusion: Chávez and the Urban Poor

Under Chávez, the links between state and society were reconfigured, as the state once more took on the role of benefactor and protector, particularly to the urban poor. Economists have shown various improvements in social indicators since Chávez has been in office. Responding to negative assessments by Francisco Rodríguez and Daniel Ortega, who conclude on the basis of the Venezuelan Households survey that the illiteracy campaigns have been an expensive failure,[67] David Rosnick and Mark Weisbrot contend that the Household Survey is an inadequate measurement tool for illiteracy, since it has only one question concerning illiteracy and thereby does not capture the great variety of change that may be taking place.[68] In a further rebuttal of Rodriguez's consequent assertions,[69] Weisbrot shows that social spending increased from 8.2 percent of GDP in 1998 to 15.9 percent in 2006, and that since 2003 the poverty rate has been cut in half and the unemployment rate has been cut by more than half.[70] Weisbrot's figures may not capture the true scope of changes taking place, as they do not account for factors such as the siphoning off of stipends that may never reach intended beneficiaries; hoarding and pilfering of goods; and underemployment, which may be the case with some who are employed in the missions but remain without a livable wage. Nevertheless, it is still the case that provision of social services has led to improvements in people's lives in ways that are also apparent through ethnographic observation, whether it is health clinics in the highest reaches of the barrios where previously people died from preventable diseases; nutritious daily meals available for children from poor families; or high school dropouts continuing their schooling during evenings in the work-study program. Chávez has won a considerable degree of sympathy from the urban poor for his social policies, which was reflected in his consecutive successes in the recall referendum and 2007 elections.

The rate of violence since 2002 has also showed considerable decline. Figures from the Centro de Estudios para la Paz at the Central University of Venezuela show that in the popular parish of Antemano the rate of homicides went from 110 per 100,000 inhabitants in 2002 to 76 in 2006. In Petare the rate was reduced during the same period from 101 to 72, and the overall rate in Caracas was reduced from 51 to 37.[71] It is likely that the improvement in social indicators—creating jobs, reducing poverty, and access to education—is breaking up the vicious cycle of crime and violence. However, the problem of violence is at the same time an obstacle to putting in place some of these programs, as community organizers find themselves subject to threats and random violence. [...] I continue to explore how social movements grapple with the issue of violence and to examine the community-based solutions to violence that they propose.

Chávez's support among the urban poor owes not only to his social programs and transfer of material goods but also to his image as an anti-establishment figure. As Yolanda Salas argues, Chávez denounces the traditional political system and the given institutional order, appealing to the masses as his allies and interlocutors. The "Chávez myth" was strengthened by Chávez's biographical connections with the llanera region as symbolic of national identity; his expressed admiration for his great-grandfather Maisanta, a general who revolted against the military leader Juan Vicente Gomez; and his coups of February and November 1992 that challenged the existing political order.[72] The renovation of the old republic and the birth of the new are based in the ideology and cult of Bolivarianismo.

Chávez draws on and elaborates the popular Bolivarian cult as it has been formulated in spaces of exclusion. The independence hero Simón Bolívar has traditionally been portrayed in official representations as part of a cult of order, patriotism, and progress.[73] By contrast, in the rural communities of Barlovento and Oriente studied by Salas, Bolívar was re-imagined in various guises as a statuesque African slave brought to the coasts of Barlovento, a saint descended from the heavens accompanied by his followers, and a common man who died poor and was betrayed by his friends.[74] From these collective popular histories emerges a Bolívar who is sanctified and mythified by those classes who feel outside the spheres of power.[75] Chávez's constant references to Bolívar and other heroes from the past are a reflection of these images preserved in popular historical memory. Chávez changed the name of the Republic of Venezuela to the Bolivarian Republic of Venezuela; the official Day of Discovery was renamed the Day of Indigenous Resistance; and the symbolic remains of the indigenous chief Guaicaipuro were moved to the national pantheon. As Salas argues, through these actions "popular consciousness has won an important space of political power."[76] Bolivarianism draws popular resonance from its appropriation of deeply rooted collective memory, legends, and histories.

On a more personal level, Chávez gives voice to the marginalized, their hopes, collective memory, and resentment. Chavismo derives much of its discursive appeal from its language of protest at political exclusion. It is associated with a newfound sense of hope, retribution for social injustices, and dignity for the urban poor. Chavismo has found strength by tapping into the deep reservoir of daily humiliation and anger felt by people of the lower classes. It is Chávez's ability to speak to the urban poor, to show that he understands their feelings of exclusion, that endears him to them. [...]

Chávez encouraged the voicing of a range of heretical and cathartic emotions in the public sphere, especially during the 2002 coup and the 2004 recall referendum, when his language of the people versus the oligarchs, and the patriots versus the *escualidos* (squalid ones), could benefit him politically. But in the post-2004 order as Chávez sought to consolidate a new state orthodoxy, he was concerned to rein in and channel these chaotic and potentially destabilizing collective emotions. A range of intermediaries has been involved in this task of political incorporation. Chavista political parties made a greater effort to penetrate and manipulate mass organizations in order to impose a leadership hierarchy and party line over these movements. María Pilar García Guadilla has noted the attempts by the Movimiento Quinta Republica (MVR) to intervene politically in the CTUs and Communal Councils, utilizing them in order to build electoral support in a similar manner to the AD and COPEI during the 1960s and 1970s. An example of this was the local elections in August 2005, when political parties mobilized community-based organizations in support of pro-Chávez candidates.[77] Cultural institutions have sponsored local cultural initiatives as a way of reconsolidating a patronage system. Some community-based organizations have also acted as brokers and mediators between the state and urban movements, using their authority at the grass roots to channel discontent and promote state directives.

But alongside renewed corporatist linkages between state and society, neoliberal logics have persisted in certain demarcated areas. Under Chávez, there has been an attempt to divide up the national territory into what Aihwa Ong calls "zones of graduated sovereignty," where "developmental decisions favor the fragmentation of the national space into various noncontiguous zones, and promote the differential regulation of populations who can be connected to or disconnected from global circuits of capital."[78] Social policy after 2002 focused on creating a protected zone where the welfare apparatus could be cushioned off from the demands and rationalities of global markets. Funds are channeled directly from PDVSA to the various missions. PDVSA manages a yearly fund of some $US2,000 million from oil revenue, and this is all channeled into social programs.[79] This considerable reserve fund, even if linked to a volatile and depleting natural resource, has allowed the state to disconnect social welfare provision from global circuits of capital.

The majority of social welfare organizations, mostly those formed under Chávez such as health committees, land committees, communal councils, and technical commissions of water, operate within this noncontiguous zone, and therefore they are protected from the demands and requirements of international markets. But other zones continue to be articulated to foreign and private capital, to different degrees, including culture and communications, mining and hydrocarbons, and the manufacturing sector. These zones are subject to market calculations, as they are tied more directly to global circuits of capital. [...]

Notes

1 Comaroff and Comaroff, "Law and Disorder in the Postcolony," 5.

2 Silva Michelena, "La política social en Venezuela durante los años ochenta y noventa," 91.

3 Buxton, "Economic Policy and the Rise of Hugo Chávez," 115.

4 Levine, "Beyond the Exhaustion of the Model."

5 Coronil, *The Magical State*, 370–71.

6 Silva Michelena, "La política social en Venezuela durante los años ochenta y noventa," 92; Contreras, "Cultura política y política cultural en Venezuela," 41.

7 Contreras, "Cultura política y política cultural en Venezuela," 41–42.

8 Ibid., 43.

9   Coronil and Skurski, "Dismembering and Remembering the Nation," 314–16. 10.

10 Ibid., 314–15.

11 López Maya, "The Venezuelan Caracazo of 1989."

12 Kornblith, *Venezuela en los noventa*, 122.

13 Buxton, "Economic Policy and the Rise of Hugo Chávez," 118.

14 See Strange, *The Retreat of the State;* Evans, "The Eclipse of the State?"; Hardt and Negri, *Empire.*

15 Robinson, *Transnational Conflicts,* 46.

16 See Meiskin Woods, "Unhappy Families"; Cox, *Production, Power, and World Order*; Panitch, "Globalization and the State"; Jessop, "Globalization and the National State."

17 El Gran Viraje: Lineamientos Generales del VIII Plan de la Nación, Enero de 1990 (hereafter VIII Plan de la Nación), Presentación al Congreso Nacional, Presidencia de la República de Venezuela, Oficina Central de Coordinación y Planificación cordiplan, 6.

18 Coronil, *The Magical State*, 382.

19 VIII Plan de la Nación, 1990, 6.

20 Mujica Chirinos, "Estado y políticas sociales en Venezuela," 241.

21 Gutiérrez Briceño, "La política social en situaciones de crisis generalizada," 226.

22 Ibid., 227.

23 VIII Plan de la Nación, 1990, 6.

24 Carvallo, "Los nuevos programas sociales," 150–51.

25 Buxton, "Economic Policy and the Rise of Hugo Chávez," 120–21.

26 Ellner, *Rethinking Venezuelan Politics*, 101–2.

27 Mujica Chirinos, "Estado y políticas sociales en Venezuela," 245–46; Gutiérrez Briceño, "La política social en situaciones de crisis generalizada," 228.

28 Silva Michelena, "La política social en Venezuela durante los años ochenta y noventa," 95–101.

29 Martínez, "Comentaristas," 221.

30 Portes and Hoffman, "Latin American Class Structures."

31 Coronil, *The Magical State*, 382–83.

32 Portes and Hoffman, "Latin American Class Structures."

33 Roberts, "Social Polarization and the Populist Resurgence in Venezuela," 60.

34 Ibid.

35 J. P. Leary, "Untying the Knot of Venezuela's Informal Economy," NACLA, December 6, 2006, http://nacla.org.

36 Buxton, "Economic Policy and the Rise of Hugo Chávez," 115.

37 Roberts, "Social Polarization and the Populist Resurgence in Venezuela," 59.

38 Wilpert, *Changing Venezuela by Taking Power*, 107.

39 Roberts, "Social Polarization and the Populist Resurgence in Venezuela," 59–60.

40 Hurtado Salazar, *Dinámicas comunales y procesos de articulación social*.

41 Leeds, "Cocaine and Parallel Polities in the Brazilian Urban Periphery."

42 Auyero, *Poor People's Politics*, 66.

43 Quinn, *Nuthin' but a "G" Thang*, 57.

44 Auyero, "The Hyper-Shantytown," 85.

45 Ferrándiz, "Jose Gregorio Hernández," 43.

46 Interview with Pancho, Centro Madre Erika, Petare, August 2005. Not more than a decade later, when a local popular clinic was opened by the Chávez government just a few blocks down, Madre Erika's intake had declined to 1,000 patients per week.

47 Duque and Muñoz, *La ley de la calle*, 161.

48 Interview with Freddy Mendoza, June 2004.

49 Salas, "Morir para vivir," 245.

50 Sanjuán, "Democracy, Citizenship, and Violence in Venezuela," 87.

51 Salas, "Morir para vivir," 244.

52 In his article "Towards a Racial Geography of Caracas," George Ciccariello-Maher notes that since Chacao attained municipality status in 1990, it is estimated to spend 25 percent of its budget on policing; it has an autonomous police force and a philosophy of law enforcement based upon constant surveillance.

53 Mujica Chirinos, "Caracterización de la política social y la política económica," 34.

54 Ibid.

55 Ibid., 35–37.

56 Ibid., 38.

57 Craig and Porter, *Beyond Neoliberalism?*

58 Ellner, *Rethinking Venezuelan Politics*, 112–13.

59 Dunning, *Crude Democracy*, 232.

60 Wilpert, *Changing Venezuela by Taking Power*, 105.

61 Ibid., 134.

62 Alejandro Botía, "Círculos bolivarianos parecen burbujas en el limbo," *Últimas Noticias*, March 20, 2005.

63 Ellner, "The Revolutionary and Non-Revolutionary Paths of Radical Populism," 24.

64 Botía, "Círculos bolivarianos parecen burbujas en el limbo."

65 http://www.infocentro.gov.ve (visited March 2006).

66 Buxton, "Social Policy in Venezuela."

67 Rodríguez and Ortega, "Freed from Illiteracy?"

68 Rosnick and Weisbrot, "Illiteracy Revisited."

69 Rodríguez, "How Not to Defend the Revolution."

70 Weisbrot, "How Not to Attack an Economist (and an Economy)."

71 López Maya, "Caracas."

72 Salas, "La dramatización social y política del imaginario popular."

73 Carrera Damas, *El culto a Bolívar.*

74 Salas, *Bolívar y la historia en la conciencia popular.*

75 Salas, "La dramatización social y política del imaginario popular," 205.

76 Ibid., 216.

77 García Guadilla, "Ciudadanía y autonomía en las organizaciones sociales bolivarianas"; García Guadilla, "La praxis de los consejos comunales en Venezuela."

78 Ong, *Neoliberalism as Exception*, 77.

79 http://www.pdvsa.com (visited March 18, 2008).

References

Auyero, Javier. "The Hyper-Shantytown: Neo-liberal Violence(s) in the Argentine Slum." *Ethnography* 1, no. 1 (2000): 93–116.

Buxton, Julia. "Economic Policy and the Rise of Hugo Chávez." *Venezuelan Politics in the Chávez Era: Class, Polarization, and Conflict*, edited by Steve Ellner and Daniel Hellinger, 113–30. Boulder: Lynne Rienner Publishers, 2003.

Carvallo, Moisés. "Los nuevos programas sociales: Notas para un balance." *Política social: Exclusión y equidad en Venezuela durante los años noventa*, edited by Lourdes Alvares, Helia Isabel del Rosario, and Jesús Robles, 141–63. Caracas: Nueva Sociedad, 1999.

Comaroff, John L., and Jean Comaroff. "Law and Disorder in the Postcolony: An Introduction." *Law and Disorder in the Postcolony*, edited by Jean Comaroff and John Comaroff, 1–56. Chicago: University of Chicago Press, 2006.

Contreras, Miguel Angel. "Cultura política y política cultural en Venezuela: Un debate sobre las reconfiguraciones de la ciudadanía y la democracia en un espacio tiempo transformativo." *Debate sobre la democracia en América*, edited by José María Cadenas, 35–70. Caracas: Universidad Central de Venezuela, 2006.

Coronil, Fernando. *The Magical State: Nature, Money, and Modernity in Venezuela*. Chicago: University of Chicago Press, 1997.

Coronil, Fernando, and Julie Skurski. "Dismembering and Remembering the Nation: The Semantics of Political Violence in Venezuela." *Comparative Politics in Society and History* 33, no. 2 (1991): 288–337.

Craig, David, and Doug Porter. *Development beyond Neoliberalism? Governance, Poverty Reduction and Political Economy*. London: Routledge, 2006.

Dunning, Thad. *Crude Democracy: Natural Resource Wealth and Political Regimes*, New York: Cambridge University Press, 2008.

Duque, José Roberto, and Boris Muñoz. *La ley de la calle: Testimonios de jóvenes protagonistas de la violencia en Caracas*. Caracas: Fundarte, 1995.

Ellner, Steve. *Rethinking Venezuelan Politics: Class, Conflict, and the Chávez Phenomenon*. Boulder, Colo.: Lynne Rienner Publishers, 2008.

Ellner, Steve. "The Revolutionary and Non-Revolutionary Paths of Radical Populism: Directions of the Chavista Movement in Venezuela." *Science and Society* 69, no. 2 (2005): 160–90.

Evans, Peter. "The Eclipse of the State? Reflections on Stateness in an Era of Globalization." *World Politics* 50, no. 1 (1997): 62–87.

Ferrándiz, Francisco. "José Gregorio Hernández: A Chameleonic Presence in the Eye of the Medical Hurricane." *Kroeber Anthropological Society Papers* 83 (1998): 33–52.

García Guadilla, María Pilar. "Ciudadanía y autonomía en las organizaciones sociales bolivarianas: Los comités de tierra urbana como movimientos sociales." *Cuadernos del* CENDES 24, no. 66 (2007): 47–73.

———. "La praxis de los consejos comunales en Venezuela: ¿Poder popular o instancia clientelar?" *Revista Venezolana de Economía y Ciencias Sociales* 14, no. 1 (2008): 125–51.

Gutiérrez Briceño, Thais. "La política social en situaciones de crisis generalizada e incertidumbre en Venezuela." *Revista Venezolana de Gerencia* 7, no. 18 (2002): 220–36.

Hardt, Michael, and Antonio Negri. *Empire*. Cambridge, Mass.: Harvard University Press, 2000.

Hurtado Salazar, Samuel. *Dinámicas comunales y procesos de articulación social: Las organizaciones populares.* Caracas: Fondo Editorial Tropykos, 1991.

Kornblith, Miriam. *Venezuela en los noventa: Las crisis de la democracia.* Caracas: Ediciones IESA, 1998.

Leeds, Elizabeth. "Cocaine and Parallel Polities in the Brazilian Urban Periphery: Constraints on Local-Level Democratization." *Latin American Research Review* 31, no. 3 (1996): 47–83.

Levine, Daniel. "Beyond the Exhaustion of the Model: Survival and Transformation of Democracy in Venezuela." *Reinventing Legitimacy: Democracy and Political Change in Venezuela,* edited by Damarys Canache and Michael R. Kulisheck, 187–214. Westport, Conn.: Greenwood Press, 1998.

López Maya, Margarita. "Caracas: The State, Popular Participation, and How to Make Things Work." Paper presented at the conference "The Popular Sectors and the State in Chávez's Venezuela," Department of Political Science, Yale University, March 2008.

———. "The Venezuelan Caracazo of 1989: Popular Protest and Institutional Weakness," *Journal of Latin American Studies* 35 (2003): 127–30.

Martínez, Santiago. "Comentaristas." *Política social: Exclusión y equidad en Venezuela durante los años noventa,* edited by Lourdes Alvares, Helia Isabel del Rosario, and Jesús Robles, 221–29. Caracas: Nueva Sociedad, 1999.

Meiskin Woods, Ellen. "Unhappy Families: Global Capitalism in a World of Nation-States." *Monthly Review* 51, no. 3 (1999): 1–12.

Mujica Chirinos, Norbis. "Estado y políticas sociales en Venezuela ¿La quinta república o el regreso al pasado?" *Revista Venezolana de Gerencia* 7, no. 18 (2002): 237–66.

Ong, Aihwa. *Neoliberalism as Exception: Mutations in Citizenship and Sovereignty.* Durham, N.C: Duke University Press, 2006.

Portes, Alejandro, and Kelly Hoffman. "Latin American Class Structures: Their Composition and Change during the Neoliberal Era." *Latin American Research Review* 38, no. 1 (2003): 41–82.

Roberts, Kenneth. "Social Polarization and the Populist Resurgence in Venezuela." *Venezuelan Politics in the Chavez Era: Class, Polarization and Conflict,* edited by Steve Ellner and Daniel Hellinger, 55–72. Boulder, Colo.: Lynne Riener, 2003.

Robinson, William. *Transnational Conflicts: Central America, Social Change, and Globalization.* London: Verso, 2003.

Rodríguez, Francisco. "How Not to Defend the Revolution: Mark Weisbrot and the Misinterpretation of Venezuelan Evidence." *Wesleyan Economic Working Papers.* Wesleyan University, Middletown, Conn., 2008.

Rodríguez, Francisco, and Daniel Ortega. "Freed from Illiteracy? A Closer Look at Venezuela's 'Misión Robinson' Literacy Campaign." *Economic Development and Cultural Change* 57, no. 1 (2008): 1–30.

Rosnick, David, and Mark Weisbrot. "Illiteracy Revisited: What Ortega and Rodríguez Read in the Household Survey." *Working Paper.* Washington: Center for Economic and Policy Research, May 2008.

Salas, Yolanda. *Bolívar y la historia en la conciencia popular.* Caracas: Universidad Simón Bolívar, 1987.

———. "La dramatización social y política del imaginario popular: El fenómeno del Bolivarismo en Venezuela." *Estudios latinoamericanos sobre cultura y transformaciones sociales en tiempos de globalización,* edited by Daniel Mato, 201–21. Buenos Aires: CLACSO, 2001.

———. "Morir para vivir: La (in)certidumbre del espacio (in)civilizado." *Estudios latinoamericanos sobre cultura y transformaciones sociales en tiempos de globalización II,* edited by Daniel Mato, 241–49. Buenos Aires: CLACSO, 2001.

Silva Michelena, Héctor. "La política social en Venezuela durante los años ochenta y noventa." In *Política social: Exclusión y equidad en Venezuela durante los años noventa,* edited by Lourdes Alvares, Helia Isabel del Rosario, and Jesús Robles, 85–114. Caracas: Nueva Sociedad, 1999.

Strange, Susan. *The Retreat of the State: The Diffusion of Power in the World Economy.* New York: Cambridge University Press, 1996.

Weisbrot, Mark. "How Not to Attack an Economist (and An Economy): Getting the Numbers Right." Washington: Center for Economic and Policy Research, April 2008.

Wilpert, Gregory. *Changing Venezuela by Taking Power: The History and Policies of the Chávez Government.* London: Verso, 2007.

Section VI: Recommended Readings

Eversole, R. (2016). *Here to help: NGOs combating poverty in Latin America*. London, UK: Routledge.

Gledhill, J. (2015). *The new war on the poor: The production of insecurity in Latin America*. London, UK: Zed Books.

Jones, N. P. (2016). *Mexico's illicit drug networks and the state's reaction*. Washington, DC: Georgetown University Press.

Pribble, J., Huber, E., & Stephens, J. D. (2009). Politics, policies, and poverty in Latin America. *Comparative Politics, 41*, 387–407.

Youngers, C. A., & Rosin, E. (Eds.). (2005). *Drugs and democracy in Latin America: The impact of U.S. policy*. Boulder, CO: Lynne Rienner.

Section VI: Post-Reading Questions

1   Discuss the role that Spain, Germany, and the United States played in the rise of cocaine as a global commodity.

2   Why did neoliberalism contribute to the rise of violence and poverty in Latin America? Include examples in your answer.